Transnational Cyber Crime and Terrorism

Transnational Cyber Crime and Terrorism

Nilesh Kumar Singh

MD Publications Pvt Ltd
New Delhi
www.mdppl.com

Published by :

MD Publications Pvt Ltd
"MD House", 11, Darya Ganj,
New Delhi - 110 002
Phone : +91-11-41563325 (Customer Service)
+91-11-41562846 (Editorial)
E-mail (orders): order@mdppl.com
Website: www.mdppl.com

ISBN: 978-81-7533-207-2

Published and Printed by Mr. Pranav Gupta on behalf of MD Publications Pvt Ltd at Times Press, New Delhi.

PREFACE

Cyber terrorism is any premeditated, politically motivated attack against information, computer systems, computer programs, and data which results in violence against non-combatant targets by sub-national groups or clandestine agents. Unlike a nuisance virus or computer attack that result in a denial of service, a cyber terrorist attack is designed to cause physical violence or extreme financial harm. Possible cyber terrorist targets include the banking industry, military installations, power plants, air traffic control centers, and water systems. Cyber terrorism is sometimes referred to as electronic terrorism or information war.

The present stage of human development is characterized by the explosive growth of information technologies, a historically unparalleled situation that is irreversibly changing people's way of life. All previous key inventions such as the telegraph, telephone, radio, television, and computer only paved the way for the unprecedented integration that is under way. In our times, global cyber space—the worldwide Internet—simultaneously represents a repository for a colossal amount of information, a means of global broadcasting, and a medium for cooperation and human communication encompassing the entire world.

The cyber threat causes emergency responders to be at risk from a common tactic used by terrorists—that is, to amplify a main attack with a supporting attack. After a main attack, terrorists might make a secondary assault on assembled emergency responders or their supporting information systems. This could reduce their ability to respond and possibly create more casualties. A secondary cyber attack may be employed before or coincidentally with a physical attack to impede effective deployment of emergency responders and thus amplify the damage from the physical attack.

The merger of transnational crime, terrorism and corruption is profound. The idea that these ideas can be discussed separately is problematic. Such compartmentalization limits our ability to analyze and address the diverse forms of transnational criminal activity. The phenomena of transnational crime, terrorism and corruption are all too often viewed as separate phenomena. These phenomena have grown in tandem because the economic and political conditions that give rise to these phenomena are quite similar. The evolution of the transnational crime-ideologically based or economically based depends on specific environmental factors that have proliferated in many developing and transitional countries that have not successfully integrated into the global economy.

Terrorists and transnational criminals use many of the same strategies to promote their operations, chief among these being the use of information technology to plan and realize their activities. The rise of greater international mobility and the proliferation of information technology throughout the world have facilitated the growth of both transnational crime and terrorism. Most transnational crime and terrorist groups are based in transitional and developing countries. The illicit businesses are now the largest and most profitable to be located in the developing world.

The widespread problem of corruption in many developing countries allows the proliferation of transnational organized crime and terrorism. The official corruption facilitating this activity may assume many different forms and is not just based on bribery. The connections between transnational crime and terrorism are not unique to developed and developing countries. As investigations in the advent of September, 11 have shown, terrorists in developed countries use criminal activity to survive. Arrests in Spain revealed that terrorists were selling counterfeit airline tickets to survive and such groups in the United States were surviving by means of money laundering and other criminal offenses.

I am very grateful to Mr. Pranav Gupta, Director of MD Publications Pvt Ltd, New Delhi, for his cooperation and support for this book.

Nilesh Kumar Singh

Contents

1

Introduction

Technology and Translation

It is an apparent paradox that to fight terrorism we maintain and solidify a life in terror. In recent years, not least after the September 11 attack in New York, the fight against terrorism has led to unprecedented steps in countering whatever possible action internationally operating terrorists may take. New national and international taskforces are set up; military forces are developing new means of intelligence, surveillance and combat; laws are enforced to allow a new level of scrutinizing and interrogating citizens; particular countries and ethnic groups are paid extraordinary attention based on terror profiles; the transport infrastructures have introduced new security measures; new patterns of behaviour have developed in everyday life, e.g. keeping an eye out for dubious bags or persons.

A statistical survey made in mid-September 2005 shows that 84% of all Danes are affected by terrorism, either in the way they behave in public spaces or in their thinking about everyday life situations. All this, to me, seems to keep us in the grips of a state of terror. Fear, anxiety and watchfulness are thus nurtured through our counter-measures against terrorism. If the initial paradox is correct, we may then involuntarily be teaming up with terrorists in achieving the intended state of terror, and consequently providing the attention they desire.

This work reflects on how terror can be seen, not just as a mental state in the minds of citizens, but also as a vast network of relations between people, technologies, laws, facts, organisations, and symbols. To discuss these interrelated issues 'terrorism' and 'technology' are discussed. Both are somehow closely tied to contemporary systems of signification, where the former is narrowed down to signify particular forms of terrorism, whereas the application of the latter seems to produce or to sustain terror. Let me begin by discussing the term 'terrorism' formally and historically.

The Methods of Terror

One all-embracing definition of terrorism, which seems generally applied, is:

"The systematic use of coercive intimidation usually to service political ends. It is used to create and exploit a climate of fear among a wider target group than the immediate victims of the violence, and to publicize a cause, as well as to coerce a target into acceding to the terrorists' aims".

According to this definition, terrorism is neither an ideology nor a movement, *terrorism is a method*. Below I will pursue that premise further. Typical kinds of terrorism are bombings, shooting attacks and assassinations, hostage-taking and kidnapping, and hijacking. It is often feared that nuclear, chemical or bacteriological weapons may be used in terror-acts, but so far few examples are found (Hussein's regime used chemical weapons against the Iraqi Kurds; in Tokyo the Aum Shinrikyo doomsday cult used the chemical substance sarin in the subway).

It is also important to distinguish between *state* and *factional terrorism*. State terrorism, like Turkey's suppression of Kurds, or Iranian suppression of non-Shiite groups, has been and is generally more lethal than factional terrorism. Often, state terrorism is an antecedent to the latter. Factional terrorism might thus be developed and directed against a state using terrorism to fight its opposition. Such fights may be cases of *internal terrorism* as opposed to *international terrorism* spreading across national borders. Today, terrorism is generally international, though, with terror groups looking abroad for weapons, supporters and shelter in friendly states.

At the level of state terrorism there is also the methodic terror created by states against other states, most notoriously by the USA and USSR in the post World War II period, during the Cold War, where the *terror-balance* became a meaningful expression of the delicate balancing of nuclear powers, and the general climate of terror-effected behaviour. Today, most acts of terrorism have the killing of innocent civilians as a basic feature. This sets it apart from *sabotage,* which is defined in a Danish dictionary as: "The destruction of things, buildings, means of transport, goods and machines, to harm a political or economical rival". The word is derived from the French 'sabot 'meaning' wooden clogs' and sabotage initially meant 'destroying something by stamping ones wooden clogs'.

Sabotage may of course lead to the killing of innocent civilians by accident, e.g. in an act of arson, but that does not undermine the distinction between terrorism and sabotage. Although the World Trade Center and other buildings were destroyed in the attack, and American finance was paralyzed, it has not been seen as a case of sabotage executed by saboteurs. Rather, it was a case of terrorism intended to spread horror and panic in the minds of large numbers of people. 'Terrorism' is thus an ambiguous term, often defined by the parties in a conflict to characterize their opponent, subsequently creating an Us-Them opposition, where we are defined by not being like them, i.e. not engaging in terrible, unjustified deeds as they do (Foucault 1988). While we now consider it a common feature of terrorism to hit civilians that has not always been a distinct feature of terrorism.

If one looks at its historical roots the term 'terrorism' has been used since the French revolution. In the years 1793-94 Robespierre's government, the 'régime de la terreur', ruled in France, using terror, including mass executions, to maintain the ends of the revolution, that is, modern democracy. Terror was then an instrument to create a revolutionary state. In the early 20th Century anarchists would use terrorism to fight governments, killing several heads of state. When the Serb Gavrillo Princip shot the Austrian-Hungarian prince Franz Ferdinand in Sarajevo in 1914, his act was characterized as terrorism although his action was directed against a specific person and not innocent civilians. Princip was seen as a terrorist because he wanted to change society through political violence. In the years following World War II a different kind of terrorism materialized around the world in independence movements fighting their colonial masters. Various nationalist movements applied terrorism as a method in their struggles to obtain this end and to become independent states, e.g. Israel, Kenya and Algeria. Usually, the terrorists went for military, structural or symbolic goals, and civilians were not a direct target of such actions.

This began to change in the 1960s and 1970s with the emergence of a new political kind of terrorism, e.g. Rote Armee Fraktion, RAF, in West Germany, and Action Direct in France. Their ends were nationally defined, e.g. to turn a government against the Vietnam war, or to force it to chose communism over capitalism, not least in light of the cold war. In Italy the Brigate Rosse kidnapped the leader of the Christian Democrats, Aldo Moro, and ended up killing him, because the Italian government did not meet the demands made by the group. A Palestinian group used terrorism in the hostage-taking at the Olympic Games in Munich in

1972. Here, innocent civilian lives were included in the use of terror, with Israeli athletes being killed, or threatened with death, if the hostage-takers' demands were not met.

In the following years, with the concurrent development of international media coverage and technologies to support police cooperation, the nationalistic focus in terrorist groups was gradually taken over by international ends and international cooperation nested in terror-networks. At this time, any one-dimensional picture of terrorism must be rejected. In 1968, 11 international terror groups were identified, and ten years later there were 55 such groups. In recent years we have seen e.g. an actor of terror over and in the Scottish town, Lockerbie, where a Pan-Am airplane exploded and crashed in 1988. Two Libyans were eventually pointed out as the terrorists, and with them a still unclear link to the Libyan government; the spreading of sarin by a cult group in the Tokyo Subway in 1995, mentioned above, was again a different kind of terrorist act with no political motive; and yet another kind was the act of terror in the Northern Irish town of Omagh, where a car-bomb exploded in 1998 during a carnival. A radical group, the Real IRA, was suspected of this act, which amongst other things led to the first condemnation of such acts from a Sinn Féin leader, Gerry Adams.

Of course, September 11 has added a whole new array of meanings to terrorism. The attack was planned and directed by religious fundamentalists, and that helped to produce a strong and easily followed polarisation between us and them. The terrorists attacked the very symbols of American values, capitalism and military super power, and they killed innocent civilians. The attackers' clear background in Islamic fundamentalism has helped solidify a strong, contemporary conception of terrorism, as a fanatic fight against our world order and religious beliefs, motivated by their - primitive - world views and dogmatic religious beliefs.

Following this, I suggest that we see any dominant definition of terrorism as a *figuration* that includes humans, institutions, artifacts, facts, organisations, symbols, ideologies, etc. To appreciate the richness of this conception, let me say a few words about its origin in the work of the American social scientist Donna Haraway.

Donna Haraway has demonstrated the merits of trying to dissolve absolute ontological boundaries between material and symbolic dimensions of socio-technical life and practices. She has identified figures and figurations as explicit expressions of "... the tropic quality of all material-semiotic processes, especially in techno science". By that she wishes to point out that a *figuration* is not just a figurative ornamentation of literal speech. Neither are pictorial utterances 'just' images or symbolic expressions of literal meaning. Rather, we live with and through such figurations. Figurations are *performative images* that one may dwell in, and there are many such figurations. In Haraway's use of images, literal and figurative modes are always intertwined. It entails that rhetorical practices are also in effect political practices.

At present, it seems that the master definition of terrorism is *global terrrorism.* This figuration has solidified around a *list*, made by USA after the September 11 attack in 2001, of all their enemies including all organisations that participate in international terrorism. To talk about global terrorism brings to life a number of figurations that are embodied and thus able to perform socio-technical work as such on top of human, verbal practice. For instance, *the axis of evil*, which very effectively and instantly positioned North-Korea, Iran and Iraq as our most, dreaded enemies. *Osama Bin Laden* may also be seen as a figuration.

We are not sure that the actual person is still alive, but the figuration is doing things in the world in symbolic, political and military contexts. In a rare video with Osama Bin Laden after the September 11 terror attack, he was seen in conversation with other Al-Qaida members. He talks about their expectations during the planning of the action: "Our hope was to destroy 3 to 4 floors" of the Twin Towers. The scale of the actual destruction, and the massive international reactions, changed the figuration of Osama Bin Laden from a dangerous terror leader to the most evil and wanted man on earth. Anti-terror programmes are fighting Bin Laden; he serves as symbol for Muslim anti-American movements and recruitment, etc.

To be included on the list of global terrorists is obviously bad, but it is equally bad to be excluded from having *access* to the list, for instance, to be able to suggest different views about international and national terrorism. Israel and Russia have demonstrated that access to the list makes a difference as to what counts as international and national issues. The Israeli government wanted Hamas and Islamic Jihad put on the list. These organisations were not there in the first edition, because US found the Palestinian problem to be a national matter. But the organisations were added to the revised list after Israeli pressure. The result has been that Hamas and Islamic Jihad are also weaved into the mesh of global terrorism.

It seems evident that a specific, modernist concept of human-technology relations is at play, sustaining the paradoxical situation suggested in the introduction, that the fight against terrorism maintains a state of terror. Narrow conceptions of technology may thus stop us from seeing the work of socio-technical systems to uphold terror in everyday life.

Combating Terrorism through Technology

In a web-based newsletter, NATO News from autumn 2004, some of the recent military leanings in the fight against international terrorism are sketched out in an article by Marshall Billingslea, who is Assistant Secretary General of NATO's Defence Investment Division, and Chairman of

NATO's CNAD and the NC3 Board. The title of the article is: 'Combating terrorism through technology.' (Billingslea, 2004). The first section sets the scene for NATO actions:

> The destructive capacity of terrorist groups is growing steadily as terrorists prove themselves adept at using modern technology for their own ends. NATO allies are working together to develop new and improved technologies to combat this increasingly sophisticated threat.

The reader is informed that at a recent NATO summit meeting in Istanbul, 2004, the leaders endorsed a 'Programme of Work for Defence against Terrorism'. The programme was put forward by NATO's National Armament Directors, who meet twice annually in a group called Conference of National Armament Directors, CNAD. The aim of the programme is to promote national expertise and research programmes to create new and improved technology in the fight against terrorism. Primarily the programme aims at facilitating systems that will help to prevent particular kinds of terror attacks in the future; to supply the military with new and sophisticated technologies to trace and prevent terrorism; and to track down terrorists.

More explicitly, the initiative is directed toward improving the capability of NATO's military systems in particular problem domains: to prevent terrorist bombs from exploding or doing harm; to airdrop special operations forces with precision; to protect airplanes and helicopters against missile attack; to protect harbours and ships against explosives carried by speedboats or underwater divers; to improve protection against chemical, biological, radiological and nuclear weapons; to implement intelligence, reconnaissance, surveillance and target acquisition of terrorists; and to combat mortar attacks.

To make the argument about an insufficient view on human-technology relations in the NATO initiative, let me take a closer look at the problem domain which aims at implementing intelligence, reconnaissance, surveillance and target acquisition of terrorists. This domain underlines the dominant viewpoint on human-technology relations. A lengthy quote will serve to underpin my argument:

> Anonymity and the ability to launch attacks at a time and place of their choosing are tactical advantages utilised by terrorists. NATO is working on reducing or eliminating those advantages. In addition to a variety of technological measures that are being explored, the NATO Research & Technology Organisation and the NATO Science Committee are jointly exploring crucial areas in the behavioural sciences, such as "human factors analysis" and the psychological aspects of terrorism.

In Billingslea's sketch of NATO's programme of Work for Defence against Terrorism a typical modernist assumption about technology is advanced. Technology and humans are separate phenomena with separate logics and logistics involved. Psychological factors are 'additional' factors to technological one. Hence, either we look into the technological realm of the fight against terrorism, or we look into the human factors including human psychology. The question then becomes: What plans are in the minds of terrorist and what are the technological means to execute those plans? How can we develop weapon systems to fight the - often - primitive technologies of terrorists, and how can we trace and calculate their thoughts? There are several good reasons to be skeptical of this stance, in spite of its dominant position today.

The Danish researcher on international affairs and terrorism, Birthe Hansen, has suggested that contemporary terrorism is "post-Fordist" in its approach to spreading terror. Fordism is used to describe the 20th century as the industrial age with Henry Ford's assembly line as a basic metaphor. That age was characterized by mass culture, standardized goods, and uniform, monotonous work controlled by top-down management. Since the 1980s, however, Fordism has been supplanted or replaced by post-industrial society, information society, individualized social formations, multi-cultural life forms, etc. Let me add, that the event of postmodernism has been seen by many as a license to subvert any given set of regularities to obtain new and unprecedented social states and events.

Hansen argues that contemporary terrorists have demonstrated proficiency in developing technology and means of productions based on the post-Fordist approach. Billingslea testifies to that in his article: Modern terrorists have shown "...the expertise to fabricate explosive devices out of a wide range of objects - from mobile phones to doorbells - and materials - from military explosives to commercial dynamite to improvised fertilizer mixes".

The September 11 attack provided evidence for this new approach on several accounts. First, an airplane is usually associated with being a huge, airborne carrier of humans and things, a fast and reliable means of transportation. With the September 11 attack, the plane was translated by terrorists (and later the world) into a highly explosive device, almost a self-contained cybernetic system with a clear, preset goal: to hit particular concrete buildings, symbolizing American values such as capitalism and military power. Humans, things, and symbols were mixed into a hitherto unknown array of practices. Furthermore, some mundane technical devices underwent the same transformation.

Stanley knives, usually associated with crafts as a means to cut into things, were turned into weapons and threats to cut into humans. Razor blades, normally used for shaving off beards, but not to cut the skin, were also turned into deadly cutting weapons. It is significant that these devices had not been considered weapon beforehand in this setting. Nonetheless, they were immediately translated as such in the hijacking situation. In other words, the translation of these technological devices from everyday inoffensive tools to murder weapons was done not only by the terrorists, but also by the passengers. If this two-stage translation had not been successful the hijacking could well have had a different outcome. The September 11 attack was marked by another fusion as well, besides the mix of tool uses. Two well-known styles of terror, hijacking and suicide-bombing, were fused into one with the crashing into the twin-towers of the World Trade Center and Pentagon.

Hansen has applied a terminology, normally related to commercial product-improvement, from the Austrian economist, Joseph Schumpeter, to reflect on the September 11 attack. That enables her to talk about the introduction of new products, so far unknown to the consumers, and the introduction of new methods of production in a domain. Hence, airplanes were turned into bombs, commonplace tools were used as hand weapons, and hijacking and suicide-bombing were mixed to become a new method of terrorism. And I would add that flight training courses and flight-simulators, usually meant to improve pilots' skills in the name of safer flying, were used by terrorists to learn to hit particular targets.

In recent years a new conception of human-technology relations, somewhat similar to Hansen's, has developed within the social sciences. I find it a convincing approach to understanding contemporary socio-technical life, including the recent acts of terror. To give an idea as to what this approach involves, it is fruitful to discuss a distinction introduced by the French sociologist, Bruno Latour.

Translating Technology

In modernist terminology new technological systems are often placed in abstract, purified categories. They may simply be classified as 'new technology' e.g. when a technical system is taken as a means to make a practical domain more efficient. This is also what NATO intends with its anti-terror programme. The 'new technology' *in practice* is an effect of a chain of complicated, dynamic processes that happen in various places and ways. 'New technology' is what is left, when socio-technical processes of delegating responsibility have ceased, to use the words of Bruno Latour.

The fight against terrorism, illustrated by the NATO approach, demonstrates both the military and political commitments to establish international standards for anti-terror technology, and the underlying modernist anticipation that 'new technology' will improve our means to fight terrorism.

To make this claim operational I suggest *diffusion and translation* as central models of technology, adapted and molded from Latour's proposals for a sociological understanding of power associations. The diffusion model encompasses the NATO view on technology, and the translation model underpins my own understanding of the dissemination of technical systems in society.

The diffusion model makes it possible to speak abut three moments in the circulation of technological artifacts and systems: 1) It is an original power or reason, that initiates the circulation of new technology; 2) This power is turned into a kind of inertia which is conserved during the entire transmission; and 3) The work of a social mediator may slow down or speed up the completed circulation. If we look out for these moments, it will be evident that there are rational human subjects, material objects and a mediating, social world, and consequently a number of a priori dichotomies to count on. Following this model, Osama Bin Laden and a few others, masterminded the September 11 attack. This very plan was transmitted in the secretive network of terror, where it was acted upon during the entire operation by those who hijacked the airplanes and used them as bombs.

In the translation model, on the other hand, one will assume that all participants, all agents - both humans and non-humans - receive and translate an original plan in accordance with their own projects and interests. What they dispatch to the next link in the chain is no longer 'the same' as that which they received, i.e. there is no simple transmission going on. The fate of the 'original' plan is always in the hands of later users, since every link will translate and transform what they receive to make it fit with their own plans and projects. One is reminded of the Italian aphorism *"Traduttore, traditore"*: The one who translates is a traitor. But you can do nothing but translate if the text is to be passed on. In the process of translating a plan to attack the World Trade Center and passing it on, people and artifacts get enrolled in the socio-technical network in which such secret plans are at work. Not just facts and artifacts, like personal identification, or Stanley knives and airplanes, but also humans are changed in the course of actions, e.g. from Al-Qaida supporters, to students in Germany with a mission, to pilot trainees in the USA, to hijackers, to martyrs.

Hence, facts, artifacts and people must be studied concurrently if we want to understand socio-technical practices. People, facts and artifacts are constantly being delegated new positions and roles in networks of politics and terror. This model cannot excuse the horrible things that were done on September 11. But it might serve to assist our understanding of the initial paradox that the fight against terror seems to install a state of terror. Instead of assuming that things and humans belongs to separate realms, we can look out for particular socio-technical associations, that keep social agency in narrow lines of behaviour, e.g. terror laws that censor critical thinking, or international harbour protection fences that stop leisure activities, or model-based predictions of possible sites of terror-acts, which scare us off from visiting foreign countries and people.

Terrorism, as such, has become a very important figuration to define normality, or us, as opposed to extremism, or them. As argued above, 'global terrorism' is the dominant figuration to set its marks on the life we lead in important ways, by guiding us around, and determining our values and political inclinations. The tragic certainty is, however, that we will learn about new meanings of terrorism in the years to come, new figurations - often the hard way. In light of that - inexpensive - prediction, it seems wise to avoid the trap of developing strategies to fight terrorism without a keen eye on the historical diversity of the concept and phenomena. Otherwise we may not be able to develop relevant strategies to relate to future cases of terrorism, simply because our conception of terrorism is too narrow to encompass such cases.

To see technology simply as a rational means to fight terrorists and their actions will probably not lead to the intended ends. If terrorists are post-Fordists in their treatment of technology, they have no problems in acting, e.g. as human missile-guides, or to crash computers to install socio-technical systems of anxiety in particular social groups. When we begin to see for ourselves, that technology is embedded in the social fabric, maintaining it, regulating it, translating it, and vice versa, then we can perhaps begin to grasp the dynamic workings of socio-technical agencies in current life, committing us to the ends of terror, by sustaining terror in everyday life situations. Hence, the initial paradox may be confronted, if we want to, and broader interpretations of social values and world orders can be made. To look out for the practical and effective work of dominant figurations, and attempting to broaden our ideas about dynamic human-technology relations, may help to frustrate the effects of contemporary terror.

2

Terrorism, the Internet and Cyber Crime

In Russia

The present stage of human development is characterized by the explosive growth of information technologies, a historically unparalleled situation that is irreversibly changing people's way of life. All previous key inventions such as the telegraph, telephone, radio, television, and computer only paved the way for the unprecedented integration that is under way. In our times, global cyberspace—the worldwide Internet—simultaneously represents a repository for a colossal amount of information, a means of global broadcasting, and a medium for cooperation and human communication encompassing the entire world. The Internet is not controlled by any state structures. According to the predictions of the public organization the Internet Society, in 2005 the number of Internet users in the world will exceed one billion, of whom about seven million will be from Russia.

Besides the multitude of positive aspects of this sort of global linkage and communication among individuals and peoples, information technologies significantly expand the arsenal of means and capabilities of criminals. Any country with computers and Internet access could, intentionally or not, become a base for users with evil intentions, any one of whom could have the goal and motivation to inflict criminal harm on other people and organizations. These people have global cyberspace at their disposal to use for criminal purposes. Crimes of such a nature are called cyber crimes (in Russian legislation, crimes in the sphere of computer information), and the people who commit them are generally called cybercriminals. Although the term cyber crime is not legally formulated in Russian legislation, this concept has taken firm root in practice.

Cyber crime may include the following:

- unauthorized access to information,
- creation, use, and dissemination of harmful computer programs, including over the Internet,
- intentional disruption of the normal operation of computers and networks,
- illegal trade in equipment for capturing computerized information,
- falsification of documents with the use of computer technologies,
- distribution of counterfeit software,
- conduct of financial swindles,
- publication of calls for violence and terror,
- publication of Nazi and fascist propaganda.

The main characteristic of these crimes is that, as a rule, they have no physical signs. Cyber criminals currently use various types of network attacks. Some use computer viruses, including network worms, which modify and destroy information or block the operation of computer systems; logic bombs, which are triggered under certain conditions; or Trojan horses, which send various types of information from infected computers back to their masters over the Internet.

The weapons of cybercriminals are being constantly honed, and their means of conducting information attacks are becoming increasingly refined. In the long term, we can expect to see the appearance of new nontraditional types of network attacks and computer crimes. On the whole, we can state with confidence that the material damage from crimes in the information technology sphere is measured in the billions of U.S. dollars and is increasing with each passing year. Furthermore, the expected growth in financial losses from criminal infringements is based not only and not so much on the increased number of computer attacks as on the growing scale of the use of network information technologies in business. In the face of harsh competition, companies are forced to shift a large portion of their business communications onto the Internet, which makes them vulnerable to criminals unless matters of information protection are handled appropriately.

The world community has fully realized the potential consequences of the threat of cyber crime, and in this regard representatives of the European Union member states, the United States, Canada and Japan signed the International Convention on Cyber crime in November 2001. In the convention, crimes committed in the information environment or against or with the aid of information resources are in fact defined as cyber crimes.

With the far lower level of development of computer networks in Russia, the situation in the Russian Federation is obviously not yet as serious as in the United States, but its intensity is increasing from year to year. We are increasingly sensing how the modern information criminal is becoming a reality.

The Criminal Code of the Russian Federation includes articles establishing penalties for computer crimes and a chapter defining crimes in the computer information sphere. This chapter includes three articles setting forth penalties for illegitimate access to computer information (Article 272); the creation, use, and dissemination of harmful programs via computer (Article 273); and violation of the rules of operation of computers, computer systems, and networks (Article 274). The number of crimes committed under these articles is increasing each year. Meanwhile, the number of crimes discovered is also on the rise. Let us look at the facts.

In 2004, 4,523 computer information crimes were discovered in the Russian Federation. Of these, 3,944 fell under Article 272 of the Criminal Code and 577 under Article 273. During this past year, the Russian Federation significantly stepped up its efforts to stop the distribution of unlicensed software, thus making a worthy contribution to the world trend toward combating computer piracy. For example, 1,483 administrative violations were uncovered in the copyright area, and 216,635 compact discs with unlicensed software with a total value of more than 9 million rubles were confiscated by court order.

Like the rest of the world, the Russian Federation is currently facing the pressing problem of so-called spam, the mass distribution of electronic messages, largely advertising, that were not requested by their recipients. Receiving spam is like an invisible tax on all users of the Russian segment of the Internet. By various estimates, financial losses from spam vary from 120 to 200 million U.S. dollars per year. In 2004 a precedent for combating this type of crime was created for the first time in the Russian Federation, with the first conviction of a spammer under the law. This person had created a computer program, sendsms.pl, and sent 15,000 mobile phone subscribers text messages with uncensored content smearing the business reputation of a cellular communications company.

Also arising last year was a trend for the use of the Internet as an auditorium to shape public opinion and exert pressure on private individuals and officials by spreading information damaging honor and impugning dignity or by disseminating citizens' personal or family secrets. In one example the authorities halted the activities of a perpetrator who had posted an Internet site with intentionally libelous materials regarding the president of the Russian Federation and statements insulting his honor and dignity. Obviously, negative press technologies adopted from the media have begun to be used on the Internet. Furthermore, in trying to evade responsibility, the ill-intentioned are claiming that laws regulating media activities do not apply to the Internet, even though its audience is often greater than that of many print publications. The Russian Federation is working actively to standardize the legislative and regulatory base for these violations, while maintaining a lack of government censorship.

An analysis of personal information about criminals arrested in the Russian Federation in 2004 shows that computer crime is mostly perpetrated by adults. Adolescents under age 20 comprise only 17 percent of the total number of criminals, the bulk of whom—70 percent—are persons between the ages of 20 and 35. It should also be noted that 63 percent of these persons attended or graduated from university, which reflects the high intellectual level of this criminal activity.

No crime, including cyber crime, can occur on its own. Crimes are committed by criminals, and in this case, by cybercriminals. People can have different motives for committing crimes. Determining the boundary between crime and terrorism in cyberspace is possible simply by determining the goals of cyber-terrorism. In practice, these goals coincide with the goals inherent in terrorism in general and political terrorism in particular. One may state that every terrorist is a criminal, but not every criminal is a terrorist.

According to the common definition of terrorism, it is a conscious and directed use of violence or the threat of violence to force society, the state, or the government to comply with the political, ideological, religious, or economic goals of the terrorist organization. A terrorist act is a crime aimed at having an emotional impact on public opinion, engendering fear and panic in society, evoking distrust of power structures, and ultimately destabilizing the political-economic situation in the country. This is a crime aimed against the security of society, the state, and each individual citizen. The cyber terrorist substantially differs from the hacker, computer hooligan, thief, or swindler. The main element of the cyber terrorist's tactics is to ensure that the crime has maximally dangerous consequences and broad public resonance and creates an atmosphere that threatens repetition of the terrorist act without specifying a specific target of attack.

The experience of the Russian Federation shows that the motives of cyber crimes are changing. Whereas computer crimes in the past were committed mainly by adolescents motivated by hooliganistic or experimental considerations, motives of greed now predominate. Intentionally false reports of terrorist attacks represent an exception. In particular, specialists have established that this was the motive of the Russian student who disseminated information about a planned New York subway bombing, accompanying his message with the words "Allahu akbar".

Means of Countering Cyber Attacks

There is no commonly accepted terminology in the sphere of information security for computer systems and networks, which makes it necessary to define certain fundamental concepts (as they are used in the Russian Federation).

Threat—A potential event, action, or process that by its effects on network components could lead to the infliction of material, moral, or other damage on network resources.

Vulnerability—Characteristic or property of the information system that if used by an intruder could lead to realization of a threat—in other words, weak points in systems.

Attack (intrusion)—An event in which a perpetrator or intruder attempts to access a system or commits any sorts of abuses with it, or any action by an intruder leading to realization of a threat by means of attacking vulnerabilities. An intruder carries out an attack in three stages: (1) collection of information about the network to be attacked, (2) implementation of attack, and (3) completion of attack. Traditional means of countering intrusions come into play only in the second phase of attack implementation. Such a situation helps to increase the damage from the attack. It would be more logical to begin active response efforts at the first stage of the attack. The most obvious example would be an attack aimed at implementing a threat to deny services or to deny access to information (a denial-of-service attack). This sort of attack is extremely difficult to thwart at the implementation stage, so it would be reasonable to suppress it at the first step in its development.

Intrusion detection—A range of methods intended to detect an intrusion (attack) on a network by means of observing various parameters, events, and subsystems for registration and network monitoring.

Intrusion detection system—Range of software and hardware network resources intended to detect intrusions (attacks).

In addition to the denial-of-service attack, which stalls a server by placing an increased load on its central processor, there are many harmful programs called viruses, which affect individual computers, computer systems, networks, and, recently, mobile communications resources, using a developed operating environment and elemental base. The number of viruses is constantly increasing, reaching 25,000 according to estimates in late 2004.

With corporate and local networks and individual users

accessing the Internet, one of the most complex problems is that of ensuring the security of information resources. A number of technologies are employed to address this problem, each of which is designed to protect against a particular class of potential security threats. These include intrusion detection systems, public key infrastructure, virtual private networks, antivirus software, cryptographic systems, identification and authentication systems, security scanners, and so forth. Firewalls hold an important place among these technologies, and their adequate application can substantially reduce risks associated with unauthorized access to data. However, comprehensively deterring cyber threats is possible by developing optimal information security policy consisting of a combination of passive and active methods of applying protection technologies.

Table 2.0 : Classification of Current Viruses

Group	Type	Characteristics
Environment	Network viruses	Spread through various networks, that is, during transmission of data between computers connected by a network.
	File viruses	Infect executable files and are loaded after start-up of the program in which they are located. File viruses can also be embedded in other types of files, but if they are placed in no executable files, they do not obtain control and lose the capacity to spread.
	Boot viruses	Install themselves into the boot sector of physical or logical discs containing boot programs.
	Mobile communication system viruses	The newest type of virus. They infect the operating environment of the latest generation of mobile telephones, which have broad intellectual capabilities.

Means of infection	Resident viruses	Leave a resident code in operating memory that intercepts communications between the operating system and infection targets (files, boot sectors of discs, and so forth) and installs itself in them. Resident viruses live in memory and remain active until the computer is turned off or rebooted.
	Nonresident viruses	Do not infect computer memory and are active for a limited time. They are activated at certain times, for example, when documents are processed with a text processor.
Destructive potential	Not dangerous	Reduce memory volume; do not disrupt the computer operations; produce graphic, audio, or other effects.
	Dangerous	Can cause various disruptions in computer operations, for example, locking up or incorrect printing of documents.
	Very dangerous	Can cause losses of programs and data and deletion of information in system memory sectors and can even cause a breakdown of moving parts of the hard disc.

The training of highly qualified information security specialists

Only a major leading university with the appropriate educational, methodological, and technical base is capable of training highly qualified specialists able to accomplish the task of ensuring comprehensive information security. The educational objectives for specialists of this type at Bauman Moscow State Technical University are as follows:

- theoretical foundations for the engineering-technical protection of information,
- methodological support for the engineering-technical protection of information,
- creation and operating principles of information systems and networks (ISN),
- methodologies for designing, building, and operating secure ISNs,
- criteria and methods for evaluating the security of ISNs,
- means and methods of unauthorized access to ISN information,
- architecture of protected computer networks,
- software, hardware, and technical means of creating protected networks,
- principles of building and managing protected networks,
- rules for the organizational, technical, and legal protection of information,
- use of software and hardware technologies for protecting information,
- construction and operation of protected databases,
- systematic approach to the problem of protecting information in database management systems,
- mechanisms for protecting information in databases, and database management systems and opportunities for overcoming them,
- conceptions of the engineering-technical protection of information,
- physical foundations for the engineering-technical protection of information,
- organizational foundations for the engineering-technical protection of information.

As a result of their training in this discipline, specialists must understand the following:

- promising areas for the development of computer security theory,
- methods for analyzing information security threats,
- architecture of secure ISNs,
- principles for constructing secure systems,
- typical attacks on secure ISNs,
- promising areas for the development of network security technologies,
- current problems in information security science and the role and place of information protection in networks when addressing comprehensive information security problems.

They must know the following:

- methodological and technological foundations of comprehensive security for ISNs, .
- threats and methods of violating ISN security,
- formal models lying at the foundation of ISN protection systems,
- standards for evaluating ISN security and their theoretical foundations,
- methods and means of building and operating secure ISNs,
- methods and means of verifying and analyzing the reliability of secure ISNs,
- methodological and technological foundations for ensuring the information security of network-automated systems,
- threats and methods of violating the information security of network-automated systems,
- physical processes in technical means and systems that lead to leakage of secure information,
- typical models of attacks aimed at overcoming the protection of network-automated systems, conditions under which they might be carried out, possible consequences, and means of prevention,

- role of the human factor in ensuring network security,
- possibilities, means, and rules for applying basic software and hardware means of protecting information in networks,
- principles for the operation of basic secure network protocols,
- foundations for the application of firewalls for network protection,
- rules for setting network security policy,
- standards for evaluating secure network systems and their theoretical foundations,
- methods and means of designing, constructing, and evaluating secure network systems,
- conception of the engineering-technical protection of information,
- basic principles and methods of information protection,
- basic guiding and regulatory documents on the engineering-technical protection of information,
- procedures for organizing the engineering-technical protection of information.

They must know how to

- analyze ISNs from the standpoint of ensuring computer security,
- develop security models and policies using well-known approaches, methods, means, and theoretical foundations,
- apply standards for evaluating the security of ISNs in analyzing and designing information security systems for them,
- implement information protection systems in ISNs in accordance with standards for evaluating ISN security,
- analyze network automated systems from the standpoint of ensuring information security,

- develop network security models and policies using well-known approaches, methods, means, and theoretical foundations,
- apply standards for evaluating secure network systems in analyzing and designing systems to protect information in automated systems,
- apply secure protocols and firewalls necessary for implementing information security systems in networks,
- take measures to counter network security threats using various software and hardware means of security in accordance with rules for their application,
- create information security systems in automated systems in accordance with standards for assessing system security,
- identify threats and technical channels for information leakage,
- describe (model) security targets and information security threats,
- apply the most effective methods and means of engineering-technical protection for information,
- monitor the effectiveness of security measures.

They must have the following skills:

- work with ISNs for distributed computing and information processing,
- work with ISN documentation,
- use of criteria for evaluating ISN security,
- construction of formal models of ISN information security systems,
- construction and operation of computer networks,
- design of secure networks,
- comprehensive analysis and evaluation of network security,
- work with means of interface support with various categories of database management system users,

- work with database management systems on various platforms,
- develop and manage databases,
- work with means of ensuring database management system integrity,
- work with means of ensuring database confidentiality,
- work as database security administrator,
- device-based evaluation of the energy parameters of side radiation from technical means and systems,
- engineering calculation of the parameters of the controlled zone.

By completing their studies at the university, the specialists acquire theoretical information and practical skills in combating computer terrorism and can independently develop enterprise information security policies based on comprehensive integrated solutions, conduct scientific research, and develop new methods for countering cyber crime.

Cyber crime is not restricted to crimes committed on the Internet. It extends to all forms of crimes committed in the sphere where information, information resources, and information technology are the targets, means, or tools of crime. With the current growth of cyber crime, which presents a danger to people's lives and welfare, threatens the security of all states, and undermines trust in government institutions, it is vitally important to ensure protection against this type of criminal activity. Therefore, we currently need to enhance the level of international coordination of scientific research on preventing and countering acts of cyber crime.

First, we need to conduct scientific research on developing a single conceptual framework. We must develop and amend legislative, regulatory, and legal documents for this type of crime, including those governing international activities. Studies on creating modern technologies for detecting and deterring network attacks and neutralizing criminal impacts on information resources are of the highest significance. In order to accomplish this, we need to develop plans for joint research on countering cyber crime. Themes for such plans could include the following:

- organizing exchange programs for undergraduate and graduate students, instructors, and researchers in the leading higher educational institutions of the Russian Federation and the United States,
- creating a single conceptual framework, terms, and definitions regarding the development of means and systems for countering cyber crime and cyber terrorism,
- creating a set of recommendations for government legislative organs on studying and amending regulations and laws regarding this type of crime, including those governing international law enforcement activities,
- creating modern theoretical methods and applied technologies for detecting and deterring network attacks and neutralizing criminal impacts on information resources.

Cyber Crime and Security

The information infrastructure is increasingly under attack by cyber criminals. The number, cost, and sophistication of attacks are increasing at alarming rates. They threaten the substantial and growing reliance of commerce, governments, and the public upon the information infrastructure to conduct business, carry messages, and process information. Some forms of attack also pose a growing threat to the public, and to critical infrastructures. Much has been said about the threat posed by cyber crime, including terrorism, but little has been done to protect against what has become the most costly form of such crime: transnational attacks on computers and the information infrastructure. Measures thus far adopted by the private and public sectors fail to provide an adequate level of security against these attacks. The Internet and other aspects of the information infrastructure are inherently transnational.

A transnational response sufficient to meet these transnational challenges is an immediate and compelling necessity. The challenge of controlling transnational cyber crime requires a full range of responses, including both voluntary and legally mandated cooperation. Both the private and public sectors are now actively pursuing transnational initiatives, ranging in form from voluntary, informal exchange of information to a multilateral treaty proposed by the Council of Europe (COE) to establish common crimes and a substantial degree of cooperation in the investigation and prosecution of such crimes. Public declarations and voluntary international cooperation have no doubt helped in dealing with transnational attacks. Funds are being made available to enhance the technological capacities of national law enforcement personnel engaged in cyber investigations, and through international cooperation, some attacks have been traced, and some perpetrators have been punished. But public pronouncements, educational programs, and voluntary cooperation are not enough.

The sources of many transnational attacks have never been determined, and perpetrators of many of the most damaging attacks, even when identified, go unpunished. A great disparity exists, moreover, in the legal and technological capacity of states to meet the challenges of preventing, investigating, and prosecuting cyber crime. An effective program against transnational cyber crime will require legal cooperation among states that involves the enforcement of agreed standards of conduct. A reasonably broad consensus exists among states concerning many forms of conduct that should be treated as cyber crime within national borders. This consensus must be translated into a legal regime in which all states that are connected to the Internet prohibit forms of conduct widely regarded as destructive or improper. In addition, much remains to be done to encourage and, as soon as practicable, to require states to adopt common positions to facilitate cooperation in investigation, the preservation of evidence, and extradition. States must establish and designate cross-patent agencies to deal with transnational issues, and to cooperate with counterparts throughout the world.

To develop and secure the universal adoption of technological and policy standards to defend against, prosecute, and deter cyber crime and terrorism, states should create an international agency, along the lines of the International Civil Aviation Organization (ICAO) but designed to reflect the particular needs and nature of the cyber world. International cooperation must include an effective program to upgrade the capacities of states that lack the technological resources to cooperate in a comprehensive international regime. These measures, though far-reaching by comparison with current policies, can be fashioned to maximize private-sector participation and control, to ensure that privacy and other human rights are not adversely affected and so as not to impinge on the national security activities and interests of States Parties.

Scope of the Problem [h]

A summary of the problem of cyber crime and terrorism was presented at the Stanford Conference by Peter G. Neumann, principal scientist at the Computer Science Laboratory, SRI International. He stated: We are becoming massively interconnected. Whether we like it or not, we must coexist with people and systems of unknown and unidentifiable trustworthiness (including unidentifiable hostile parties), within the U.S. and elsewhere. Our problems have become international as well as national, and cannot be solved only locally. Computer-related systems fall on their own, even in the absence of intentional misuse.

However, misuse by outsiders and insiders and the presence of malicious code . . . present some enormously difficult challenges that are not being adequately addressed at present. . . Computers and communications are increasingly being used in almost every imaginable application. However, our computer-communication systems are not dependably secure, reliable, or robust. Reliability, fault tolerance, security, and overall system survivability are all closely interrelated.

There are fundamental vulnerabilities in the existing information system infrastructures, and serious risks that those vulnerabilities will be exploited—with possibly very severe effects. Our national infrastructures depend not only on our interconnected information systems and networks, but also on the public switched network, the air-traffic control systems, the power grids, and many associated control systems—which themselves depends heavily on computers and communications. Global problems can result from seemingly isolated events, as exhibited by the early power-grid collapses, the 1980 ARPANET collapse, and the 1990 long-distance collapse—all of which began with single-point failures. Our defenses against a variety of adversities—from intentional misuse to hardware flaws and software bugs to environmental disturbances—are fundamentally inadequate. Our defenses against large-scale coordinated attacks are even more inadequate. . . . The risks of cyber terrorism and cyber crime vastly outweigh our abilities to control those risks by technological means, although technology can help and should be vigorously pursued. There are many important problems, such as providing better defenses against denial of service attacks, outsiders, and insiders. Socio-politico-economic measures must also be considered.

The costs of cyber crime are difficult to measure, but by any reasonable standard they are substantial and growing exponentially. The most comprehensive available source of data on costs is compiled annually by the Computer Security Institute (CSI), with the participation of the FBI's Computer Intrusion Squad. The CSI survey for 2000, edited by Stanford Conference participant Richard Power, is based on 643 responses from computer security practitioners in U.S. corporations and government agencies. It establishes that computer security breaches are widespread, diverse, and costly. Respondents are investing heavily in a variety of security technologies, at a cost estimated by the International Data Corporation to grow from $2 billion in 1999 to $7.4 billion in 2003.

These investments are dramatic evidence of the huge costs being inflicted by cyber crime. To these amounts must be added the costs of cyber crime insurance, a new coverage for an expanding market. In spite of the costly defensive measures thus far adopted, CSI/FBI survey respondents experiencing unauthorized use of their computer systems increased from 42 percent in 1996 to 70 percent in 2000; those not experiencing such events declined from 37 percent to 18 percent in the same period. Only 37 percent of all attacks reported in 1996 involved Internet connections; in 2000 this proportion increased to 59 percent, with a corresponding decline in insider attacks. So far, the most serious category of reported financial loss has been through "theft of proprietary information", which appears to include attacks that result in the theft of financial data. Other categories of substantial losses include fraud, virus attacks, denial of service, and sabotage.

Estimating the monetary damage inflicted by cyber crime is difficult but worth attempting and particularly valuable for tracking relative costs from year to year. The CSI/FBI surveys for the last four years report total losses of about $100,000,000 in 1997, increasing to some $266,000,000 in 2000. Stephen J. Lukasik has found a pattern reflecting a trend in which costs have essentially doubled each year. This progression has been shattered by costs associated with the "I Love You" virus of May 2000, estimated at between $1 and $10 billion. Although the costs reported by respondents include lost time, and may be exaggerated, the reluctance of companies to acknowledge losses tends to result in underreporting. The overall numbers are useful indicators when these uncertainties are taken into account. At a purely technical level, all messages on the Internet are broken down into "packets" that separate and travel through available routers and servers located throughout the world.

Cyber crime goes beyond this technical, transnational dimension and involves senders who deliberately fashion their attacks and other crimes to exploit the potential weaknesses present in the infrastructure's transnational nature. These weaknesses include: (1) a worldwide target pool of computers and users to victimize, or to exploit in denial-of-service or other attacks, which enables attackers to do more damage with no more effort than would be necessary in attacking computers or users in a single state; and (2) the widespread disparities among states, in the legal, regulatory, or policy environment concerning cyber crime, and the lack of a sufficiently high degree of international cooperation in prosecuting and deterring such crime. The most damaging cyber attacks thus far experienced have been transnational, originating in many different countries and aimed at computers everywhere. Here are some prominent examples:

- The so-called "Phonemasters", a "loosely-knit", "12-member" international "hacking ring" headed by Jonathan Bosanac of Rancho Santa Fe, California (near San Diego), who, using the online name "The Gatsby", developed a method for gaining access to telephone networks (such as MCI, WorldCom, Sprint, and AT&T), credit-reporting databases (such as Equifax), and even the FBI's own National Crime Information Center, which they utilized in a number of countries.

"The breadth of their monkey-wrenching was staggering; at various times they could eavesdrop on phone calls, compromise secure databases, and redirect communications at will. They had access to portions of the national power grid, air-traffic–control systems and had hacked their way into a digital cache of unpublished telephone numbers at the White House. . . . They often worked in stealth, and avoided bragging about their exploits.... Their customers included ... the Sicilian Mafia. According to FBI estimates, the gang accounted for about $1.85 million in business losses".

- David L. Smith, a New Jersey programmer, pleaded guilty in December 1999 of creating the "Melissa" computer virus and using an xrated website to spread it through cyber space via e-mail in March 1999, where it "rampaged personal, government, and corporate computers around the world", "caused worldwide devastation", and was estimated to have done $80 million (or more) in damages.
- From December 1999 through April 2000, five hackers in Moscow stole more than 5,400 credit card numbers belonging to Russians and foreigners from Internet retailers, pocketing more than $630,000 until arrested. The incident pointed up the threat that "Eastern European fraudsters continue to pose . . . for all card issuers, even those with no direct business in the region.
- In 1995–96, from his home in Buenos Aires, a twenty-one year- old Argentine student, Julio Cesar Ardita, "slipped through the security of . . . systems at Harvard University's Faculty of Arts and Science, the U.S. Defense Department, the U.S. Naval Command, the San Diego-based Control and Ocean Surveillance Center, the Washington-based Naval Research Lab, NASA's Ames Research Center and Jet Propulsion Laboratory, and the Los Alamos National Laboratory

in New Mexico". His actions were not criminal in Argentina, and his extradition to the U.S. was refused, although he later surrendered voluntarily.

- Reports of persistent, international attacks on official government websites throughout the world in 1999–2000 appeared with great frequency. Some of the notable ones include: (1) Hackers breaking into the website of the Ministry of Finance of Romania in November 1999 to introduce bogus taxes and to change the official exchange rate of the national currency. (2) Recurrent Taiwan-China "hacker" wars in 1999 and 2000 in which attackers broke into various government and business websites, penetrating protective firewall software with seeming ease. (3) Frequent transnational attacks on sensitive military and other national security networks of many governments, as well as public service websites/ infrastructure at the national and local levels.
- The "I Love You" virus was propagated from the Philippines in May 2000. Estimates of the damage it caused range up to $10 billion, mostly in lost work time. U.S. investigators pressed to have the suspects in the attack—computer programming students from the Philippines — arrested and prosecuted and Filipino investigators attempted to do so under a 1998 law prohibiting the use of "access devices", such as credit cards, to defraud. The Chief State Counsel concluded, however, that this law could not be used, since "the intention of a computer hacker . . . is not to defraud but to destroy files". The Philippines adopted a law punishing those who spread computer viruses with up to three years' imprisonment and fines from $2,350 to a maximum "commensurate" with the damage caused.

The new law will not apply retroactively, however, so this costly act has gone unpunished. The open and defiant manner in which hackers currently operate reflects the weakness of the legal, defensive, and investigative capacities of the current system. They plan and discuss proposed forms of attack on websites, exchanging ideas and comments. These activities enabled Thomas A. Longstaff of the Computer Emergency Response Team (CERT)/Coordination Center (CC), Software Engineering Institute (SEI) at Carnegie Mellon University to predict at the Stanford Conference that a new and very harmful, distributed form of denial of service attack was the next likely threat. He described precisely the method that was used by hackers in the subsequent worldwide February 2000 attacks—on CNN, eBay, Amazon.com, and others—to plant programs in computers around the globe that enabled hackers to send so many messages to particular IP addresses that they were rendered inoperable.

Though law enforcement personnel were able to anticipate this type of attack, they were not able to prevent it, and security personnel at CNN, Yahoo!, Amazon.com, and others could not defend against it. After several months of investigation, in April 2000, the Royal Canadian Mounted Police (RCMP) arrested a Montreal teenager on suspicion of having caused the CNN and other shutdowns, but the extent to which the culprit (or culprits) may be successfully prosecuted is in doubt, and deterrence of those not caught and punished, as well as of other would-be attackers, seems unlikely. These troubling failures stem from serious weaknesses in the authority and capacities of states to protect cyber systems from attacks.

Escalating Dangers of Attacks

New forms of denial-of-service and other destructive types of attack, such as the "I Love You" virus, have been openly discussed, or uncovered, and cyber copycats continue to be active, replicating or modifying attacks into yet more dangerous forms—such as the "Killer Resume" follow-on to "I Love You"—with virtually complete impunity. Knowledgeable individuals have anticipated new forms of cyber attack that may be even more costly than prior ones. For example, a virus similar to "I Love You", called "Timofonica" (Spanish for "phone prank"), that has been intercepted in Europe is designed to attack cell phones, and can easily be altered to attack pagers and other hand-held devices such as Palm Pilots and Microsoft Pocket PC computers. Vincent Gullatto, director of the AVERT antivirus lab at the San Jose, California–based Network Associates, which makes McAfee antivirus software, has noted that, once hand-held devices become sophisticated enough to use "miniature automation programs known as macros, the potential to wreak havoc will grow".

Similarly, as reliance on wireless transmission increases, the danger posed by forms of jamming will grow. An even more threatening development is predicted by Israeli computer security expert Ofer Elzam. In addition to "an increasing number of viruses, worms, and vandals" he expects will populate the cyber world, he anticipates "something far more lethal and threatening—the Trojan horse". These devices, Elzam states, "are smart spying machines or engines that can sit in a PC for years and give anyone access to the most personal information stored on the computer", without creating any sign of damage: "Things are going to get much, much worse in every field of Internet security", in part because "the more complicated things get the more holes there are". It was reported on June 18, 2000, that an undisclosed number of America Online (AOL) employee accounts had been compromised by a Trojan horse. The trend toward increasingly dangerous attacks is well established. The danger of cyber attacks extends to matters of intense public concern.

Cyber terrorism has not yet resulted in any public disaster, but attacks on the websites and cyber systems of public agencies are common. Favorite targets include defense and intelligence agencies. Although for the most part these attacks are amateurish and are blocked successfully or result in only superficial damage to websites, a significant number have shut down websites, and some have penetrated much further. To classify such attacks as pranks merely because they seem politically aimless is mistaken. Politically aimless conventional attacks on public infrastructure are an established form of terrorism—the hallmark of anarchists. Where such attacks are intended to, and do, causes serious damage, they should, and will, be treated as terrorist acts. Furthermore, when states sponsor such attacks, they take on an additional political dimension; the FBI's National Infrastructure Protection Center (NIPC) appears to believe that state-sponsored acts have already been undertaken. Among the nation's critical infrastructure most vulnerable to cyber attacks are transportation (especially air travel), power, defense, water, and medical care. The Stanford Conference focused on the dangers to civil aviation as exemplifying this danger.

A significant weakness in the current system is the disparity among individual states in the laws and practices necessary to permit them to investigate and prosecute cyber crime effectively. Though states may have agreements in place to cooperate against and extradite or prosecute for conventional crimes involving the *use* of computers, no international agreement yet exists on such cooperation for criminal attacks on computers and the information infrastructure. In several highly significant cases, investigations and prosecutions have been stymied by this deficiency. In 1996, Argentine hacker Julio Cesar Ardita escaped relatively unscathed after having compromised numerous sensitive and proprietary computer networks, including some in the U.S. Department of Defense (DOD), from his Buenos Aires home. Argentina refused to extradite Ardita to the U.S., because his intrusion did not constitute an extraditable crime. Another very serious series of attacks on national security sites in the U.S. and Israel—subsequently code-named "Solar Sunrise" by the DOD—was conducted by "a trio of teenage hackers" in February 1998.

These individuals were identified and were ultimately prosecuted for their criminal conduct, but not without significant difficulties encountered by U.S. and Israeli investigators owing to the lack of established commitments and procedures. Boaz Gutman, chief superintendent of Computer Crime Division, National Anti-Fraud Investigation Unit, Israeli National Police, detailed some of the difficulties at the Stanford Conference. He noted that, though voluntary cooperation is better than none, the lack of national commitments led to confusion and resentment in the Solar Sunrise case, especially when U.S. personnel became intensely involved in the Israeli investigative and judicial processes. In spite of encountering difficulties like these, the U.S. and other states were no better prepared when the "I Love You" virus was propagated from a state where deliberate computer attacks were not even illegal. Even states with advanced economies, and heavily reliant on information technology, have failed to take steps necessary to protect themselves and others from attacks, thereby becoming weak links in the chain of security, or places where criminals and terrorists are able to attack other states with impunity.

In his keynote presentation at the Stanford Conference, Raisuke Miyawaki, chairman of Ochanomizu Associates in Tokyo, explained how and why Japan had failed to take Internet security seriously, and the risks this created for Japan's economy and for users worldwide: The ease with which the origins of cyber attacks can be hidden, and the fact that cyber attacks on one nation can come from anywhere on the globe, mean that cyber crime and cyber terrorism are truly international threats. And Japan's relatively lax cyber defenses mean that Japan is a potentially weak link in the global economic and security architecture in the event of a major cyber crime, cyber terrorist, or cyber military attack on Japan.

Miyawaki reviewed the rapid increase in illegal network access cases in Japan, as well as several unexplained or unsolved incidents involving breakins at the national computer research centers, a shutdown of parts of Japan Railway's system in Tokyo, and several shutdowns of the Tokyo Stock Exchange, all caused by computer problems of unknown origin: The uncertainty surrounding many of these incidents is troubling. When such network systems crash, they are restored by the company that installed the system, and the problem is not examined by a third party with a special interest in cyber security. Also, unless the crash affects an ATM or other highly visible network that affects customers or everyday citizens, companies don't publicize their computer problems— and, it is said, there are many such incidents that companies don't publicize.

The program Miyawaki recommends to deal with Japan's cyber security deficiencies includes the passage of laws making unauthorized access to computer networks illegal (adopted in 1999) and authorizing wiretapping in computer cases (effective August 2000). He also supports Japan's increased involvement in the private-sector and voluntary government programs under way. At the Stanford Conference, he stressed the need for international cooperation, through harmonization of laws and technical issues, emergency response mechanisms, and intelligence sharing.

He concluded that, to act effectively against the growing cyber threats, states must in effect form a cyber-defense alliance: The goals and tactics and behavior of cyber rogue nations, cyber criminals, and cyber terrorists are threats to all the world's nations. We of the world's leading democratic nations must examine what has helped us work successfully together in the past, and take lessons from that in preparing for the new era of cyber crime and cyber warfare. Perhaps, we must even create a technologically linked "cyber-defense alliance". And as in so many other matters, the day-today sharing of intelligence and information on cyber-security, and the steady building of trust between nations and national officials, will be the bedrock on which international cooperation against cyber crime and cyber terrorism must be built. The pertinence of Miyawaki's warnings about Japan's vulnerability was fully borne out in January 2000, when a series of humiliating raids on government websites by hackers prompted emergency conditions. His insights are universally applicable.

Vulnerability of Existing Programs

Several participants at the Stanford Conference observed that current computer systems are inherently vulnerable. Robert E. Kahn, president of the Corporation for National Research Initiatives (CNRI), explained that existing systems are unstable and subject to spontaneous failure, even as they are increasingly relied upon for sensitive functions, requiring ever higher levels of complexity. SRI's Peter G. Neumann believes that the unreliability of current technology is by far the greatest danger to cyber security. Vulnerabilities are regularly exploited by hackers and other criminals, and the widespread dominance of highly vulnerable Microsoft programs and services has created a situation of grave risk. Most software designers, concentrating on satisfying customers seeking greater ease of use and functions requiring greater complexity, regard reliability and security as secondary matters. Enhanced security in cyber systems requires enhanced reliability and stability, not merely quick-fixes in which vulnerabilities to specific types of attacks are eliminated on a case-by-case basis through design modifications.

The vulnerability of the information infrastructure also stems from the insufficiency of current security measures. The costly "I Love You" virus was "a relatively simple Visual Basic script" that operated much like the "Melissa" virus of the year before, according to Michael J. Miller of *PC Magazine:* "Melissa was enough of a warning. We shouldn't be going through this again". Microsoft provided a fix for the "Melissa" virus, but since it did not change the components targeted by "Melissa", it was still relatively easy to run scripts affecting the settings in Microsoft's widely used Outlook, Outlook Express, Exchange, and Windows. Microsoft left these components unchanged for the same reasons they were designed to be accessible: "convenience for users and letting corporations create complex scripts that tie Outlook together with other Microsoft applications".

As Miller points out, while antivirus makers found the "I Love You" virus and came up with a fix "fairly quickly", this was "not good enough in this era of Internet time. By the time the virus definitions were ready, the virus had already spread. The antivirus makers must come up with a more generic way of blocking suspicious-looking scripts before they've spread all over the world". Miller also observes how many computer users have failed to implement even the limited security measures that are available for their protection, creating dangers not only for themselves, but also for others, from attacks designed to exploit their inadequate protections.

"Cultural" Vulnerabilities

A subtle aspect of the "culture" of businesses that operate in cyber space is their reluctance to cooperate openly in efforts to suppress cyber crime. The business sector, as Donn B. Parker of Atomic Tangerine (a spin-off of SRI International) explained in his submission to the Stanford Conference, although increasingly reliant on cyber commerce and support, has significantly different incentives from law enforcement with regard to the handling of cyber crime, and consequently with respect to the sharing of information concerning such crime: Security is a fundamentally different issue for business than it is for government because the goals of business and government are fundamentally different. Business survives and grows by managing risks, including security risks, to achieve profit and productivity and views security as a necessary enabler to achieve its goals. Security is balanced with other objectives and made as transparent as possible to avoid interfering with or constraining these objectives. Greater security is often promoted and implemented in businesses when it is needed to meet customer expectations or regulator requirements, when losses are occurring, or in attempts to meet standards of due care to avoid negligence.

Competing businesses have hidden agendas and sensitive security and loss experience information that would cause them harm if revealed. Business organization public affairs experts reveal cyber crime and security information to the public only when necessary and beneficial under controlled well-timed circumstances that minimize the negative impact on business objectives. Governments, and especially military and law enforcement departments, in contrast to business, have security as their goal, and it is enforced by law and motivated by significant rewards and penalties. Legislatures, watchdog groups, and news media discover and publicly report losses and security failures within governments, and incidents are vigorously prosecuted. The relationship between business and government organizations is not on a level playing field. Businesses are allowed to fail; governments are not. Governments have hidden agendas that include criminal investigations of businesses and their staffs. Governments may be sued only with their consent. Many government people are sworn officers of the law, have security clearances, and must keep their crime-fighting activities and intent secret.

Governments also have the duty to protect their indigenous infrastructure businesses in the support of commerce and national security and are often frustrated in their efforts to assist reluctant businesses in achieving more effective security. For example, businesses learn from experience that reporting a suspected hightech crime to law enforcers may result in taking great amounts of valuable employees' time away from business goals to assist in gathering evidence, giving depositions, and acting as witnesses in court appearances. As Parker concludes, "It is necessary to understand the cultures of businesses and governments to achieve effective security information sharing and usage among them".

One clear implication of Parker's insights is that cooperation between private and public cyber security experts should occur through voluntary affiliations of businesses, at the national and international level. Parker noted several such efforts, including the International Information Integrity Institute (I-4) and the Information Security Forum (ISF), which serve the information security staffs of many of the world's largest corporations and several governments. Significantly, many of these organizations include present and former government officials, including former law enforcement personnel, who participate in what Parker observes is in effect an "old boys network" and have a high degree of mutual trust. In addition, other more explicit alliances have been developed between business and government.

Parker considers these groups—especially those providing informal exchanges— as the most effective vehicles available for partly overcoming the conflicting interests between businesses and governments, which otherwise limit the likelihood of robust cooperation. He believes they should be allowed to evolve internationally, as a supplement to more formal methods of communication: The informal method partly solves or at least sorts out the international dichotomy problem of global businesses interacting with national governments' entities. It provides a means for citizens of each country that are employed by international infrastructure businesses to interact with their own governments that may, in turn, share the information obtained with other governments. The reluctance of private-sector cyber users to cooperate with governments also suggests that governments cannot responsibly expect the private sector to solve the cyber security problem. Speeches and congressional testimony by U.S. Attorney General Janet Reno and FBI Director Louis J. Freeh called upon businesses for assistance in dealing with cyber crime.

The response of the Internet Alliance, among others, makes clear that the private sector will reject any effort to overreach and enlist businesses in law enforcement. Businesses will cooperate, but the private sector cannot be expected to perform roles traditionally performed by law enforcement. The cyber world's culture in fact includes a very significant element of users and participants who strongly oppose virtually any form of government activity. As Stephen J. Lukasik explains, the Internet is largely fashioned and run by private-sector experts, some of whom look upon a government role in creating standards mandating or enabling cooperation in law enforcement as a cure more dangerous than the disease of cyber crime.

Even as established an organization as the Internet Alliance, composed of representatives from large and powerful cyber and cyber-related businesses such as AOL, AT&T, eBay, Microsoft, Netscape, and Prodigy, has argued that all transnational efforts to control cyber crime should be based on *voluntary* cooperation. In testimony before Congress, businesses have emphasized what Congress should *not* require: We must not pass laws of dubious enforceability, risking erosion of the public's confidence in law enforcement and in the Internet. We must resist overreaching, even in the name of security, and make certain that constitutional and statutory protections in the investigation and prosecution of Internet crimes are observed. . . . Industry cannot and must not be made an agent of law enforcement.

The notion that voluntary activity alone can create adequate security for cyber activities is simply untenable. First, it is likely that at the national level cyber crime would be even more prevalent and costly had the U.S.

government left the area unpoliced; the domestic laws so far adopted that make cyber attacks criminal have at least provided a vehicle by which to arrest—and thereby to stop, punish, and deter— cyber attacks designed to steal, defraud, and destroy. The great majority of users—commercial, educational, individual—favor such laws. Effective government on the international level also depends on adopting laws setting universal standards for misconduct, authorizing investigatory cooperation and extradition, and developing and standardizing technologically advanced methods for detecting, blocking, tracking, and deterring prohibited conduct.

A much broader attack on the regulation of cyber space than that advanced by the business community is based on the notion that cyber space cannot or, in any event, should not be regulated by government. John Perry Barlow's claim in "A Declaration of the Independence of Cyberspace" is that cyber space is "an act of nature", based on collective actions, and beyond the borders of any state. This philosophical effort has been supplemented with legal arguments based on a claimed lack of jurisdiction to regulate cyber space. Both the philosophical and the legal claims are thoroughly addressed by Neil W. Netanel, who explains how "courts and legislators have increasingly applied real world, state promulgated law to cyberspace activity, steadily constricting the domain of semiautonomous cyberspace rulemaking", and why these developments, in principle, reflect sound results based on traditional liberal democratic theory.

Legislators and courts are rapidly coming to regard cyber activities as analogous to other activities already regarded as permitting prescription, investigation, and enforcement on any of the traditional bases for legal regulation. Resistance to government involvement in cyber regulation is not, however, entirely based on anarchistic preferences or paranoid fantasies; U.S. government actions have undermined trust and strengthened the case for purely voluntary initiatives. The U.S. government has, for example, exerted much effort in attempting to restrict the effectiveness and distribution of advanced encryption, though encryption is widely regarded as one of the most effective tools available for the protection of cyber security and privacy.

When the government appeared to have lost its battle to prevent the free transfer and use of encryption, it tried to convince Congress, and later the Internet Engineering Task Force (IETF)—which establishes voluntary standards for Internet Protocols (IPs)—to include "trap doors" in computer security programs so as to enable the government to pursue criminal investigations more easily. The IETF refused to do so. The implementation of a search engine injudiciously called "Carnivore "enhanced distrust, although the system seems potentially consistent with legal standards. Distrust on the international level has been generated by the COE's Draft Convention on Cyber crime, the most recent version of which (at the time of this writing) was released on November 19, 2000.

This draft—the twenty-fourth since the exercise was initiated—includes coverage of copyright offenses, despite the lack of international consensus on the scope and forms of protection of the many types of works potentially covered. The draft also specifies the types of cooperation that may be required under it, not only from States Parties, but also from Internet Service Providers (ISPs) and other entities and individuals. Among other things, ISPs may be required to conduct real time surveillance of customers (an earlier draft had required them to store at least forty days of customer data), and all entities and individuals could be required to provide passwords (an earlier draft would have used technology to identify each computer on the Internet).

Criticisms of the COE's draft convention, which has been substantially revised in recent months, are in many respects unwarranted, and fail to take into account that all the measures it proposes are "subject to the conditions and safeguards provided for under the domestic law of the Party concerned, with due regard for the adequate protection of human rights and, where applicable, the proportionality of the measure to the nature and circumstances of the offence". But the COE's effort has evoked negative reactions because of its scope and because it seeks to establish standards without allowing for an open process in which the private sector is able fully to participate.

Widespread distrust of the intentions of commercial entities and merchandising groups with regard to privacy also exists among experts and consumers. Commercial entities and service providers have unilaterally developed and used intrusive software and practices that fail to inform consumers adequately or to provide effective methods for opting out of information-collecting programs. Congress and the Federal Trade Commission (FTC) are considering restrictions on merchandising and consumer tracking aimed at protecting privacy.

Finally, private-sector decisions to maintain proprietary systems and programs designed for user convenience and accessibility rather than for security are themselves a root cause of cyber vulnerability; the private sector could greatly enhance cyber security by reordering design priorities, without any government involvement. An enhanced government role need not, however, be one that requires significantly greater domestic powers or more intrusive measures; rather, the need is for international cooperation to create common standards and practices. In attempting to satisfy these objectives, it is imperative to take into account the legitimate concerns of those who seek to avoid conferring inappropriate or unnecessary powers on governments to regulate and to intrude upon cyber systems, to preserve as far as practicable private-sector control of this uniquely productive and dynamic sector, and to avoid impinging upon national security interests and activities.

As Lawrence Lessig has explained, it is illusory to believe that the cyber world cannot be regulated, and to expect that it will not be regulated, for purposes of facilitating commerce, enhancing security, and—one hopes—protecting freedom and privacy. Regulatory power exists in the "code" that governs all cyber activities. But the scope of regulation will depend on the measures adopted, and it is on that front that the battle over the future of the cyber world must be fought.

Fashioning a Solution

A program to deal with cyber crime should be based on its characteristics and be limited to the steps needed to address identified weaknesses. The Stanford Conference made clear to many of us the need for some form of international cooperation. Our effort here is to determine what sort of cooperation is called for, and how best to provide it. First, the transnational nature of cyber crime calls for a transnational response. The actions of individual states are insufficient. Affected states need to agree on the kinds of conduct that should be proscribed and adopt laws making such conduct criminal.

Considerable consensus also exists on problems of regulating some conventional crimes in which computers are used, including cyber-related child pornography; but as points out, on many such crimes major differences of political outlook would make a universal agreement impossible. Still, the exclusion of many conventional crimes involving the use of computers from an international agreement is less important than ensuring comprehensive coverage of harmful conduct aimed at computers and their operation, with a commitment to impose substantial penalties. In addition to ensuring universal condemnation of serious forms of misconduct, any effective system for punishing cyber crime will require the full range of cooperation afforded by states to each other in mutual legal assistance and extradition treaties.

The nature of cyber crime also requires national commitments to undertake special efforts to search for, secure, and preserve usable evidence. The speed with which cyber-related evidence can be lost, and the frequency with which it will be located in foreign jurisdictions, makes it necessary to have the consent of states in advance to some forms of searches that reach into their territories, as well as agreements to assist in seizing equipment and other assets and to provide usable evidence and other forms of cooperation. It is insufficient, moreover, for states merely to agree to perform conventional services for each other. They will have to be prepared to implement technologically adequate measures, as these are developed. Participants at the Stanford Conference described efforts under way to enhance the capacity of users, providers, investigators, and prosecutors to deal with the challenges posed by cyber attacks.

Securing agreement from all states connected to the international information infrastructure for these far-reaching forms of cooperation will certainly be more difficult than securing agreement on the conduct to be proscribed. No multilateral consensus yet exists on providing legal assistance and extradition in cyber cases. States must be convinced that such cooperation is in their best interests, as in the areas of civil aviation, international banking, money laundering, and narcotics. To overcome claims or fears of improper extraterritorial activities, states should agree that all measures undertaken in pursuing a cyber investigation will be performed in a manner consistent with the law of the state that is asked to perform such services. To overcome claims or fears that cyber investigations or prosecutions could compromise domestic constitutional protections, no state should be required by the international commitments it undertakes to compromise its national standards of conduct.

In addition, some states, owing to the so-called "cyber divide", will be unable to provide the assistance required by an international agreement. It is very much in the interests of all states to guard against "weak links" in cyber crime enforcement (that could be exploited by attackers). States should agree to a program to assist those states with legitimate needs in this regard, as international agencies do in a number of other arenas requiring technological expertise. Because cyber systems and programs are designed with efficiency and ease of use rather than security as the primary objective, states should consider adopting technological measures that go beyond investigative cooperation. Technological breakthroughs to enhance protection against and to improve investigation and prosecution of, cyber crimes should be encouraged and widely implemented.

To achieve such cooperation will require overcoming the antiregulatory perspectives of private-sector participants who have built and continue to develop the information infrastructure. One necessary response to this resistance is to build private-sector control into the process of developing solutions and formulating standards and practices for enhancing cyber security. In addition, the proposed convention seeks to ensure not only that national standards of state conduct related to human rights are preserved, but also that States Parties will provide certain minimum due process rights in the arrest, charging, prosecution, and extradition of suspects, analogous to protections widely regarded as required by international law.

Finally, the Draft Convention explicitly makes it in applicable to national security activities. U.S. officials are justifiably concerned that an international agreement might lead to unwarranted restrictions on defense-related activities. This possibility can be successfully averted, however, as in other treaties potentially bearing upon national security. A program based on these principles and proposals should eventually overcome resistance to a multilateral convention to deal with cyber crime and terrorism. Escalating damage and the inadequacy of current efforts are increasing the pressure on governments—and through them on ISPs, major companies, and private standard-setting bodies—to respond effectively.

Efforts by governments reacting to recent major attacks have focused on seeking (or in the case of legislators offering) new powers, such as stiffer sentences, the right to arrest and/or search without prior judicial approval, and other inadequate and damaging measures. Knowledgeable legislators and industry leaders should eventually turn to more useful and appropriate options.

Apart from the dangers of increasing police powers, relying on prosecutors to plan and implement solutions in a highly technical area in which private control is regarded as a substantial advantage may well be ineffective even in satisfying the need for better security. Those who support adoption of a multilateral approach to deal with this quintessentially transnational problem must be encouraged by the fact that states have consistently adopted multilateral solutions to deal with technologies that affect populations across national boundaries. As technology advances, new technologies with transnational impact that require transnational controls have repeatedly led to multilateral arrangements; agencies have been created to deal with such international areas as air travel, shipping, and telecommunications.

Transnational needs have demanded transnational solutions, which have been satisfied through international agreements on principles, standards, and practices, often developed and proposed by specialized international agencies. States make such arrangements based not upon ideological considerations but on considerations of safety, productivity, and efficiency. They have done so, moreover, with no sacrifice of national sovereignty, and almost entirely on the basis of consensus decisions determined by both self-interest and reciprocity. It may, in fact, be a mistake to continue to place primary responsibility for coping with cyber crime within the scope of agencies oriented toward criminal investigations, such as the FBI. Prosecutorial agencies are concerned with developing information for their own use, and tracing and capturing criminals. They are not necessarily going to use information to warn the public of attacks or to develop policy and/or technological solutions aimed at making successful attacks less likely.

The information infrastructure faces analogous challenges. Its security and efficiency will be materially increased through international implementation of principles, standards, and practices specifically designed for this field of activity. The optimum manner of achieving these objectives in this particular field is a multilateral treaty with the necessary commitments to cooperate in investigating and prosecuting an agreed range of conduct, and an international agency with authority to accomplish (through measures analogous to those widely in use by other agencies) the legal and technological objectives essential to create a more secure cyber world.

3

Cyber Crime and International Responses

Concerned technical experts well understand that information security issues are inherently and unavoidably global in nature. Judicial and law enforcement officials equally well understand that the means available to investigate and prosecute crimes and terrorist acts committed against, or through the medium of, computers and computer networks are at present almost wholly local and national in scope. The material for this chapter is drawn largely from papers prepared for, and presentations made at, Session Two, "International Response to Cyber Crime", of the challenge therefore is how to regulate a technology that permits rapid transactions across continents and hemispheres using legal and investigative instruments that are fragmented across jealously but ineffectually guarded national and jurisdictional borders.

When one adds to this the rapidity with which the technology itself continues to evolve and the difficulties this poses for designing, updating, and disseminating effective technical security measures, the full complexity of the problem begins to come into view. Recognition of this state of affairs points toward the desirability of arrangements at the international level to overcome these procedural barriers. However, in the short to medium term such efforts will need to build upon, or at least take into account, existing national and regional efforts to combat cyber crime and terrorism. The International Convention to Enhance Security from Cyber Crime and Terrorism presented in this volume aims to formalize, in the near term, the highest degree of multilateral cooperation feasible.

Points of similarity across national-level laws already promulgated by concerned lawmaking bodies in different countries should indicate where, both in substance and scope; efforts to bring about a multilateral arrangement are most likely to succeed. To this end, this chapter will survey a number of existing national laws that establish criminal penalties for various categories of behavior in cyberspace. It will consider whether and to what degree apparent similarities reflect an emerging international consensus1 on the need for cyber law, on the types of conduct that should be treated as computer crimes, and on the conditions of pursuit and punishment of cyber criminals. In the second part of the chapter, we turn the focus on a brief examination of other multilateral initiatives to combat cyber crime and cyber terrorism, most of which have yet to reach fruition.

The objective is to 1. "Consensus" as it is used in this discussion is defined broadly as a state of "general agreement". To find consensus on an issue, therefore, does not demand an identity of opinion on every aspect of the question; rather, it merely suggests that there is enough agreement among enough states to permit consideration of a multilateral effort. Demonstrate why a multilateral initiative that can be implemented over the short term, such as the proposed International Convention, is both necessary and desirable in spite of the ongoing parallel efforts of a number of international and regional organizations. National Responses to an International Problem as argued in the preceding chapter, a growing number of states appear to have recognized that cyber crime and terrorism pose a significant threat to the infrastructure, commercial interests, and public policies of highly industrialized and highly computerized societies.

This emerging recognition is reflected most directly in the national legal codes of concerned countries. An examination of the legal codes of fifty countries conducted in mid-1999 by Ekaterina Drozdova, with the help of Marc Goodman, Jonathan Hopwood, and Xiaogang Wang, revealed that nearly 70 percent of the countries for which data were readily found have promulgated, or are planning to promulgate, laws prohibiting a reasonably comprehensive state of computer-related crimes. The remaining roughly 30 percent of states surveyed had few or no laws against computer-related crimes.

Countries in the Drozdova survey found to prohibit, or to be in the process of promulgating legislation to prohibit, most of or all of the computer-related offenses specified as "consensus crimes" in the Draft Convention are: Australia, Austria, Bulgaria, Canada, Finland, France, Germany, Greece, India, Israel, Italy, Japan, Malaysia, Mexico, the Netherlands, Norway, the People's Republic of China, Portugal, Romania, Russia, Singapore, South Africa, Spain, Sweden, Switzerland, the United Kingdom, and the United States. In regional terms, the Drozdova survey encompasses 60 percent of the European countries, 100 percent of the North American countries, several countries in Central and South America and the Middle East, but fewer in Asia and the Caribbean, and very few in Africa. The survey covered roughly 50 percent of world population, including many populous nations such as China, India, Japan, the United States, Russia, and Brazil.

These countries are: Argentina, Brazil, Chile, Costa Rica, the Czech Republic, Denmark, El Salvador, Equador, Hungary, Iceland, Ireland, Jordan, Luxembourg, New Zealand, Oman, Panama, Peru, Poland, Saudi Arabia, Trinidad and Tobago, Tunisia, the United Arab Emirates, and Venezuela. The actual state of legal coverage for cyber offenses is, in all likelihood, considerably lower than 70 percent. Although The Draft Convention discussed in this volume takes an "inductive" approach to determining what kinds of conduct should be considered cyber offenses? That is to say, it seeks to codify on an international scale conduct that all (or nearly all) states that have enacted criminal statutes against cyber crime *already* include among their criminally punishable offenses.

The Drozdova survey found that, of the thirty countries identified as having laws against computer misuse, each prohibits, in some statutory form all, or most, of the following acts: (1) unauthorized access; (2) illicit tampering with files or data (e.g., unauthorized copying, modification, or destruction); (3) computer or network sabotage (e.g., viruses, worms, Trojan horses, denial of- service attacks); (4) use of information systems to commit or advance "traditional" crimes (e.g., fraud, forgery, money laundering, acts of terrorism); (5) computer-mediated espionage; (6) violations against privacy in the acquisition or use of personal data; (7) theft or damage of computer hardware or software. These seven acts will be referred to throughout the chapter as "consensus crimes".

Clearly, the Drozdova data indicate at least some measure of international consensus on the desirability of punishing a small but significant group of acts perpetrated against, or by means of, computers and computer networks. But a great deal of national-level variation at the margins underlies this broad finding. Although points of legal difference in the substantive definition of cyber offenses, and even country-specific gaps in legal coverage, do not necessarily preclude the survey conducted by Drozdova et al. includes a high proportion of the most highly industrialized and most highly computerized countries, its coverage of the developing world is less thorough owing to limitations on the availability of information about the criminal codes of many of those countries.

Insofar as more highly computerized societies have a greater incentive to promulgate laws against computer-related crime, the absence of data for much of Africa, Asia, and the Caribbean is not surprising. Note that throughout this chapter, the term "unauthorized entry" (the formulation used in the proposed International Convention to Enhance Security from Cyber Crime and Terrorism) is used interchangeably with the term "unauthorized access", the preferred formulation in many national cyber laws and international documents. Countries where law conduct on consensus sufficient to sustain a multilateral effort, the existence of such differences at the very least counsels for closer examination.

A country-by-country examination of cyber law on a global scale is, unfortunately, beyond the capacity of a single chapter. Therefore, in this section we examine cyber laws on the books in three geographic regions—the United States, East Asia, and Western Europe— to compile a handful of comparative snapshots of how different countries and regions have responded legislatively to the threats posed by computer and network misuse. The United States Code contains a number of statutes and statutory provisions to regulate the use of computers and computer technology. Chief among them is the Computer Fraud and Abuse Act, enacted in 1984, which was "designed to deal specifically with unauthorized use of computers and the alteration and destruction of the records they contain".

Unauthorized access to a computer or network without a further offense (e.g., system impairment, obtaining protected information) is per se illegal only with respect to computers used exclusively by the Government of the United States. Unauthorized access to all other computers — for instance, those used nonexclusively by the federal government, including computers containing national security records, and those containing financial and credit records—require some further act or damage to occur in order for criminal penalties to apply. In addition to these offenses, the Act also prohibits use of a computer in interstate commerce to "transmit a program or command which damages a computer system or network", or interrupts the use of a cyber system; "trafficking" in passwords to U.S. Government computers; and the use of interstate commerce to transmit passwords with the intent to defraud. Under the U.S. federal system, each of the fifty states of the United States is also permitted, within the constraints imposed by federal law, to pass additional substantive criminal laws to regulate computer use at the state level.

As Susan Brenner described in her overview of state cyber crime statutes at the Stanford Conference, a number of state legislatures have exercised their ability to further criminalize a wide range of acts involving computers and computer networks. In so doing, these legislatures have provided an interesting demonstration of the degree of substantive variation possible in cyber law, even among entities that share many similarities in their general legal environment. At least as instructive, however, is the degree of coincidence evident particularly with respect to legislative activity on many of the "consensus crimes" identified above? According to Brenner's research, "crimes involving intrusion and damage" are responsible for "by far the largest number of [state] substantive criminal statutes" related to computer crime.

Almost all states have trespass and vandalism statutes. Many of these statutes make unauthorized entry a more serious offense when it occurs with the intent or effect of harming data. A substantial number of states outlaw "computer invasion of privacy", which generally entails gaining access to a person's personal financial, medical, employment, or academic information. A handful of states have also added statutes to cover the subsequent use or appropriation of illegally obtained data. Many states also have separate statutes covering use of computers and the Internet to "devise or execute" fraud, theft, and embezzlement. But, as Brenner observed, few states have outlawed computer "forgery", or falsification of data in computer systems; U.S. state legislatures distinguish themselves from the international norm in their uncommon degree of concern with sexual crimes involving computers, which constitute the second-largest body of criminal cyber crime statutes at the state level.

In this category, the majority of statutes concern use of the Internet to solicit, entice, or lure minors into a sex act. On the other hand, few U.S. states currently have statutes that criminalize potentially destructive acts of computer "mischief", such as the creation of viruses, worms, or "malicious logic" programs that can harm the information system or, in many applications, damage the equipment it controls. A handful of states have enacted legislation criminalizing the disruption or denial of essential services, including "a public or private utility, medical services, communication services, or government services". In Brenner's opinion, the lack of activity in this area at the state level is due to a considerable degree to the small number of such incidents reported in the media.

In practical terms, a large-scale attack against public or private infrastructure would fall squarely within the purview of federal law enforcement and federal criminal prosecution. However, Brenner argues, there is still room for state legislatures to act effectively in the criminalization of infrastructure and service attacks. First, state law is necessary for state courts to be able to deal directly with small-scale attacks (that is, those confined to the territory of a single state or portion of a state) against essential services. Second, state law may, under some circumstances, also function as an adjunct to federal prosecution.

Asia-Pacific

George Chen identified categories of computer and network misuse that approach the status of consensus crimes in Asia. These include: unauthorized access; unauthorized use; modifying or damaging data stored on a computer system; theft of money, financial documents, assets, and services by means of a computer; theft of computer software, data, and other forms of information; and damaging or destroying a computer system. Chen cautioned that apparent parallels in the black-letter laws being promulgated in many Asian countries may conceal vastly different modes of interpretation and patterns of enforcement.

In 1997 the Taiwanese criminal code was revised and laws prohibiting computer crimes were added. After a long debate Taiwanese lawmakers decided that merely accessing a computer system without authorization would not be considered an offense unless there was also proof of an additional crime, such as modification or destruction of data. However, the bar on what constitutes an additional offense was set quite low, to include, for example, acts such as reviewing, without consent, e-mail not intended for the intruder. Since 1997, electromagnetic records have been accorded the same protections under Taiwanese law as written documents, including provisions against forgery and theft, and are likewise regarded as movable property.

This feature of the code can be applied broadly in the future to cover everything from transactions involving electronic currencies to interference with the processing of electromagnetic files through, for example, the release of viruses into a system. The Taiwanese code makes it an offense to perpetrate fraud by means of "input [of] false information or commands into a computer or related device, to infringe on copyright, or to appropriate the possessions of others". Other acts that have been criminalized include "libel", "business disparagement", "obscenity", "making threats", "gambling on the net", and "disclosure of secrets". Under Japanese law, unauthorized access to a computer in which an individual may view secret information is itself a criminal offense, even if there is no damage to the system. The disclosure of secrets that may result from unauthorized access falls under the Business Secrets Act Against Unfair Competition.

Also criminally punishable under Japanese law are "offenses against e-mail", "damage and destruction", "disruption of operations", "computer forgery of electromagnetic documents", and "interception of computer data or files". The current legal trend in Japan is toward making interception of electronic records an offense against movable property, as in Taiwan. In Singapore, computer crimes are covered by the Computer Misuse Act. Under this Act "unauthorized access", "disclosure of secrets", "destruction or damage of computer systems or electronic data", and "computer fraud" are all prohibited. Although Singapore has no special provisions against defamation or libel, business disparagement, or obscenity perpetrated by means of cyberspace, these offenses are covered under the standard Penal Code. In Malaysia, a Computer Crime Act issued in 1997, though not yet entered into force, covers essentially the same offenses as the Singapore Computer Misuse Act.

However, Chen noted, in Malaysia, defamation and libel, business disparagement, and obscenity offenses are subject to civil liability only. In Hong Kong, computer crimes are, as a rule, governed under the Telecommunications Ordinance. Exceptions include the crimes of "defamation" and "business disparagement", which are covered under the Defamation Ordinance together with Common Law provisions, and also computer obscenity, which is covered by the Control of Obscene and Indecent Articles Ordinance. Under Hong Kong law, "offenses against e-mail", "damage and destruction", "computer fraud", and "theft of electronic data" are all criminal offenses. In the People's Republic of China, computer-related crimes are covered by Articles 285–287 of the Criminal Code. As Chen explained, the Chinese provisions of which he is aware are notable both for the breadth of their drafting and the severity of the penalties attached.

Offenses such as "illegally interfering in the operation of a computer system", for example, are punishable by a minimum sentence of five years in prison, but in 1998 two brothers from Jiangsu Province were sentenced to death after having been convicted of breaking into a bank's computer system pursuant to a robbery. The PRC is also concerned about possible subversive content in network communications, and has undertaken to monitor and criminalize such communications. This effort goes beyond the norms of most other states and is unlikely to find its way into any international agreement. Finally, in Vietnam and Thailand no law specifically targeting computer crime has been propagated or proposed at the time of this writing.

Apparently it is up to prosecutors to stretch provisions in the Criminal Code to cover Internet-related offenses. The general approach has been to attempt to persuade courts in these countries that electronic data should be treated as movable property, thereby extending the protection of existing penal laws against offenses such as theft, fraud, disclosure, defamation, and "mischief". This type of legislative inaction will in all likelihood leave important legal gaps that cannot be papered over with existing statutes. Even supposing that law enforcement and judicial officials in these countries were to take a highly assertive approach to the pursuit of computer crime, the successful prosecution of so-called "pure" computer crimes under existing statutes would demand a high degree of legal creativity and massaging of definitions. In civil code countries lacking a strong tradition of judicial discretion, the chances that such a strategy will prove effective are quite remote.

Europe

The legislatures of Western and Central European countries have been active in promulgating laws prohibiting unauthorized access, computer sabotage, computer espionage, data manipulation, and computer fraud. Though the diversity of national cultures and legal traditions in Europe all but guarantee variation among national laws in this group of states, the European Union (EU) operates in this, as in other fields, as a force for legal harmonization across national approaches. A thorough account of the national laws of all fifteen Member States of the European Union is beyond the scope of this chapter.

For more information, consult All EU Member States, with the exception of Austria, have enacted laws prohibiting some form of unauthorized access to computers and computer networks. Although most EU Member States have statutes prohibiting "mere access" of systems without authorization, some states attach further requirements in order to trigger criminal penalties. In Germany and the Netherlands, for example, the law against unauthorized access protects only "secure systems" for which some effort has been made to inhibit open access. In Spain, some damage to the penetrated system must occur for criminal sanctions to apply. Ulrich Sieber has noted that some general anti hacking provisions, such as those in the United Kingdom and Finland, have a builtin progression from a "basic" hacking offense to more serious forms of conduct implicating "ulterior" offenses.

One area in which the national laws of European countries are significantly in agreement is that of computer sabotage, which encompasses purposeful damage to the integrity of computers, computer networks, and computer data. Variation in the extent of protection afforded to computer-stored data (CSD) among the criminal laws of European states is, according to Sieber, rooted in varying requirements of intent and degree of damage caused that underlie vandalism or criminal mischief statutes more generally. States with statutes specifically protecting CSD include Austria, Denmark, Germany, Finland, France,

Luxembourg, the Netherlands, Spain, Sweden, and the U.K.; so far in Europe, the enactment of laws prohibiting computer sabotage and the destruction of data includes only a small number of national provisions directed specifically against the creation or distribution of destructive programs, such as viruses, worms, or Trojan horses.

Italy, Sweden, and the Netherlands are among the handful of countries that have included such provisions in their respective criminal codes. Only Germany and Italy have promulgated laws directed specifically against forms of computer sabotage "leading to the obstruction of business or national security". The degree of protection afforded by national laws of EU Member States against computer espionage has in many cases been achieved by extending the coverage of laws protecting trade secrets to computer and data processing. Denmark, Germany, the Netherlands, Sweden, and the U.K. have all enacted provisions to reinforce trade secret protection.

Civil provisions aimed at discouraging unfair competition in Europe have attained a significant measure of harmonization through First Pillar initiatives in the European Union. By contrast, the criminal sanctions that underlie those policies are anchored in varying national traditions relating to the legal protection of various types of property, including intellectual property, and thus exhibit greater variation. Sieber notes that, whereas intellectual property is an established category in the common law tradition, the civil law (or "continental law") tradition "does not regard information as per se protectable".

The situation is similar with respect to computer fraud and computer forgery. While all Member States of the European Union criminally sanction fraudulent acts in general terms, not all have statutes specifically directed against computer fraud. European states that have promulgated laws against computer forgery include Germany, Finland, France, Greece, Luxembourg, and the

U.K. Sieber explains that Sweden, and the U.K. Sieber notes that the absence of a computer fraud statute can complicate catching fraud by means of financial manipulations, because many national statutes, including those of Italy and Germany, require deceit of a "person", which leaves untouched a host of offenses involving electronic misappropriations.

The fraud statutes in Belgium and France require an "abuse of confidence" as a trigger. Normally, abuse of confidence is understood to apply only to actors in high positions and may not extend to low-level programmers and operators many of the remaining states have forgery statutes that can be extended without difficulty to cover computer forgery. However, in Austria, Belgium, and Italy—none of which has computer forgery statutes— the traditional forgery statutes in force limit protection to "visually readable" documents, thereby excluding electronic and computer stored data from protection. A survey of national legal initiatives in Europe would not be complete without a few words regarding European Union–level initiatives that increasingly place important limitations on the legislative autonomy of EU Member States.

The Council of the European Union has been the most important engine driving EU Member States toward a harmonized approach to combating computer-related crime, but combating computer-related crime inside the European Union is complicated by the fact that the issue straddles important divisions in the EU structure. Issues mainly commercial or economic-regulatory in nature, including, for example, telecommunications, fall within the purview of the European Community, which forms part of the First Pillar of the EU's three-pillar structure. Harmonization in the criminal legal sphere, together with questions of law enforcement and judicial cooperation, are handled under the Third Pillar, Justice and Home Affairs. Whether a matter is handled as a First Pillar or a Third Pillar issue is the key to determining the available mechanisms for attempting to bind Member States to a common course of action. The situation is further complicated by the fact that one and the same body, the three components, the most important of which is the European Community (EC) (formerly the European Economic Community).

The other two components are the European Coal and Steel Community (ECSC) and the European Atomic Energy Community Council of the European Union, can operate under either set of rules, depending upon the question at hand. Under the Third Pillar, the Council of the European Union acts as an intergovernmental body of national representatives, and not in the legislative capacity it serves under the First Pillar. This means, for example, that when acting in a Third Pillar capacity, the Council operates under a "unanimity" decision rule, as opposed to the "qualified majority" rule normally used for First Pillar affairs. In addition, under the First Pillar, the Council is empowered to issue, in accordance with the rules of co-decision with the European Parliament, Directives and Regulations that are binding upon Member States and enforceable by the European Court of Justice.

By contrast, under the Third Pillar constraints, Council decisions are more akin to traditional international agreements and are therefore not directly enforceable through First Pillar mechanisms. However, the gulf between First and Third Pillar capacities is narrowing slowly as European integration progresses. Under Article 34 of the Amsterdam Treaty adopted in 1997, the Council, acting in its Third Pillar capacity, acquired the power to issue legally binding framework decisions. With regard to the national laws discussed above, this means that the Council may now affirmatively require Member States to bring national legislation into concordance with EU standards in areas where the EU chooses to "occupy the legal field", thereby overcoming at least those points of national difference that inhibit realization of the EU policy.

And the EU has chosen to act in this area. Dietrich Neumann explained that the work undertaken in the European Union in the field of cyber crime has not been directed toward drafting a unified legal instrument. Rather, the EU approach has sought to take into account and, where possible, to complement initiatives in the Council of Europe, the OECD and the G-8. Neumann points out that one way forward could have been to formally associate EU efforts with work in other international forums, without developing separate EU initiatives in order to avoid a duplication of effort.

However, he argues, "the legislative and regulatory system of the EU allows much more effective action than would have been possible in other forums". Accordingly, the strategy adopted is to associate with existing initiatives where it makes sense and to develop EU instruments where necessary". In concrete terms, these efforts have ranged from the promulgation of new legislation, to funding law enforcement training for investigation of hightech crime, to initiatives to encouraging more regular coordination between First Pillar and Third Pillar institutions (for example, between telecommunications and law enforcement).

Common Concerns

States in the international system differ widely in their vulnerability to criminal activity perpetrated against or by means of computers and computer networks. They also differ widely according to the degree of threat they face from criminal and terrorist attacks, both domestically and internationally. To a considerable extent, the observable variation in states' reactions to the growing potential for cyber criminal and terrorist activity can be explained with reference to these two dimensions. The sizable group of states that have, or will soon have, laws directed specifically against cyber crime include the most highly industrialized countries, which, as a rule, are also the most dependent upon computers and computer networks. This group also includes a number of countries less dependent upon information technology (IT) that nevertheless share important economic and trading relationships with the IT giants.

Not surprisingly, the least computerized societies have been the slowest in passing national legislation against computer crime. Among countries in the Asia-Pacific region, for example, the toughest and most detailed cyber crime laws have been passed in states with the most highly industrialized and highly computerized economies, as exemplified by Taiwan, Japan, and Singapore. States with little or no legislative action on cyber law have low levels of computerization and low reliance on network infrastructures, and they face little or no internal vulnerability from acts of hightech crime and terrorism. But the very lack of vulnerability to cyber attack among states with low IT dependence is cause for concern in states that perceive a high threat of cyber attack, since the absence of internal vulnerability to cyber attack correlates strongly with a failure to take national legislative action to criminalize such offenses.

Network attack Arena pointed out in his Stanford Conference paper that even within this group, consensus on the recognition of the threat is quite new. He related that "only a few years ago, as the United States attempted to discuss the need for protection of critical infrastructure from cyber attack with colleagues from other very developed (but not as IT-dependent) countries I was often politely told that our concern was reminiscent of those who worried [in 1968] that student radicals would spike U.S. urban water supplies with LSD". Although the cyber laws in the People's Republic of China are notable for their "toughness", as Chen pointed out, they are drafted more broadly than those of Taiwan, Japan, and Singapore, which makes them applicable in a wider set of potential circumstances.

This difference in approach is probably explained by the greater degree of direct control maintained by the PRC government over most forms of private and public communications. Note that no information on South Korea was included in Chen's research can be launched from virtually any geographic location against any other with an international telephone connection, and some countries can become legal operating bases and safe havens for cyber criminals in their attacks against IT-vulnerable states. Addressing the failure of some states to respond to the threat of cyber crime and cyber terrorism will almost certainly demand differentiated tactics and incentives. In some instances, traditional political pressures at the regional or international organizational level may be sufficient to prompt legislation to bring the laws of less IT-dependent states into line with international minimum standards.

Among the least economically well-off states, forging policy may require more tangible incentives along the lines of development assistance and technological transfers already familiar in other areas of international coordination. Even among states that have chosen independently to adopt legislation criminalizing cyber offenses, effort is needed to coordinate national responses both in terms of specifying offenses and in applying the laws that are enacted to cross-border illegal acts. Without measures that actively coordinate national actions and policies at the international level, the amalgam of national cyber laws and policies is unlikely to result in a coherent framework for the identification, investigation, and prosecution of computer crimes occurring within or affecting multiple jurisdictions at any time in the near future.

In Search of a Working Consensus

How, then, is it possible to recognize when consensus is present to a degree that could lead to an internationally acceptable but nevertheless substantive prohibition regime?

The search for a working consensus demands both finding specific points of agreement and determining an overarching structure within which to frame those points. The purpose of the following survey is to suggest what the points of existing consensus might be and to contextualize them within a larger view of what, ideally, has to be done so that the level of consensus that exists can be put into effect.

In this section we identify two areas in which some level of consensus is necessary if law enforcement and judicial actors working from within various national jurisdictions are to be effective in identifying, investigating and prosecuting computer offenses. The first area is that of specifying what conduct will be treated as a criminal offense. Because this area shows the most potential for formal agreement in the short term, it is the main focus of the Draft Convention. The second area concerns points of existing consensus on what rules and procedures should dictate the scope and extent of operational powers enjoyed by law enforcement and judicial authorities inside their respective spheres of jurisdiction.

Condemnation of Specific Conduct

To cooperate across national borders, whether at the level of bilateral contacts in the course of an actual investigation or in the context of multilateral negotiations to establish a framework agreement, legal systems must agree that certain acts should be prohibited and punished. Particularly in the criminal sphere, international law enforcement and judicial cooperation depend upon at least general agreement on what conduct should be regarded as punishable offenses. The principle of double criminality, for example, prohibits extradition of a fugitive to a requesting state unless the offense charged is a crime in both states. In practice, this principle also extends to mutual legal assistance in gathering evidence in the course of a criminal investigation, particularly when the acts of discovery in question are considered intrusive. Without a minimum basis for agreement, therefore, multijurisdictional computer crimes will not be fully investigated, and, as a consequence the perpetrators of those crimes will in many cases go unidentified and unpunished. Several multilateral efforts to coordinate national responses to the threat of cyber crime have devoted considerable attention to the specification of offenses.

The Council of Europe (COE), the Organization for Economic Cooperation and Development (OECD), Interpol, the United Nations Committee on Crime Prevention and Criminal Justice, and the European Union has all been active in various capacities. Additional organizations are becoming involved at a rapid rate: the Commonwealth Secretariat, the Organization of American States (OAS), and the Association of Southeast Asian Nations (ASEAN) have all recently initiated projects on international harmonization of law relating to computer crime among their members. Drew Arena points out that these groups, many of which have overlapping memberships, have taken some pains "to exchange views and avoid duplication or conflicting approaches" in addressing international shortfalls associated with computerrelated crime.

The Council of Europe is so far the only organization to have made considerable progress toward negotiating an international multilateral agreement for the specification and criminalization of an enumerated. The Council of Europe was formed in 1949 as a standing forum for the promotion of democracy, human rights, and the rule of law among its members. In 1989, the organization's membership began to expand from the original ten Western European states to its current total of forty-one states, which includes many of the newly independent former Soviet republics and former Eastern bloc states. The COE should not be confused with either the European Council or the

Council of the European Union, both of which are components of the entirely distinct European Union treaty structure. Unlike EU bodies, the COE has no power to issue binding instruments for its members.

Instead, the COE operates primarily through negotiated conventions, roughly 160 to date, that its members are encouraged to adopt and implement. According to Drew Arena, the primary contribution of the UN Committee, to date, has been the publication of its "Manual on Computer-Related Crime" in 1994 set of cyber offenses. The Draft COE Convention on Computer-Related Crime concentrates largely on crimes directed against the "confidentiality, integrity and availability of computer data and systems"—"c.i.a.-offenses" for short. These offenses, which Arena also refers to as "pure" computer crimes, are qualitatively "new" offenses that are not readily classifiable under old statutory categories, particularly in countries without some experience in dealing with offenses against non-tangible forms of property.

The five "consensus crimes" discussed by COE members are: (1) illegal access, (2) illegal interception, (3) data interference, (4) system interference, and (5) the production and distribution of illegal devices that may be used in the commission of any of the first four acts. Offenses against the possession (that is, taking without violating confidentiality), authenticity, and utility of information, although not spelled out explicitly in the Convention, are covered under Article 7 (computer-related forgery). A consensus has also emerged among COE members condemning certain offenses related to child pornography. The aiding and abetting of The UN General Assembly has also created an Ad hoc Committee to draft a Convention on Transnational Organized Crime before the end of 2000.

Arena notes that "in addition to certain references to computer-related issues in the draft text (for example in the context of mutual legal assistance) many states feel that eventually a protocol to this convention specifically addressing cyber crime should be negotiated". Offenses such as "computer fraud" and "computer forgery" essentially entail the application of a new technology to commit an old crime and are therefore easily caught by existing fraud and forgery statutes, but the fact that so many lawmaking bodies in cyber law states have seen fit to promulgate statutes specifically outlawing *computer* fraud suggests that there may be some merit in a distinctive approach. As noted in the *U.N. Manual on the Prevention and Control of Computer-Related Crime*, "the criminal codes of all countries have, up to the present, predominantly protected tangible and visible objects".

Protection for intangible forms of property, such as "intellectual property" and copyright evolved over the course of the twentieth century but has been robustly enforced only in a relatively small number of countries. Even in jurisdictions accustomed in regulating intangible property, the extension of those protections to electromagnetic data and the integrity of information necessitated new legislative responses. Dietrich Neumann observed that even this modest degree of consensus around a content offense is rather remarkable given the range of opinion regarding the boundaries of free speech among Council Member States and around the globe.

Content-computer offenses are also punishable under the Council of Europe Draft Convention, as is the attempt to commit a criminal act, although detail regarding the contours of these latter offenses has yet to be enumerated. Still, after more than three years of negotiation, the Draft Convention on Computer-Related Crime has yet to reach final approval. Thus, although there is much to recommend the thorough approach of the Council of Europe's Draft Convention, the effort will require several additional years of negotiation before entering into force. In the meantime, the threats posed by cyber criminals and terrorists will continue to mount internationally as the vulnerability to attack grows.

The Council of the European Union, 36 in its ongoing effort to bridge Council of Europe efforts, issued its "Common Position of 27 May 1999 on negotiations of the European Union relating to the Draft related offenses are particularly difficult to standardize and harmonize because they implicate some of the most closely held values on which different nations are constructed. For example, in Germany and Italy, both states with fascist periods in their past, legal tolerance for hate speech is low. By contrast, in the United States, the First Amendment to the Constitution establishes an extremely high barrier against government censorship on the content of speech, so much so that it protects the dissemination of information (scripts, codes, and the like) needed to perpetrate many of the crimes under discussion.

The project was launched in 1997 on the initiative of the Council's Committee of Experts on Cyber Crime. Committee members include Member States of the European Union, Central and Eastern European states, and also a number of active observer states, including the United States, Canada, and Japan. The Council of the European Union, also known as the Council of Ministers, is a body of officials holding ministerial positions within their states who are empowered to commit their governments on policy matters. The Council of the European Union carries out its work mainly through specialized subcommittees. It holds primary control over approval of the EU budget and also has the power to conclude international agreements between the EU and third states and international organizations. It functions as the coordinating body for police and judicial cooperation among EU Member States.

As noted earlier the Council of the European Union should not be confused with the European Council, which is the body consisting of the heads of state of the EU members, plus the president of the European Commission and the European Parliament that meets only at "European Summits" held biannually. In this document, the Council articulated what it perceived to be specific points of emerging consensus, including agreement on features most in need of future inclusion in the Council of Europe Draft Convention. The Council of Europe/ European Union effort has sought, in Neumann's words, "ways to overcome, or at least reduce procedural obstacles that hamper international computer crime investigations and which partly relate to the principles of territoriality and national sovereignty".

This effort is helped by a number of general measures instituted by the EU to facilitate police cooperation at the operational level and to simplify requirements for the extradition of criminal fugitives among Member States. The European Union has also encouraged its Member States to enact national legislation to facilitate mutual legal assistance in the search and seizure of evidence from organized crime and hightech crime. The OECD has also been an active player in efforts to achieve harmonization in the cyber laws of its Member States. Like the approach adopted by the Draft Convention presented in this volume, the OECD initiative has sought to identify and build upon existing areas of international consensus.

However, the OECD has not attempted to draft a formal agreement, instead confining its efforts to issuing recommendations and guidelines for action. In 1986 the OECD released its first report on cyber offenses, "Computer-Related Crime: Analysis of Legal Policy", which surveyed existing laws and proposed a minimum list of five substantive offenses that it recommended strongly for criminalization by OECD members. Those offenses are (1) unauthorized access, (2) illegal computer transfer of data or funds, (3) forgery, (4) interruption of service, and (5) illegal appropriation and exploitation of data or software. In 1992 OECD issued "Guidelines on the Security of Information

Systems" together with a mandate for a periodic review of those guidelines every five years.

The most recent set of guidelines, issued in March 1997, is a set of Cryptography Policy Guidelines, together with an extensive comparative report on cryptography policy. Several of the Stanford Conference panelists cautioned that apparent patterns of coincidence in the choice of rules and terms may not represent a true consensus but may instead mask widely varying patterns of practice. Laws that appear to be similar or identical from a drafting perspective may be enforced differently by law enforcement and criminal justice officials acting entirely in good faith, owing, for instance, to differing interpretations of key terms or different views regarding the law's intended scope.

The potential for variation in practice, they argued, is heightened by the absence of a common vocabulary with which to discuss issues of cyber crime and cyber terrorism. Marc Goodman noted in his conference presentation that because many national laws do not define basic terms, such as "computer network", "protected system", or "data interference", the laws in which those terms appear have uncertain scope of appiication. But since this condition obtains in virtually every multilateral legal agreement between sovereign states and it is not preclusive of a functional international regime. Given the relatively small number of major cyber attacks to date, we simply do not know whether and to what degree these ambiguities may pose problems for international cooperation.

Nevertheless, we do know that similar obstacles have been successfully overcome in regulating international intercourse on the open sea and in international air traffic. More problematic from the perspective of international consensus building are laws that define the scope of their coverage very narrowly. This point is illustrated by comparing some laws that prohibit "unauthorized entry" into computer systems. In the People's Republic of China, for example, the relevant law makes it a criminal offense to "access computers without permission", particularly computer systems important to state security; in India the law makes it an offense to enter "protected systems" only.

In the United States, the federal law has broadened over time from protection of "government computers", to protection of "federal interest computers" and eventually to protection of "computers involved in interstate commerce". It is not difficult to imagine how loopholes and gaps can arise—for instance, in translating the American concept of a "federal interest computer" into a Chinese or Indian equivalent for purposes of extradition, or to request permission for search and seizure of data. In some cases, the narrowness of a formulation chosen by a national legislature is intended to stimulate a particular response among private entities claiming protection under the law.

Germany's statute against unauthorized access criminalizes only the penetration of "specially protected computers". Statutes of this kind are drafted to induce system owners to take proactive steps to protect their systems against outside access, rather than placing the entire burden of deterring criminal acts on *post hoc* legal remedies, as is the case under federal law in the United States. The Draft Convention proposes a definition that would require system users to make clear they intend to restrict access. Finally, the narrowness of statutes may in some cases be due to practical considerations of enforceability rather than to failure to appreciate wider levels of threat.

More broadly drafted laws would in many cases implicate, on a systematic basis, actors and assets located in other jurisdictions, thereby complicating the process of application and enforcement. This suggests that actual levels of consensus regarding computer-related crime may be broader than is immediately apparent from a textual survey of legal codes.

Administration and Operation of Cyber Law

As difficult as reaching consensus on issues of substantive law appears to be, the difficulties multiply when the discussion turns to administration and procedure. Whereas the purpose of substantive law is to delineate what private citizens may or may not do, the purpose of procedural law is to regulate what law enforcement and judicial officials may or may not do in administering and enforcing substantive law. Sec. 202 Penal Code Computer espionage: Unauthorized procuring of data not meant for the offender or specially protected against unauthorized access; penalty is up to three years' imprisonment or a fine. (Attempts not punishable.) The term "data" is explained in the comments on Sec. 303a of the Penal Code. "Procuring" data does not imply knowledge of the data. The offense also covers procuring data for a third party.

The offender must have acted without the necessary authorization by the party entitled to dispose of the data. The "specially protected" criterion (required to constitute the offense) is not defined by the law. The victim must make his interest in keeping the data secret clear by providing a certain level of access security. Prosecution is subject to a complaint lodged by the victim. The provision protects not only stored data but also data in the course of transmission or processing. In practice, procedural issues are never entirely detached from the substantive specification of an offense. The specification of the elements and seriousness of the offense are important in determining whether the system in question will take cognizance of a suspected violation, and, if so, what level of intrusiveness will be permitted during investigation.

Though encouraging a country to incorporate a small number of computer-related offenses into its criminal code is unlikely to have a large impact on the character of the system as a whole, the altering or carving out of exceptions to procedural rules in order to facilitate the identification or investigation of computer-related crimes may have important implications for the national legal systems in question. The enforceability of laws against cyber offenses enacted at the national level becomes complicated when, as is frequently the case, the source, object, or path of an attack has its physical nexus in more than one country.

The main procedural difficulty is not, as some early commentators suggested, the absence of territorial *nexi* in crimes committed via cyberspace, but rather the *plurality* of national connections, each of which may carry its own jurisdictional claims. Even among the several United States, Susan Brenner found that questions of who has jurisdiction to do what with respect to investigating and prosecuting computer crimes in which state lines are crossed in cyberspace are hotly contested. Arena illustrates the types of issues that may crop up even in a relatively straightforward scenario: Consider a corporate Internet [host] used by employees of a foreign company in a U.S. city with the system server in another country. U.S. agents obtain a valid warrant to search the computers at the U.S. office for particular evidence of fraud.

If the evidence was entered from the site in the U.S. and is still accessible from there, does or should the location of the server matter? What if the location of the server is unknown? This is not to say that such questions are entirely unsettled. A large body of jurisprudence, termed the "Conflict of Laws", is directed precisely at resolving jurisdictional contests in a rule-bound fashion in situations where a number of entities have colorable claims to jurisdiction. However, the Conflict of Laws is a notoriously muddy area of the law, in both its domestic and international application, not easily distilled into a set of reliable general guidelines. Should the U.S. authorities have to seek help from the authorities in the country where the server is located through an international letter rogatory or a Mutual Legal Assistance Treaty to obtain the evidence?

Or may they rely on their U.S. search warrant to access and download [the information] at the U.S. site? Arena points out that the scenario could be easily complicated by the addition of other common considerations, notably "the number of nations involved, the presence or absence of extreme urgency, the existence of consent and its voluntariness, and the extent to which the data sought is protected by firewalls, passwords or encryption". He argues further that a government's opinion as to whether a particular search should be allowed quite frequently depends upon whether it is part of the "searching" state, or the state on whose territory the search will take place. Again, although Arena rightly identifies these factors as impediments to law enforcement and judicial action, such impediments do not, in many respects, constitute new problems for transnational law enforcement.

Officials at the national level have developed mechanisms, in the form of mutual legal assistance treaties (MLATs), to facilitate transnational law enforcement and judicial cooperation generally. Experts at the Stanford Conference agreed that standard mutual legal assistance procedures designed for access to paper documentation are necessary but insufficient for conducting investigations in cyberspace. Dietrich Neumann explained that under the standard approach, formal requests must be addressed to the relevant authority in the home country, which then forwards the request to the appropriate authority in the recipient country, which must then approve and execute the request. Depending on the circumstances, the process can take weeks, months, or even years to complete.

By contrast, traffic data and other potentially important sources of information about particular cyber attacks are stored only temporarily in most servers and may become irrecoverable if not seized quickly. For example, identification of the source of a cyber attack can be made most efficiently while the criminal is still online, thereby necessitating an extremely rapid response on the part of investigators. Two possible remedial approaches have emerged. The first is to find ways to accelerate traditional mutual legal assistance processes for the investigation of computer-related crimes in which rapid response is key factors.

The second approach anticipates a qualitatively new regime of mutual legal assistance that would, for example, permit law enforcement officials limited powers of direct, cross-border search and seizure, subject to the post-search notification of the searched state. Although attractive in theory, solutions that would require a drastic overhaul of the existing structure of mutual legal assistance may be beyond political reach, at least in the near future. Even in Europe, with its fairly robust consensus regarding substantive offenses, the COE Committee has made no significant progress on the search and seizure issue, leaving its draft article on transborder search "to be determined".

Neumann summarizes the European situation succinctly: "Consensus has emerged where the more traditional concepts of mutual legal assistance were used for drafting provisions of this [COE] Convention. Agreement could also be reached when it came to defining consensus crimes. Difficulties arise, however, where the Convention tries to widen the traditional concepts and therefore enters into conflict with principles such as national sovereignty and territoriality". Thus, the COE has limited itself to constructing the obligation to cooperate "to the widest extent possible" on procedural matters out of broad formulations. These include the "General principles relating to international cooperation" (Art. 20 of Draft No. 18) together with specific provisions on "Extradition" (Art. 21), "Mutual Assistance" (Art. 22), and provisional measures for the expedited preservation of stored computer data (Art. 24).

In the European Union, the Council of the European Union's Common Position of May 27, 1999, took a further extraordinary step of endorsing, in general terms, the need for a provision permitting, in exceptional cases, transborder computer searches with post-search notice to the State Party. However, attempts to negotiate this point reportedly became ensnared by differing visions regarding the details and conditions of its use. Outside the European context, the Group of Eight (G-8), and in particular the High-Tech Subgroup of the Senior Experts on Transnational Organized Crime, have been at the forefront of the multilateral effort to improve international cooperation in obtaining evidence of computer-related crimes. In October 1999 the G-8 ministers adopted "Principles on Transborder Access to Stored Computer Data".

The first section of this document requires states to react quickly to requests for the preservation of electronic data, "in particular data held by third parties such as service providers, and that is subject to short retention practices or is otherwise particularly vulnerable to loss or modification". The second section concerns expedited handling of requests to search data thus seized. The idea, in Arena's words, is a "quick freeze, slow thaw" arrangement by which law enforcement and judicial bodies can fulfill their procedural obligations under domestic law for release of information to foreign law enforcement or judicial officials without risking the loss of critical data. Although the principles may appear "fairly modest" in terms of resolving the overall problem, Arena maintains that the G-8 principles lay the basis for an effective interim international regime for the preservation of electronic data.

The third section of the G-8 Principles, "Transborder Access to Stored Data Not Requiring Legal Assistance", addresses the question of whether *any* direct penetration of foreign jurisdictions via cyberspace is permitted by outside law enforcement officials in the context of a criminal investigation. Arena notes that the Subgroup was created in 1997 at the beginning of the U.S. Presidency of the G-8, and was chaired initially by Scott Charney, then chief of the Computer Crime and Intellectual Property Section (CCIPS) of the U.S. Department of Justice. The group of Senior Experts antedates the Subgroup by only two years. It is often called the "Lyon Group" on the basis of a group of 40 Recommendations on Combating Transnational Organized Crime that were adopted at the group's 1996 summit in Lyon, France. In 1998, a set of Ten Principles and a Plan of Action were announced by the Justice and Interior Ministries of the G-8 members at the Washington meeting, and were subsequently ratified at the 1998 Birmingham Summit.

Arena notes that "the Subgroup is currently working on the problem of locating and identifying computer criminals in a global environment, and will hopefully be able to develop principles in this area". The answer in the affirmative specifies that "a State need not obtain authorization from another State when it is acting in accordance with its national law for the purpose of: a) accessing publicly available (open source) data, regardless of where the data is geographically located; b) accessing, searching, copying, or seizing data stored in a computer system located in another State, if acting in accordance with the lawful and voluntary consent of a person who has the lawful authority to disclose to it that data".

The sole procedural requirement that attaches to such searches is a postsearch notification of the searched State that a search has occurred. In sum, the progress achieved by the G-8 demonstrates that significant steps can be taken to facilitate the investigation of computer-related crimes within the context of traditional mutual legal assistance. At the same time, the third section of the October 1999 G-8 Principles suggests that incremental advances toward a more ambitious transnational investigative regime are possible even now. The information surveyed in this chapter suggests that a significant degree of consensus exists regarding certain types of prohibited conduct in cyberspace.

The roster of prohibited acts enjoying a measure of de facto international consensus runs the gamut from "pure" offenses against the confidentiality, integrity, and availability of computers and computer networks to traditional offenses like fraud and larceny in which computers are a material element. The level of consensus identified in this survey is not particularly "deep" in the sense that, in many instances, it probably does not extend to a detailed specification of computer-related offenses or to common definitions of the "objects" or instruments involved. However, in the opinion of the authors of the Draft International Convention, it is enough to permit formalization on a meaningful level.

The successes and failures apparent in the ongoing efforts of international and regional organizations, considered together with the cyber crime laws that have been promulgated by concerned states, reveal a great deal about where short-term agreement may be possible, and where it is not. If ratified by a significant number of States, the proposed International Convention to Enhance Protection from Cyber Crime and Terrorism could constitute a meaningful step in coordinating the promulgation and enforcement of existing laws against computer crime and in further closing off legal loopholes and eliminating safe havens for cyber criminals.

Indeed, the most persuasive argument in support of a formal, multilateral effort at this juncture is the magnitude of the threats and vulnerabilities against which these measures are directed. In this recognition lie the seeds of effective international action, even as differences in national law and traditional repertoires of transnational law enforcement and judicial cooperation constrain the menu of short-term responses. Experience is showing that national governments are increasingly willing to cooperate in foreign investigations. Director of the National Infrastructure Protection Center Michael A. Vatis reported that in the investigation of the February 2000 e-commerce denial of service attack, "for the first time . . . investigators had sought and received cooperation from foreign governments".

As for the multitude of offenses that fall outside the set of "consensus crimes" identified here, Arena maintains that a lack of consensus may for the present actually be a desirable state of affairs. Absence of consensus lends itself to legal and technical experimentation, which in turn increases the likelihood of happening upon effective solutions that may be foreclosed by premature formalization at the international level. Although this chapter has dealt primarily with proposed short-term steps in the legal sphere, the legal-deterrence approach can and should be reinforced by further developments on the technical side. In the technical realm, harmonization is likely to be helped by the fact that the technology of security and enforcement is likely to have its source in only a few states.

Arena echoed the arguments of Peter Neumann and Richard Power at the Stanford Conference, in positing that the way through the international political maze will probably be found in the free market. Increasingly reliable measures of how much hightech crime in electronic commerce is costing at the enterprise level have already begun to drive demands for better IT security. Improved cost measurements will also increase awareness of the costs associated with the inefficiencies of transnational fight against computer crime due to outdated agreements for mutual legal and judicial assistance. In the meantime, progress on the difficult questions can be helped along by demonstrated successes in areas where consensus already exists.

Experimentation in transnational law enforcement and judicial cooperation will undoubtedly proceed by means of bilateral agreements among states with similar interests, and through practical lessons learned from investigating and prosecuting cyber offenses. It is to be expected that the de facto regime of multilateral cooperation and consensus will continue to expand and may, over time, pave the way to more comprehensive international legal solutions.

The Civil Aviation Analogy

One of the most frightening images of cyber terrorism is a scenario in which terrorists take over the air traffic control system to cause an aircraft to crash or two planes to collide in flight. H. H. Whiteman, director general for Security and Emergency Preparedness of Transport Canada, places this possibility at the worst-case extremity of a wide range of ways in which information systems could be used to interfere with civil aviation operations. Transportation systems are important national and international infrastructures that are especially attractive targets for malicious or reckless attack with potentially serious casualty and economic consequences. They have been favored targets of terrorists and criminals for decades. They are also becoming increasingly dependent on information systems, and this dependency is a source of vulnerabilities for hostile information operations.

For four important reasons, civil air transport could be singled out for particular attention with respect to international cooperation to combat cyber crime and terrorism:

1. Civil aviation is one of the most widespread and extensively interconnected international infrastructures. It is one of the primary industries for interconnecting and integrating the world, and it spans almost every country on earth. In the United States alone, according to Vidyut Patel of the U.S. Federal Aviation Administration (FAA), almost 300,000 passenger aircraft took flight during 1999, not counting cargo, military, and noncommercial private planes. Each day, this transportation sector is entrusted with millions of lives.

The direct and indirect—that is, as a supporting infrastructure for the activities of businesses and governments—economic value of this sector is enormous.

2. The civil aviation infrastructure is extraordinarily dependent on computer-telecommunications information systems. Some of the most prominent and widely used systems include those for air traffic control, navigation, reservations, and aircraft flight control. Others are used extensively for airport and airline management. Individual flights can now be tracked on the Internet in close to real time. Patel stated that more than 180 different information systems have gone through the FAA security certification process. Increasingly, these information systems have become critical to the complete spectrum of activities in this industry. Peter Neumann of SRI believes many of these systems are poorly designed with respect to security and are at risk to GPS jamming, electromagnetic interference, denial of service, Trojan horses, disgruntled employees, and other threats.
3. Civil aviation has a long history of being a target of terrorists. Aircraft and airports have been threatened and attacked all over the world over the course of decades. The extensive vulnerabilities and dramatic consequences of attacks against civil aviation make for very high profile events. The extensive use and dependence on information systems provide the potential for new forms of both crime and terrorism. Although few well-known events have occurred so far, they include a range of prospective failures from chaos created in baggage handling systems to an inflight collision. Industry and governments are extremely sensitive even to the appearance of threats and vulnerabilities. A collapse of public confidence in civil aviation safety, and a failure to manage public expectation, may have serious and widespread economic and social consequences.

4. There are near-universal international forums for cooperation already in existence concerning air transport. Prominent among these are international agreements that go back to 1919, with the dawn of international commercial aviation immediately after World War I. Even then, the unique vulnerabilities of aircraft and the potential for the loss of life resulted in cooperative agreements to improve safety.

As Mariano-Florentino Cue´llar, of Stanford's Consortium for Research on Information Security and Policy (CRISP), describes, these ultimately have expanded to include a major new focus on the intentional acts of criminals and terrorists to interfere with air transport either in the air or on the ground. Around 180 sovereign countries are signatories to these agreements, putting them among the most universally accepted of international agreements. They have arguably been very effective in that they have denied havens to attackers and served as umbrella agreements for other cooperative efforts that have collectively done much to curtail physical terrorism and to apprehend and punish people who engage in attacks against civil aviation.

For all these reasons, we believe that it would be timely and prudent to devote attention to developing explicit forms of international cooperation to deal with the vulnerabilities of and prospective threats to this infrastructure. It is a good example of an important sector whose protection can be pursued quickly and within the context of an existing and near-universal international regime that has already proved itself effective against similar problems over a long period of time. Dealing with the problems of cyber crime and terrorism in one major sector may also serve as a useful example and precedent for others or for international cooperation more generally.

The Civil Aviation Analogy

To these ends, Whiteman presents a comprehensive

overview of the problems of security in civil aviation. These include an overview of threatening information operations and a description of important forms of international cooperation, including the constructive roles played by the International Civil Aviation Organization (ICAO), which was created under the 1944 Chicago Convention and now operates under the United Nations. He pays particular attention to issues of prevention. Cue´llar then reviews the existing international agreements for the protection of civil aviation against terrorist attacks.

He identifies some problems related to attacks via information systems that are not covered by existing conventions and, in keeping with a focus on international agreements elsewhere.in this volume, proposes a draft extension to the 1971 Montreal Convention to rectify these problems. Both Whiteman and Cue´llar make it clear that civil aviation safety and security have greatly benefited from an effective and sustained regime of de facto cooperation under the framework of an extensive international treaty structure. We would hope this will be explicitly extended to cover information systems.

4

Current and Future Technical Capabilities

Information systems are vulnerable to attack, as evidenced by the rapidly growing number of system intrusions. Current protection capabilities allow for relatively limited degrees of defense or deterrence, making attack relatively easy and defense relatively difficult. This chapter outlines technical measures that could help to identify and track intruders into computer systems and networks. But in addition to deploying specific technologies, a new international regime will be required to reduce the ability of intruders to hide behind the frequently slow and incompatible processes under which defenders must operate when different sovereign nations are involved in the investigation of an intrusion. Some of what is suggested will require explicit agreements among nations, but there are other steps that, without government-to-government agreements, will fit naturally into the open and cooperative environment that has characterized the Internet to date.

Such measures, undertaken directly by the users who, by definition, live in "Internet-time", can be accomplished more rapidly than those where formal international agreements must be agreed to and implemented. Thus, in spite of the rapid rate of growth of system intrusions, there is the prospect of being able to make significant improvements in system security on a time scale that matches that of the problem. The focus here is on criminal violators, including terrorists who seek to attack and destroy elements of society. A different, and potentially more severe, threat is where the attacker is a sovereign state.

The Internet and its Governance

The Internet provides the basis for the global information infrastructure, and it increasingly provides connectivity for a wide range of other infrastructures. To the extent that the Internet manifests vulnerabilities that cannot be addressed through unilateral measures, changes in its governance may be desirable. This requires examining existing mechanisms that can effect change. To the extent that these change mechanisms prove to be incapable of protecting the Internet, other approaches will be needed to protect this global resource. The Internet is governed through the voluntary activities of the technical people who develop and extend its functionality.

Internet users adopt its protocols to be able to communicate with others; vendors implement its protocols in their hardware and software products because the user market requires it; technical experts extend the Internet based on their research and analyses. Thus, although the provision of Internet services has become a major business, the Internet's core specifications and their implementations are maintained and developed by its users acting through a governance structure that is little changed in concept from the way its founding academic researchers preceded thirty years ago.

Even the businesses that use the Internet or provide its communication facilities are not, as organizations, part of the group that develops and maintains the Internet's technical specifications, although those specifications must change to keep up with new technologies that are deployed. This may be changing, as more constituencies demand to be heard, but the fundamental processes through which the Internet operates have stood the test of time and are not likely to be abandoned lightly. It runs on the basis of network protocols, agreements on how information should appear in a message, how that information is to be interpreted, and the format of that message.

The Internet is managed, developed, and operated by a hierarchy of volunteer organizations. The Internet Architecture Board (IAB), the Internet Engineering Task Force (IETF), the Internet Engineering Steering Group (IESG), and the various IETF Working Groups are the primary groups responsible for the development of the Internet. The IETF, the engineering, development and standardization arm of the Internet Architecture Board (IAB), is a self-organized group dedicated to the continued development of the protocols and standards that form the basis of the Internet.

The IETF's mission includes: identifying and proposing solutions to operational and technical problems in the Internet, specifying protocols and architecture to solve such technical problems, making recommendations to the Internet Engineering Steering Group (IESG) regarding the standardization of protocols and protocol usage in the Internet, and providing a forum for the exchange of information within the Internet community. The IETF is organized into eight areas of interest, one of which is security. Each area is headed by an Area Director, who oversees the various working groups—the creators of Internet specifications—that consist of all parties having a stake in the protocol under consideration.

A charter sets the agenda and timetable for the group's work. Working groups focus on developing a protocol specification, but sometimes they serve to delineate some current practice. Working groups are established based on a recognized need and they terminate when the work called for by their charter is completed. The IETF standardization process is well defined. The process starts with a working group producing a series of documents called Internet Drafts that are posted on the Worldwide Web with notification to the IETF mailing list. Based on comments received, the working group can decide that an Internet Draft reflects a consensus view. At this point the working group asks the IESG, through its Area Director, to make the Internet Draft a Proposed Standard RFC.

A Proposed Standard specification is advanced only if it is stable, represents the resolution of known design choices, is well understood, has received significant community review, and appears to enjoy enough community interest to be considered valuable. Thus a Proposed Standard RFC is viewed as the initial specification from which implementations should be developed. After a minimum of six months the working group can ask that the Proposed Standard RFC be moved to the level of Draft Standard RFC.

The requirement for such a change is based on the existence of two independent and interoperable implementations from different code bases and on sufficient successful operational experience. Such implementation experience may well uncover the need for changes to the specification. It is the implementation and experience requirement that differentiates the Internet standardization process from other standards activities. Implementations are used to prove the utility and precise operation of the specification.

After a minimum of four months a Draft Standard can be moved to an Internet Standard. Internet Standards are characterized by a high degree of technical maturity and by the understanding among its developers that the specified protocol or service provides significant benefit to the Internet community. Security issues were not of concern for the original Internet specifications. Cyber crime per se is not currently an IETF agenda item. Addressing cyber crime would have to be stated as an issue in protocol design.

Physical and Information Architectures

There are two views of Internet architecture. The most common is that the Internet is a set of linked computer hardware, software, and communication facilities. In this view, security is a matter of protecting that hardware and software against theft, damage, or denial of service. A second view is that the Internet links a collection of information. Though not as easily understandable as that of physical architecture, certain features of its information architecture are becoming clearer. First, just as the physical Internet embodies a meta-architecture that embraces the interconnection of heterogeneous networks through the processes described above, so does the information system embody a meta-architecture that embraces heterogeneous information systems.

Robert Kahn and Robert Wilensky in their introduction to this general notion describe the digital object as the basic architectural element in the global information system, with each object having a unique and persistent identifier. Finally, the architecture assumes the existence of certain systems that can speak with authority on specific information issues. For example, is the following digital object subject to a claim of copyright in the United States? Or, regarding authenticity, what is the following organization? Or, are the bona fides of this organization accurate? While some entities may have their authority conferred by law, others will develop it by superior performance in the marketplace.

Given the existence of a meta-architecture for information systems, the Internet will embrace many of them, all different in some aspects. Today, the most widely used information systems are those that rely on access to files on specific machines. The older File Transfer Protocols (FTP) and the current Web protocols are examples of information system protocols, but because neither one allows for persistent access over time through unique identifiers, one can expect the spectrum of information systems in the future to range from those that are strictly informal, with possibly transitory information, to those that have more formality.

Defining the Internet

The broad term "information infrastructure" covers a range of private, public, and national capabilities. I focus here on the information systems that constitute the Internet and exclude separate national systems used by sovereign nations for the operation of their government, and facilities owned or operated by private entities that are separate from public facilities. I do, however, include both physical aspects and the information and service aspects that are not necessarily physical.

Within the United States, the Federal Networking Council has adopted the following definition of the term "Internet": Internet refers to the global information system that: (i) is logically linked together by a globally unique address space based on the Internet Protocol (IP) or its subsequent extensions/ follow-on; (ii) is able to support communications using the Transmission Control Protocol/ Internet Protocol (TCP/IP) suite or its subsequent extensions/follow-on, and/or other IP-compatible protocols; and (iii) provides, uses, or makes accessible, either publicly or privately, high level services layered on the communications and related infrastructure described herein. An important element of this definition is the reference to "subsequent extensions/follow on".

The dynamic character of networking technology suggests the need for a continuing review mechanism to ensure that basic conceptual underpinnings are not inadvertently changed with the passage of time. A second important element is the inclusion of high-level services within the definition. More than simply the physical devices and telecommunications capabilities that constitute the underlying network, one must view the global information system in its totality.

Abusing, Misusing, and Attacking the Internet

The Internet, after undergoing a twenty-year period of development and use by academic researchers, took on a different aspect when it was opened up to commercial users in the late 1980s. The environment quickly changed from one directed to the open and cooperative use of its information resources and services by a narrowly defined set of users to one where the new users sought privacy in their communications, and protection of their intellectual property, and expected to receive a choice of reliable services at costs set competitively. The new users display a varied set of behaviors. Some are business competitors or bargain-seeking consumers who are not above stealing intellectual property or services. Others are irresponsibly playful, and they set loose viruses and other malicious code or they deface web sites or destroy data files.

Still others are criminals who use the Internet to perpetrate fraud, theft, and extortion. Terrorists, noting the increasing dependence of many societies on the Internet, may use it as a target or channel for the expression of their views, or to harass, coerce, or destroy social institutions. National security analysts translate these same concerns into the domain of strategic attacks on sovereign states. Such abuses and attacks may use the Internet to reach other targets, or they may target the Internet itself. The first category uses the Internet to attack defined entities, such as a particular computer, the information contained within it, or the service it provides, thereby causing harm to those dependent on those entities. The second category, attacking the Internet itself, intends to degrade or deny parts of its contents and capabilities to large numbers of users.

Compounding these difficulties are several related factors. As information technology becomes increasingly powerful, so do the attack tools that become available. These tools are distributed to would-be attackers using the Internet itself, much in the way that poisons spread through an organism in its bloodstream. By increasing the power of their users, the tools allow a larger number of individuals, less skilled than the tool creators, to damage information systems. Excluded from the concept of network abuse are failures that inadvertently result from acts of nature, wear and tear or other usage, approved maintenance and operations status monitoring, and diagnostic activities of network operators.

These are considered part of the normal operational environment and part of the terms and conditions for use of the network that are made explicit in either employment contracts or service agreements. The focus of this discussion is on deliberate acts, not accidents, although the possibility of civil or criminal negligence cannot be excluded. At the current level of networking technology numerous problems will arise from the inherent lack of robustness of the system and even of incompetence on the part of its users and operators. These unfortunate realities can have consequences as harmful and costly as those caused by deliberate conduct, but they are not addressed.

Protecting Individual Computers

As with any form of private property, protecting a single computer is primarily the responsibility of its owner. An owner may seek assistance from appropriate government agencies and jurisdictions, according to the national laws applying to the locations and the activities involved. The broader the impact of such attacks, the greater will be the case for public involvement. Where the information, operation, and impact of an attack involve entities from more than a single sovereign state, which is often the case, the appeal for help may extend to the international community of nations and organizations. International actions can be as simple as supporting the resolution of civil contract disputes.

In other cases they may involve the exchange of information relating to computer crimes, or suspected crimes, or to anomalies in computer operation. It is conceivable that personal information relating to the citizens of one nation might be provided to entities in other countries, such as alerts, warnings, modes of penetration, identities and aliases, and the like. In some cases assistance in the resolution of attacks on individual computers can involve disclosures of personal information that may raise concerns about the requirements of privacy. A balance between property rights and those of personal privacy must be achieved. A possible approach to this problem, involving the use of automated techniques, is discussed later.

Protecting the Global Information Infrastructure

A very different circumstance arises when the information infrastructure itself, in whole or in part, is the target of attack. In this case, the jurisdiction in which such attacks occur is more complicated than for attacks on individual targets, and international agreements become increasingly important. Infrastructure "capabilities" are abstractions, substantially different from their physical manifestations; they depend on multiple locations and jurisdictions (including the oceans and space) and, most important, have properties and capabilities that, rather than being simply resident in any of its parts, grow out of their collective existence. Without explicit agreements dealing with the protection of the network, global protective actions may be limited to those common to all jurisdictions taken together.

This least common denominator will not, in general, provide the greatest amount, or even adequate amounts, of global protection. For protection to be adequate, the shared global system should have the capacity to detect and identify violators with sufficient accuracy to deter them through the prospect of being indicted, prosecuted, and punished, or otherwise caused to pay a price for having initiated an attack. To achieve this degree of effectiveness will require creating appropriate tools, procedures, and organizations, not only to satisfy these aims but also to satisfy national authorities that their sovereign rights and the rights of their citizens are protected.

Although in some situations bilateral international interactions may be all that is required to deal with an attack on the Internet itself, in many others multinational action will be required. Certainly a global attack on the entire information system would require a coordinated worldwide response, and such a prospect is properly a subject for political consensus on how best to respond. At a minimum, the governing policies and processes will need to be established in advance.

Defending Information Systems

Against Cyber Attack

For a realistic assessment of future prospects for the defense of information infrastructures against cyber attack, the current state of practice provides a starting point. In addition to the art and science of system defense, we should examine those areas that security professionals feel could provide the greatest leverage in blunting future attacks. In the case of a prepared defense there is a secured network with a perimeter involving, for example, firewalls, virtual private networks, and/or challenge response systems. This perimeter is monitored by an information protection staff using a combination of automated and semi automated tools.

An effective perimeter defense implies that the modes of possible attack are known a priori and that methods are in place to detect the signatures of these attacks. Early warning of an attack might, for example, come from monitoring the TCP, UDP, and ICMP activities occurring on inbound packets. Early warning could also come from automated searching for key words in the internals of network traffic that would generally indicate an attempt to gain access to systems or privileges not permitted from outside the secured perimeter. This could in addition include the routine scanning of attached files in e-mail, which can contain known viruses or suspicious executable programs.

A potential attack may be indicated to the information protection staff via e-mail, pager, or other means. At this point, the information protection staff must ascertain whether the alert is real or a false alarm. This is done in several ways, and is somewhat dependent on what information is captured or buffered at the firewall. Essentially, the team must look manually at the information collected by the automated monitoring system in order to make an initial assessment. Adequate evidence may or may not be available, but in either case, in By contrast, "externals" refers to the routing information that is contained in the message that identifies the source and destination without providing detailed information of the message content order to support both evidence collection and better situation assessment, the security staff will increase the amount of auditing and data collection being done at the perimeter.

If the increased monitoring and auditing process confirms a suspected attack on the network, rapid engagement of additional processes is necessary. Engagement typically will require disaster preparation and warning, contingency plan execution, system isolation, and ultimately denial of access to the attacker. The security staff must move quickly to determine the nature of the intrusion, as well as to intervene to deny access to the attacker. During this period of the engagement, security personnel will trace the origin of the attack. In most cases, a serious attack will not have originated from the source that has been monitored; the real attacker will be located one or more "hops" away. That means that the defenders must attempt to contact security personnel at the apparent attack source to see if the attack is originating from that location or from some other "hop".

This tracing period may take time, and prove difficult, since the only contact information that is usually available is from the personnel at the point of initial contact and the attack may not occur during business hours. For these reasons, it is usually difficult for security staffs to trace a multiple "hop" attack, and the urge to deny the attacker access, either through the operating system or the firewall/router, is hard to resist. Having an automated way of tracing such attacks would be of great use, for it would increase the number of successful traces and would thus enhance deterrence.

Denial of access to attackers results in the immediate ending of any intrusion, but attackers frequently eliminate the evidence of their activities on some number of the intervening "hops", or they may place confusing or contradictory evidence in log files that would suggest to investigators that the attack came from somewhere other than the true origin. Sometimes the various "hops" along the way are outside the country boundaries of the computers under attack, creating the further difficulty of additional barriers such as different laws, languages, and time zones. For most practical purposes, the average security staff that is well prepared for an attack of this nature will be in the position to detect, investigate, and terminate the intrusion, yet because of the "network of networks" nature of the Internet, detailed investigation leading to the location of an attacker is not likely to take place without the involvement and cooperation of law enforcement, Internet Service Providers (ISPs), and telecommunications providers.

Unfortunately, this seldom occurs simply because the amount of work necessary to coordinate and carry out an investigation outweighs the value of finding the attacker— or at least it would require the group attacked to admit publicly that it had been attacked. These issues could be practically solved if we had an automated method for tracing attacks, particularly one that would protect the identity of the institution under attack.

Hasty Defense is More Difficult

In many cases, the attack as launched has not been prepared for, and so the defenders must mount a hasty defense—not an easy task. Though the defenders know that something has happened, they may not be sure what, how, when, who, or why, but in all likelihood, speed is of the essence because evidence may be lost at any time. Usually the first step in such situations is to analyze what systems and/or networks may have been affected so that computer backups for those systems can be immediately secured and duplicated. A team may set to work analyzing the data contained on those backups, looking for clues to how the attack occurred. Additionally, the security staff may make duplicates of audit and transactions logs, as well as network traffic and/or firewall logs.

At this point, the security staff will increase the level of auditing and monitoring conducted on the network, in order to collect improved evidence in the event of further attack. This may best be done with computers that are dedicated to "sniffing" packets off the network and storing the packets on removable media. Unfortunately, in the case of the hasty defense, it may or may not be clear whether the attack occurred from outside or inside—that is, the attacker may possibly be an authorized user, operating inside the network. In the process of analyzing the attack, defenders may discover some unique aspect that is characteristic to the attack—for example, certain accounts are used, a particular time of day, and so on.

That may be difficult, however, since many computer networks are complicated interconnections of heterogeneous equipment with numerous ways in which they can be accessed. In addition, it is necessary to characterize the attack, and this characterization will form the basis by which investigators will review data, looking for possible intrusions or unauthorized accesses. The process of analyzing the network topology (how computers interact or interconnect with others on the network) may also be of assistance. This correlation must lead to the development of a profile for the intruder that can be used to search through the large volumes of historical as well as current data, looking for further evidence of intrusion. Ultimately, the endgame in the hasty defense is locating the attacker through a more and more detailed approximation of the "attack signature".

Continued refinement of this signature through the collection of a significant number of intrusions helps to identify the attacker, even when normal means to gain access to the computer systems in question are used—such as signing into the system using a stolen user name and password. Once a sufficiently discriminating signature has been developed, the hasty defense takes on the nature of the prepared defense, and defenders can continue to investigate and/ or terminate the attacker's access.

Automated search tools are important to detect intrusions in the large volumes of data involved in normal network operation. Since this produces a number of sessions that contain possible events that must be reviewed individually by investigators, review at this level requires the detailed reading of interactions between users, computers, and other users. Most of these sessions, as one would expect, are those of legitimate users so technology could be of enormous value here, if it could provide a means to detect and track unauthorized users without requiring investigators to read message internals.

Tracking Packets

One mechanism to identify tracks through the network could be facilitated by routers and the Internet service providers who operate them. If every time a packet left a router, the packet contents were fingerprinted, for example, by a check summing or other mechanism implemented in hardware, one network could verify with its neighboring network that a packet with a specific fingerprint passed through the network at a given time. This fingerprint could also be passed to the next network or destination system, which could then use the fingerprint to identify a specific packet, and each network on a hypothetical reverse path, could then be queried to determine if it carried that particular packet.

This, of course, could generate a very large amount of auxiliary data, which would, depending on how long it would be retained, have to be logged and stored, either by the routers or in repositories associated with them. A variant on this approach would keep statistical track of packet fingerprints over designated time frames, for example, over ten-minute periods, so that, with relatively much less storage, it could be determined with certainty that a given packet fingerprint did not pass through that network during that time frame.

Although such a system would not be able to determine whether a given packet actually did pass through a network, it could be used to establish the negative. Networks en route from host A to host B at a given time that might be sufficient evidence to require disclosure of service-level information retained by host B that is correlated with the specific packet fingerprint, assuming it still existed. This information could then be used to correlate with the corresponding information in host A, which never had access to the packet fingerprint in the first place and therefore could not have initiated the inquiry. However, host A could initiate a reverse query based on received packets from host B, whose packet fingerprint host B was not privy to.

This would let host A take the lead in identifying the reverse channel, and let host B take the lead in identifying the forward channel. If executed effectively, this would have an impact similar to the impact that accessing billing records has in tracing use of the telephone system and would be a useful tool for enabling cyber attackers to be identified and located. A similar suggestion is made by Stephen Rizzi, who notes that technology for privacy-protecting packet tracing would also be desirable. All too often an intrusion event is not investigated extensively because current manual methods do not allow for timely or privacy protected tracing of multihop attacks.

Technology is needed to support near-realtime automated tracing of multihop attacks. Such technology should protect the identity of the institution requesting the trace, to avoid undesired publicity, and in addition, the tracing algorithm should not directly use internals of the message to trace the origin. Such architecture could be accomplished by the installation of a "trace server" on each registered domain subnet. With time, such a server could be as important as a firewall. To be useful, all networks willing to support a trace capability would have such a server. The trace server would keep track of all incoming and outgoing traffic, and reduce those exchanges to time-stamped records with origin, destination, and a message digest, such as the fingerprint mentioned above.

All this information would be encrypted using the public key of a clearinghouse. A tracing request would originate from a subscriber to the clearinghouse, again, encrypted using the public key of the clearinghouse with a query stating the perceived origin of the attack, the date/time range, and a message digest of suspect communications. The automated system at the clearinghouse would then begin a series of queries to trace servers of networks implicated in the attack. The automated clearinghouse matches up the outgoing traffic of one network with incoming traffic of another, tracing the communications until the point of origin is reached.

The communication channels and information resources used for coordinating investigation of attacks must be separate from the information resources that are the targets of attack, and they must receive special protection. This can be accomplished through an overlay on the network, but its functionality and points of origin must be limited to avoid compromise of the overlay itself. Clearly, the design and operation of such channels is a matter for international cooperation. As noted earlier, a need exists for anonymous communications between incident responders under some conditions, which suggests that care be taken in implementing such "back-channel" facilities.

Integration of Defensive Technologies

Current defenses against a cyber attack include prevention mechanisms such as firewalls, intrusion detection and response components, and security management applications, but a lack of communication and coordination between vendors' security components limits their effectiveness in large heterogeneous environments. Key technical and organizational issues limiting coordinated cyber defense across administrative and national boundaries can be identified, and challenges in achieving agreements between international organizations on how these technologies can be integrated are substantial.

A clearinghouse is an objective third-party organization that is considered a trusted recipient of information from member parties. A clearinghouse makes relevant information available to all parties without divulging source information that could violate the privacy of participating members. Automated response to intrusions is a major need for defending critical systems. Vendors have developed products that support intrusion response. These products use proprietary protocols and are limited by an architecture that requires all response decisions to be made at a central controller. Because an adversary can take actions at computer speeds, systems must react at comparable speeds, implying the absence of human intervention.

Current tracking mechanisms have significant limitations, especially when applied to large heterogeneous environments such as the information infrastructure. First, intrusion detection systems detect local intrusion symptoms and can only react locally, for example, by reconfiguring local boundary controllers and hosts. Because an attacker may cross many network boundaries, a local response by the target cannot identify or mitigate the true source of the attack. Second, even if intrusion detection systems were capable of communicating with boundary controllers near the attacker, there is no common language for remotely instructing them to handle selected traffic. It is also unlikely that intrusion detection systems would know enough about all such devices to be able to reconfigure them remotely using low level, device-specific commands.

Nor is it likely that the owners of such devices would allow it. Third, if intrusion "symptoms" are detected in different areas of an internetworked environment by different intrusion detection systems, current technology lacks the infrastructure and protocols for pooling this information to allow intrusion correlation and to develop and promulgate a coordinated response. Current research is providing a framework that allows the integration of detection and response components, thereby enabling experimentation with automated response strategies.

The Intruder Detection and Isolation Protocol (IDIP) has been shown to be capable of providing cooperative tracing of intrusions across network boundaries, blocking intrusions at boundary controllers near attack sources, using device-independent tracing and blocking directives, and centralizing reporting and coordination of intrusion responses. Each network in an administrative domain—for example, a company intranet—has an intrusion detector. Networks are connected through boundary controllers. In the example shown, an attacker, having legitimate access to his own network, intrudes upon two more remote networks where he is noted as an intruder. Intrusion reports are forwarded to a central discovery coordinator who is able to discern the attack path.

The discovery coordinator issues a response instruction to the boundary controller closest to the attacker. The attacker is thereby identified and either an automated or a manual response can be initiated. To support communication between the varied IDIP components requires a flexible and extensible language. IDIP uses the Common Intrusion Specification Language (CISL) developed using the Common Intrusion Detection Framework (CIDF) as the language for describing attacks and responses. This language includes terms for describing the blocking actions used in the current IDIP implementation, and it can be extended to support additional responses as they are developed. Currently, IDIP uses only two actions: block and allow. These can be used with various objects (for example, users, processes, messages, or connections) to cause a number of different responses.

A "block user" message, for example, is interpreted as a request to stop that user from doing anything; a "block user and connection" message is interpreted as a request that the user be prevented from using the specified connection. Connection information includes protocol, source address, source port, destination address, and destination port. Response messages can also include a specification of when to start and stop such actions. An IETF working group is currently investigating standards for communications between intrusion detection components. One of the proposed standards is CIDF.

The major modifications needed are a limitation of the type of information communicated, definition of data formats and exchange procedures for sharing information of interest with intrusion detection and response systems and the management systems that may need to interact with them, and the integration of the protocol into the TCP/IP suite of protocols. The requirements specification is currently an Internet Draft and has been forwarded to the IESG for publication. Other documents to be produced relate directly to the protocol: a definition of the data items desired in the messages to be exchanged; a definition of the message format; and a protocol for communicating the messages.

Coordinated Response to an Attack

Responses should be in proportion either to the damage already done or to the potential for future damage. Thus damages need to be assessed. When the attacker is inside, no external aid need be solicited, unless domestic law enforcement or other investigatory organizations are brought in. If the attacker is outside, the first question is whether he is located in the target's country; for if the attack is from or through another country, international cooperation will be needed. Furthermore, if the foreign country is the point of origin of the attack rather than a pass-through country, response will be different, because the required investigation can impinge on its sovereignty. Greater cooperation can be expected if the foreign state is itself a victim or is an uninvolved transit country.

Need for a Global Incident Response Capability

Clearly, information exchange and interaction among many parties is necessary for producing comprehensive approaches and solutions to system intrusions. The need is to support a global incident response effort and thereby to reduce the number and extent of computer security incidents. The Computer Emergency Response Team Coordination Center (CERT/CC) at Carnegie-Mellon University provides one basis for such a capability. This Center, established by the U.S. Department of Defense in the late 1980s, has extensive practical experience in the conduct of violations of computer security.

Incident response and computer security teams consist of practitioners and technologists who have operational experience but may lack authority to make policy and security decisions for their organizations. A response team may not have sufficient staff to respond effectively to all security incidents. At this time there is no infrastructure to support a coordinated global incident response effort, although there are some components that could form the basis of such an infrastructure. A variety of issues must be addressed when considering how to promote an effective global incident response infrastructure. These include which organizations will coordinate and participate in the development effort, how current groups and forums can fit their missions and objectives into an agenda to create a global infrastructure, and what possible structures and mechanisms might be required in the future.

The 1999 Melissa virus attack underscores the lack of such a global response structure for incident response. Because individual teams focused on individual or national response needs, there was no operational global response effort. Although the Forum of Incident Response and Security Teams (FIRST) played an essential role in the early identification of the problem through reports shared among its member teams and was therefore able to notify others, it lacks the operational mission and funding necessary to facilitate further responses; almost four days elapsed from the initial activity report to solicitation and receipt of status reports and generation of the global activity summary. Even so, the resulting summary provided the needed global perspective on impacts and spread of remedial activity. A global response capability can be achieved by building on existing incident response and security teams. Successful resolution of international incidents has been possible when the following elements were in place:

- A common terminology between parties involved in the incident to include identification of the intruder's modus operandi, the technical attack details, and the identification of the targets,

- Knowledge of the technical skills of all parties involved in resolving the incident,
- Existing agreements on how incidents of a variety of types will be handled,
- An understanding of the common and conflicting societal issues surrounding the incidents.

Such an approach is not necessarily dependent on international agreements or treaties between governments, but government-to-government agreements can significantly improve the effectiveness with which incidents are resolved. FIRST is a possible basis for such an expanded international technical cooperation. Organized in the early 1990's, FIRST consists of more than eighty incident response and security teams from nineteen countries. It provides a closed forum for these teams to share experiences, exchange information related to incidents, and promote preventive activities.

Although other teams exist that are not yet FIRST members, and new teams are constantly being established, the labor intensive nature of incident response and the growing number of incidents leave the world with a dearth of capability. FIRST is a voluntary organization that provides an introduction service and meeting place for teams to establish trusted interactions, but since it lacks operational elements it cannot provide the necessary coordinated global effort or meet other needs, such as a more open flow of sensitive information and close collaboration to respond to widespread events.

Overcoming these shortcomings will require appropriate policies and procedures, formal contractual agreements among its member organizations, and documented procedures to serve as guidance for new entrants. Beyond formal structure, what is needed is a way to build on personal trust relationships to achieve organizational trust. Gaining entry to the incident response community can be a difficult and lengthy process; the community is ready to embrace new members, but it is wary of interacting with new teams until an existing member of the trusted community can vouch for them.

A global incident response capability is difficult to build rapidly, but national boundaries, which provide a demarcation for policies, procedures, and jurisdiction for information exchange, are a natural starting point. Response teams that cross national boundaries, such as incident response teams for multinational corporations, are another useful basis for international cooperation. Above all, there must be participation and cooperation among governments, law enforcement agencies, commercial organizations, the research community, and practitioners who have experience in responding to computer security incidents.

Different Viewpoints of Victims and Law Enforcers

Rapid collection of forensic evidence is needed by both victims and police. Police seek to identify the attacker; the victim has the task of cleaning the attacked hosts and getting them back into operation. With limited technical resources, the defender's efforts must be divided among learning the extent of the invasion, reconfiguring hosts to be resistant to future attacks, getting the hosts back online, and helping law enforcement agents track down the attackers. Even though the evidence gathered at these first steps is often too vague to prove a defendant's guilt, it can provide probable cause for further investigation. Rarely does an attacker explicitly give away his or her identity.

Either the "smoking gun" evidence is found on the attacker's own computer, or is observed through interception of a data stream while a crime is being committed. Once law enforcement agencies have collected evidence from the scene of the crime, the evidence must then be combined with the evidence collected by the defender. This should show that the evidence collected from the crime scene is directly tied to evidence collected from the intrusion site. Items found at the scene such as lists of usernames and passwords, computer and network addresses, help screens from attacked applications, and so on, can be correlated with evidence stored by the defender that documents the intrusions.

To be usable in court, evidence collected by the defender must be properly collected and stored. Usually law enforcement and the victim will keep a write-locked copy of each disk image dump. A growing number of tools are available for examining and processing image dumps. Speed is essential because ISPs generally keep their logs for only a few days. In the U.S., ISPs generally require a subpoena before supplying log data to law enforcement agencies. But they will preserve log data, which may normally be kept for only two or three days, in anticipation of a subpoena. Evidence collected at the scene of the crime will provide additional clues for what to look for in the defender's historical data, so that eventually, a comprehensive profile can be developed to reanalyze the data, documenting information to support prosecution.

Log-keeping is an important part of dealing with the Internet. Logs help identify usage patterns, administrative and configuration errors, misuse, and attacks. Mailers keep logs to help identify sources of spam mail. Firewalls log rejected packets. Authentication server's record account usage, and DHCP server's record caller ID information, accounts, and IP addresses assigned. ISP records of this sort are particularly important in tracing attacks back to their source. Such logs, kept in the ordinary course of business, are admissible in court. However, since nearly all computer forensic evidence is machine-readable, it is subject to easy and undetectable editing. Governments have to deal with this obvious possibility. Providing access to logs is a source of tension for ISPs, particularly those who do not wish to become involved in legal actions.

If logs are discarded routinely, without backup, the investigatory process will have less information to utilize. Logs to handle routine problems such as mailing errors are seldom needed for more than a week. On the other hand, firewall logs of suspicious activity are preserved on a WORM drive, where they remain available indefinitely. Bulk backups and disk image copies may provide usable and admissible evidence if the chain of evidence is preserved. CD-ROMs are useful for preserving evidence, though they lack the capacity to deal with current online storage technology. Newer technology such as write-once DVD disks should help. Image backup tapes need a write protect switch to prevent inadvertent overwrites that can be sealed at the time of the dump.

Although a switch can be defeated with a modified tape reader, there are cryptographic solutions to this problem as well, since cryptographic checksums verify that data have not been tampered with. There are also time-stamping services that can verifiably time-stamp a checksum without revealing the actual data. Possession of username and password files is illegal in the U.S. Password files are access devices, and the mere presence of several of these files on a defendant s computer is illegal, even if there is no evidence that they have been cracked. However, the use of a username/ password pair is not proof that the owner is at fault, since accounts are easy to steal and many sites offer free e-mail accounts with user selectable account names.

Nor is possession of code evidence that it has been used. Although idiosyncrasies of code may be suspicious, it has been difficult for law enforcement agencies to prove that particular code was actually used. This has been a crucial problem in prosecutions. Code idiosyncrasies may strengthen a case, but software is often widely known. Further complicating prosecution is the fact that cyber crime usually involves innocent third parties. Internet Service Providers are the entry point to cyberspace. On one side of the ISP is the "user", the arena of private property, civil rights against unreasonable search and seizure, rights to privacy, and due process. The other side of the ISP can be characterized as "commons", something shared, and hence something where the rights of various entities are not absolute but must be balanced against the common good. Damage to the commons affects all who use it.

This balancing of rights and responsibilities is a matter of process, which can be voluntary or may be subject to various domestic and international laws and agreements. Law enforcement agencies need help from ISPs, regardless of their location. They will want real-time access to packet streams and authentication to tap specific sessions, giving stronger links between the user and criminal activities. Some ISPs assist in these matters when they can, but it is a difficult job. The growth of the Internet leaves hardware running at full speed, with few spare facilities for this activity. For a busy router, some kind of hardware assist will be necessary, and this can only be provided by the router manufacturers, and only in response to ISP or legal requirements.

Since this would increase the costs of the router, it may take legislation similar to the CALEA requirements for the telephone system. Such requirements would have to be international to be effective, and in the long run they will probably not work, for the ubiquitous encryption that is coming will frustrate many of these efforts. The new generation of CPUs, driven by such needs as voice recognition and game graphics, has adequate power to apply strong encryption to network traffic streams, and there is little hope that even a government will have the resources to penetrate these sessions directly. Even weakened or broken cryptography presents a large economic obstacle to real-time wiretaps; 40-bit encryption is considered weak, but it is not easily amenable to real-time cracking. High-performance hardware is required to extract even plaintext packets from packet streams.

The Fifth Amendment to the U.S. Constitution complicates the question of whether a defendant can be forced to reveal passwords and unlock cryptographic keys. Other complications arise when an ISP is itself under investigation. Specific circuit identifications can be obtained from telephone companies to determine connectivity, but the extent to which one can trust the logs of an ISP that may itself be compromised, possibly inadvertently, is unclear. Given an IP address, there are still questions about the actual location of the computer at the time of the alleged crime, and the identity of the actual user. From the standpoint of the ISP, it must, as a first priority, protect its own hardware, software, and databases from compromise, meet contractual commitments to its customers, maintain the continuity of its business, and guard against liabilities arising from allegations of negligence.

Attacking routers and switches can compromise the entire network infrastructure, and such attacks are heavily defended against, though how effectively remains to be established. In addition, ISPs must help protect their customers from accidental and malicious actions on the Internet. Finally, they may be seen to have some sort of responsibility, at least implied, to the global community to protect it from the accidental or malicious actions of their customers. These responsibilities are difficult to fulfill in the face of rapidly changing technologies—which imply frequent upgrades in systems; rapidly growing market demands that require frequent upgrades in capacity, rapid changes in the ability of hackers and criminals to compromise networks and computers, and rapid changes in security technology that must be assessed and in which investments must be made.

ISPs cannot ignore security issues, but selecting and implementing appropriate security measures in a timely manner while maintaining high traffic throughput to the Internet nevertheless requires a high degree of cooperation among ISPs and communication providers. The open management environment in which the Internet operates and the dedication of its vendors and operators to meeting the needs of its users requires the balancing of these opposing tendencies of cooperation in protecting the commons and in competition among themselves. The maintenance of this environment is under severe pressure, however, as the Internet and the number of its users expands.

A central consideration, as we move to protect the Internet and its users, is that while doing well, we should also do nothing that will limit its potential for continued growth. Given these considerations, a statement of best common practices for ISPs is needed. Such a document, or family of documents addressing recommended practices to various degrees of depth, should be prepared and updated to reflect current business and technical trends. This is the proper task of an industry or trade association. Adherence would be voluntary, although in view of the tradition of service to Internet users, one might expect it to be adopted for reasons of efficiency and economy. Should risk management through insurance become widespread, such best common practices could naturally assume the role of minimum standards for insurability and protection against allegations of negligence. Security research and product development is undertaken by ISP hardware and software vendors and this can be expected to increase the level of protection in deployed information networks.

A desirable result would be for differences in security to become a market differentiator for ISPs, much as price, quality and reliability of service and ease of use are today. There are a number of vendor roles including close interaction of router vendors' operations staff with those of ISPs; providing personnel for product support emergency reaction teams; having product development staff working with customers on new features; providing security consultants for assistance with countering attacks, undertaking audits, and prosecuting intruders; and staff who track hacker communities. Labor-intensive approaches to computer and network security can use automated tools and techniques to improve their speed and efficiency.

Timeliness will minimize losses due to attacks; efficiency will enable more protection to be provided for a given level of resources applied; scaling to accommodate the growing number of attacks can, in principle, be achieved; and privacy for innocent users can be enhanced to a degree through automated rather than manual screening of traffic. All too frequently, the requirement for privacy conflicts with the need for protection; once people have exhausted their ability to protect themselves, they must appeal for assistance, and this inevitably involves some sacrifice of privacy. Nevertheless, it is reasonable for victims of cyber intrusion to expect their protectors to tread as softly as possible, and that those seeking protection have options as to how much protection they will receive and what price, in terms of loss of privacy, they are willing to pay.

Tools to Automate Protection

Automated tools can improve protection in various ways. For example, if information is only accessible by reference to its unique identifier or handle, the ability to collect and analyze data on system use can be greatly augmented. At a minimum, the ability to establish the presence of a user at a given place in the global information system will be critical for evidentiary purposes, recognizing also that the ability to challenge such evidence and contest differing points of view or interpretations will also be needed. One class of tools noted earlier, are those that detect intrusion and other unauthorized uses of network and computer systems and highlevel services.

These will range from the more obvious tasks of checking logins to be sure they match authorized users, to running software agents on the machine to detect other software agents that may arrive without authorization. Agents that are able to detect the presence of, and oppose, other agents may be a possible countermeasure. Another class of tools for protection would monitor current usage of all relevant machine resources and look for unusual patterns. Periodic checks of user identity might be warranted. Compared with traditional password protection schemes, cryptographic login systems provide considerable increases in protection against unauthorized access.

Unlike the traditional password systems, cryptographic logins are not vulnerable to playback attacks and other attacks that involve stealing passwords. Alternate systems based on public key encryption can be used to authenticate users. Automation of protection could be implemented in the network, tracking patterns of usage in real-time and alerting system operators to unusual conditions for manual or semi automated review. Another automated approach to preserving privacy would be to package suspected sessions and e-mail them to the user to verify that it was indeed that user who was actually at the keyboard for that session.

Timely Tracking

Pursuing an attacker can reduce future exploitation of system vulnerabilities. Rapid response will minimize compromise and contain damage that may have occurred. This would require the cooperation of automated software modules en route from and at the attack source. It would also require trust among the cooperating organizations and technical activities that are in place to facilitate such automated communication among software modules. There are several meanings of "timely". One is "session time", the time during which the intruder is logged-in. Information collected during this time will enable tracking most easily since all the links in the attacker's path are open, but this sort of tracking requires not only an unusual degree of readiness but also technical capability.

Once the intruder is no longer online, traces of the surreptitious activity, other than any changes made or code purposely left behind are—if the intruder is skilled—likely to have been erased. A second time period of importance is the transaction clearing time, that is, the time between the online action by the intruder and when the intruder's desired goal is achieved. This will depend on such things as the organizations and business processes involved, the calendar date, and the objectives of the attack. In some cases, the intruder can achieve the goal while still online; in others, actions will be required by other organizations to bring the act to fruition.

Another time period is the "revisit" interval of the attacker. From penetration experiments, we recognize that attacks are not single isolated events but frequently consist of multiple intrusions to collect information about the system, to undertake various test and practice actions, or to exploit a vulnerability repeatedly. For the intruder, success means achieving the objectives of the attack and remaining undetected. Though one may have multiple opportunities to detect an intruder, one may have to sustain repeated successful intrusions before succeeding in plugging the hole. A fourth measure is the time needed by the attacker to evade pursuit, such as to shift from one location or jurisdiction to another. There might also be an explicit threat time, such as occurs with an announced deadline.

The output of the IETF working groups in the security area may have positive effects on protecting information systems. A major development that will help is the implementation of IPv6, the next generation of the Internet Protocol. IPv6 addresses several issues that can have a significant impact on network security. First, IPv6 expands the address space for network device addresses from 32 bits to 128 bits. A problem with the depletion of addresses in IPv4, the current version of IP, is that in order to support new network hosts, various workarounds have been required, resulting in a situation where not all hosts have unique IP addresses. IPv6 has another feature likely to prove powerful in tracing the origin of a message: the "hop-by-hop" header, which allows each of the routers along the delivery path to exercise certain options. An obvious option that would enhance tracing activities is to have each router that has forwarded the message record its address in the message header.

The problem with using "hop-by-hop" in this manner is that each packet will be modified by a number of devices enroute, with the distinct possibility that one of those devices, for example, controlled by an attacker, and could change the routing history. Another approach that could be used is controlling the interconnection of routers to the point where routers will only accept traffic from certain other "trusted" routers or users.

Although this changes the way routing is currently done, it could provide enhanced security over the current practice. Encryption is another method of securing network activities from cyber crime. In an environment where each transaction between hosts is encrypted, there is a guarantee that the source and destination are known. This allows trace back, but only if we are willing to support strong encryption and incur the overhead of encryption on network interactions.

Facilities for Internet Monitoring

There is also a need to enhance security by monitoring for persistent but marginal internal network problems from locations outside the network. For example, a network that consistently loses one percent of all packets sent over it may appear to be working well, but the small loss can be important. The loss may be due to a failing component in the network, but it could also be caused by an insider who has altered the network without authorization. Collectively, other networks connected to such a network could federate to detect and report the problem if they had access to all its inputs and outputs, or the network itself could detect the problem if it insisted on the equivalent of double entry bookkeeping.

Some of these problems can be alleviated with more effective cooperation among ISPs, as is happening within the Internet operators (IOPS) organization. IOPS consists of many of the largest national and international ISPs who collaborate to prevent or alleviate problems in the Internet and routinely share information on a confidential basis. In addition, they seek to improve performance and efficiency where such improvements require collaboration. Whether part of tagging and tracking or as passive observation in a statistical sense, monitoring Internet traffic statistically will require an embedded data collection infrastructure that does not currently exist.

Modification of router and switch hardware and software is technically possible, although it is unclear whether vendors would be interested. Because of concerns over privacy, it will be even more difficult to secure user buy-in. Regulation is one way of addressing user reluctance; market incentives, such as insurance, are another. Even granted that Internet monitoring is politically and economically feasible, much detailed technical work must be undertaken. Requirements must be defined, monitoring facilities must be designed and deployed, and an organized data collection operation must be managed.

Scaling and the Need to Provide Information

Providing international assistance involves more than a potential incursion on a nation's sovereignty and on its citizens' privacy. It will require human and technical resources that are often in short supply. If cyber attacks continue to increase, and if the number of affected countries increases, and as all equip themselves with intrusion detectors, the number of requests for assistance will grow substantially. Furthermore, owing to the presumed time urgency of the requests, responding to such requests will have disruptive effects on the nations involved. It is believed that in 1995 there were roughly 250,000 penetrations of computer systems owned by the U.S. federal government alone. Based on controlled penetration testing, it is estimated that 64 percent (160,000) of these were successful.

The GAO also estimated that only 1–4 percent of these attacks were detected, and only a quarter of those detected were reported. Based on a database of 30,000 incidents, Thomas Longstaff notes that 40 percent have a foreign component. This would suggest that 600 attacks per year might qualify for requests for foreign assistance in tracking intruders. If, as estimated by the GAO, the number of such attacks is doubling annually, that many more of those detected could be reported, that many more penetrations could be detected with the deployment of new intrusion detection technology, and that these numbers only cover the intrusions into U.S. government computers, the obvious conclusion is that the number of requests in the future for assistance from other countries could easily exceed the ability of those called upon to respond.

Therefore nations will need some kind of criteria for assessing the impact of attacks in order to evaluate the seriousness of intrusion events in the light of available investigatory resources. Reconciling the positions of those who see governments as part of the solution and those who see governments as part of the problem will not be easy. Making Internet protection architectures and operations public will reduce the anxiety of some, but possibly at a certain cost in the effectiveness of the protection offered, and it may complicate the collection of forensic evidence. Since much of the burden will fall on ISPs, we have to evaluate both the economic cost-benefits and the social cost-benefits in deciding how best to strengthen the protection of the commons.

The common situation, where the victim and the attacker are in different sovereign jurisdictions, or where the attacker has transited other sovereign jurisdictions, will require agreements on a variety of subjects. In light of the speed with which computer-mediated events unfold, the processes employed by those seeking to understand the nature and source of the attack will require prior agreements if the operation of systems is to be restored in a timely manner and damage minimized. Since, unlike jurisdictions based on national boundaries, the digital information infrastructure does not have a central location in the physical world, responding to attacks not only is difficult technically, it also limits the use of accepted methods for practicing law enforcement.

Recent G-8 and OECD activities are examples of increasing recognition of this international problem. Improving critical information infrastructures requires involvement of diverse parties, including governments, policy- and lawmakers, law enforcement, software vendors, the research community, and practitioners, such as FIRST members, who have experience responding to computer security incidents. Attempting to address the problems in one group without input and feedback from the others can result in incomplete solutions. For example, recent U.S. legislation, the Digital Millennium Copyright Act, results from the World Intellectual Property Organization (WIPO) treaty, generated concern within the Internet security community.

Practitioners, researchers, software vendors, and incident response teams noted the legislation could limit some aspects of their efforts to address security flaws and reduce risk to critical infrastructures. Though this was clearly not the drafters' intent, it is an example of the need for ongoing communication among policymakers, technologists, and others to ensure that future policies and agreements on national and international scales are practical and effective. Frequently, information is reported to incident response teams that does not involve a specific victim or computer security incident but does indicate that some activity may be ongoing in some part of the community. Currently, there is no standard way of sharing that information, although sometimes this information is posted to a shared list of FIRST members.

The sharing of information relating to emerging technical threats is increasing and this trend is to be encouraged. The technical forums that FIRST sponsors on a periodic basis to discuss recent developments in technical threats and vulnerabilities been effective for the incident response community, but they are not open to other international experts to relate the technical trends to broader international concerns. The tracking of sources of even small amounts of traffic is likely to be important in locating perpetrators of crimes. Hints of activity in the form of programs left behind, usernames assumed, methods of operation, and so on are all likely to be of significance in determining identities and locations of attackers.

Systematically checking for such information, as well as other best practices is required. Exploiting these understandings of attacker behavior can assist in defending against them, a technique Raymond Parks refers to as "dynamic defense". Therefore it is important to exchange both general and specific information on attacker modus operandi to provide the greatest degree of protection for the greatest part of the global information infrastructure.

A best-practices document prepared by an international group of experts and updated periodically would assist in establishing de facto standards. Conforming to best practices should be a part of justifying international cooperation in obtaining redress. A database of attacks and known viruses has been compiled by organizations such as the CERT/CC at Carnegie-Mellon University's Software Engineering Institute. It would be helpful to restructure this information so that it can be used directly by automated tools to detect patterns of criminal activity.

Prioritizing Requests for Assistance

Not every case of cyber crime will require international cooperation, nor will every case be equally deserving of such cooperation; it will be necessary, as Kahn and Lukasik have suggested, to establish priorities, with each request that is made being subject to some form of evaluation. As a minimum, and assuming assistance is merited on the basis of the magnitude of the attack or the extent of the loss, the following questions are likely to be raised:

1. Due Diligence. Has the requesting organization conformed to best practices as formulated for its industry?
2. Rapid Response. Has the requesting organization implemented near realtime monitoring and auditing of its information systems?
3. Potential Impact. Has the potential impact of the intrusion been evaluated and ranked in terms of importance to enable an assessment of the degree of international cooperation that is justified?
4. Probable Cause. How has the requesting organization established that the intruder used the facilities of the country whose assistance is sought?

Although all signatories to an international agreement will have a right to assistance under its terms, there are practical limits on what can be reasonably provided. If information systems continue to remain poorly protected and if their vulnerabilities are increasingly exploited, the need for assistance will greatly exceed what can be made available, and the necessary expertise will become a rate-limiting factor in the resolution of intrusions. In such a case, some form of rationing or prioritizing of assistance can be expected. It will be useful to factor such prioritizing criteria into an agreement to encourage improving the state of self-protection throughout the world. Thus, apart from the direct assistance that can arise from an international agreement, the long-term systemic improvement that can be thereby facilitated is an important goal.

Certificates can be used to authenticate information as well as users. A piece of information in digital form can be cryptographically "fingerprinted" and the result attached to the information or stored separately from it. The certificates can be used to verify packet fingerprints, which in turn will verify the underlying information. Another method of validation could rely on encrypted archived "snapshots" of critical information provided by or taken from key locations in the net or even from user systems. The archive could be run by a trusted third party, who would warehouse the information for whatever period was deemed appropriate.

This information could be retrieved and decoded after the fact to provide insight into problems and to corroborate other evidence. Global cyber defense will involve the sharing of cross-organizational intrusion information and arriving at cooperative responses. The mechanisms for doing this must be capable of being tailored to protect sensitive information and must allow organizations to manage their trust relationships. An essential part of such cooperation is the ability to recognize when multiple parts of the global infrastructure are simultaneously under attack.

The Defense Advanced Research Projects Agency (DARPA) program in Multi-Community Cyber Defense (MCCD) is directed to identifying the primary barriers that limit effective sharing of attack-related information with neighboring organizations and mounting a coordinated defense against detected attacks. This work seeks to extend the IDIP by focusing on three key areas:

1. Providing local administrative control over the release of their internal attack-related information, including sanitizing data prior to release;
2. Establishing and maintaining trust relationships between organizations; and
3. Developing higher-level capabilities for conducting attack analyses and data fusion.

These capabilities will be integrated into the IDIP framework by adding additional functionality to the IDIP components and by extending the message language used to communicate between components. To provide strategic defense of critical infrastructure requires that organizations that do not normally share information are able to cooperate in responding to attacks. In the DoD, problems arise when communication occurs between classification domains or across coalition force domains. In the commercial arena, organizations are mutually suspicious. Even when organizations work together as partners, they must protect various types of proprietary information. In either case, there are problems in both releasing data to, and accepting response directives from, remote domains.

In a cooperative environment, the following potential types of information could be sent between administrative domains to improve intrusion detection, correlation, and response: (a) Near real-time information and requests, including (1) attack notification, and (2) response recommendation, (b) Slower, but still immediate information and requests, including (1) correlation results concerning an immediate problem, and (2) discovery coordinator requests for immediate action and (c) Human-speed information and requests, including (1) policy information, (2) correlation results, and (3) other information to be used by higher-level correlators, and alerts from higher-level strategic warning systems.

All but the human-speed actions are intended to be sent automatically between administrative domains. The last type would instead be handled by a "trusted" third party that would provide a global situation awareness and response capabilities. In addition to enhancing the IDIP framework to include this type of message, each domain must have the ability to establish a policy for information sharing and for verifying that the policy is implemented.

The likelihood that remote organizations will not

completely trust each other, or will not be able to share information fully because of policy, requires more constrained information flows at organizational boundaries—such as, for example, the IDIP requests for severity and certainty fields. The severity field indicates the degree of potential damage the requester might suffer if the attack continues, the certainty field indicates the degree of confidence the requester has that its detection mechanisms have detected a bona fide attack. Together, these fields may reveal the power of the domain's detection mechanisms and the extent to which it can protect itself against various kinds of attacks.

That information may need to be sanitized at a domain boundary. Because the remote domain may have fewer safeguards than the local domain, releasing this information can result in giving attackers additional data to be used in an attack. Executing remotely generated response directives requires trusting the originator, or at least establishing controls that limit the damage from untrusted originators. For example, one might take action only if attack information can be corroborated locally. Blind trust in the results of intrusion-detection algorithms could enable a serious attacker to cause the detection and response system to misbehave by first penetrating the detection component.

Unquestioned erroneous reports from a penetrated detection component could have a number of effects, including shutdown of critical subsystems in response to nonexistent attacks, claims that other detectors have been penetrated and therefore should be ignored, or changes to the state of other detectors, causing them to reduce their warning levels. These issues are being addressed by investigating mechanisms for determining: (1) the current trust in a remote domain, (2) changes in detection and response policy based on the current trust relationships between domains, (3) changes in trustworthiness, and (4) the point when trustworthiness has been reinstated.

Research on cryptographic trust models and fault-tolerant systems can be applied to this area.

Results from the cryptographic trust model community can be applied to establishing authenticated identity, but the trust computed for what appears to be authentic data must be modified based on intrusion-related data from other sources. Techniques used in fault-tolerant systems for voting, diagnosing components, and redundancy are directly applicable. The MCCD architecture, based on an enhanced IDIP framework and integrated with high-level analysis and correlation techniques, should provide the capabilities necessary to enable organizations to implement cooperative agreements on sharing attack-related information, analyzing and identifying serious threats, and executing coordinated responses to detected attacks against global information systems.

The global research and development community must be heavily involved in efforts aimed at protecting information systems and their users from cyber attack. As information technology rapidly evolves, threats, vulnerabilities, and protective measures are also changing. Hence continuing R&D activities are required in order to be able to meet the still evolving threats. In addition to currently available technology, a number of areas of industrial and academic research that might yield novel paradigms for addressing the rising challenges of information assurance and survivability have been noted:

- Economic, financial, and market-based paradigms. Tapping the checks-and-balances, which are used by the financial community in order to reduce unauthorized activities, and using market incentives to promote proper use of cyberspace.
- Biological immunology paradigms. Some paradigms that make the human body successful in identifying and fighting invading bodies, in spite of the complex nature of the biological systems involved.

- Public health paradigms. Computer viruses, and perhaps even the computer-based attack, can be considered an invading disease in the multinational body of the Internet. In public health practice, nations participate collaboratively in the exchange of infectious disease information, and concepts such as quarantine, immunization, and treatment may apply.
- Reliability paradigms. Using experience gained in complex process systems, such as chemical and nuclear plants, should be considered. The large number of dynamic variables and the delicate interplay among them might provide insight for dealing with complex cyber scenarios.
- Correlation paradigms. The defense against coordinated attacks that use large enterprises to execute multiphase complex attacks requires correlation of different attack components in order to detect and defend successfully. The development of fast correlation algorithms and their implementation in systems will be important.
- Expert systems paradigms. Learning algorithms are very useful in studying the normal behavior of a system and achieving the ability to detect abnormal and anomalous behavior that can occur during a cyber attack.
- Data mining paradigms. Obtaining useful information from voluminous audit logs and event records requires expertise in data mining.
- Control science paradigms. Ability to generate an effective adaptive response to combat the attack in progress.

Feedback to the response policy could stabilize and move the system to a healthier state. A distributed international facility for experiments, tests, and demonstrations of security products and services could speed the transfer of R&D advances. The IDIP technology developed to date can be inserted in a number of commercial off-the-shelf (COTS) components, including intrusion-detection products, firewalls and filtering routers, security management components, and clients and servers. The IDIP software was designed for portability and is currently executing on Solaris, BSDI, Linux, and Windows NT platforms.

Operating system dependencies were minimized during the development and have been encapsulated. This design provides an easy, low-cost integration path into COTS products, enabling vendors to adopt the technology with minimal investment. Both widespread integration and acceptance of this framework, and agreements on the international use of this technology, are needed to protect global information systems.

Agreements are on paper, and they are necessary for the reasons suggested. But agreements are implemented by people and people tend not to accept matters at face value; they do not trust people with whom they have not previously interacted with satisfactory outcomes. Thus agreements, while necessary, are not sufficient. Trust is another necessary dimension. One can expect that self-protection technologies, agreements, and trust together will provide both necessary and sufficient conditions for global security.

Ultimately, some trust must be placed in parts of the system—for example in the authentication systems or encryption systems. But because, as with any human system, even those parts could be compromised, we shall still need trust at the individual level as well as at the organizational level. An international treaty, by facilitating increased interactions among all stakeholders can be expected to help in this process.

Clearinghouses, or other impartial third-party nongovernmental organizations, will be important as security risks become more pervasive and more complex. Having a mechanism whereby anonymous interactions and cooperation can take place through a trusted third party would help in these circumstances. This trusted-third-party construct would be part of a larger "trust network" in which communications can be passed without conveying identity. Institution of a "hot line" concept for computer attack might also reduce risk.

Such a secure and redundant system could provide signatory nations in a multinational regime with the means to communicate assessments of the intent of detected activities. It could also provide states the confidence needed to collaborate against a common threat. Those nations that do not recognize the realities of cyber vulnerabilities— or wish to exploit them—will ultimately become safe harbors for criminals and cyber terrorists.

The international community should seek incentives for all nations to participate in international conventions to combat these threats. Such a convention should put "teeth" into what is expected of signatory nations: signatory nations would put pressure on other nations to meet minimum standards for the deterrence of cyber crime and for investigation, prosecution, and extradition, so that, ultimately, nations that refuse to sign the convention could face sanctions, possibly extending to "disconnection" from international networks—a sort of cyber isolation. The international convention proposed in this volume would satisfy these requirements.

Implementing Cooperative Actions

Most of the above suggestions, such as exchanging intrusion data and attack profiles, undertaking cooperative R&D, and establishing clearinghouses for anonymous communication, do not require broad international agreements; specific actions could be implemented on bilateral or multilateral bases. But if global changes in the security of information infrastructures are to be achieved, some larger international framework can assist in facilitating cooperation. Elements of such a framework for international cooperation, drawn from various international contexts, are:

- Broad membership, consisting of both the world's most technologically advanced nations as well as developing nations, all of whom share the benefits and the risks of global information architectures.
- A voluntary and non-coercive environment based on concepts of consensus and practical experience.
- Open technical standards that prevent the manipulation of information technology for unilateral gain.
- An open organizational structure that provides opportunities for all constituencies to express their concerns.
- A mechanism for providing continuous monitoring of actions that can adversely impact privacy.
- Mechanisms for reviewing the state of information technology and its practical implementations to enable the international framework to remain relevant in the light of changing capabilities and requirements.
- Mechanisms that can assist in building trust relationships globally.
- Funding arrangements that can assist less developed nations in meeting their responsibilities to protect the information commons.

The problems addressed here derive from a confluence of factors: an increasing social dependence on information-based infrastructures, an increasing complexity of those infrastructures that makes it difficult to anticipate all their failure modes, a growing number of people versed in information technology that can harm information systems, and tools readily available to assist in carrying out malicious acts. These have resulted in alarming rates of growth of system malfunction and system intrusion.

The Internet operates by means of a voluntary but structured process that provides the capability, in principle, to respond to changing technology and user needs, including enhanced security. But since the process is driven by its developers and users, the incorporation of security features in the Internet is not assured, however valuable that may be from a public policy standpoint. There are a number of existing techniques computer and information system owners and operators can utilize for their protection. These include firewalls, virus protection software, one-time passwords, encryption, and virtual private networks. They also include instituting and enforcing security policies, real-time and offline auditing of system operation and use, penetration testing, and implementing data and system backup practices at all levels.

But enhanced security brings associated financial and operational costs that can result in lesser levels of security than are technically feasible. Intrusion detection systems are available today and are increasingly being deployed, but at the same time the number of system attacks, already large, continues to grow. Furthermore, tracking intruders is difficult, slow, and uncertain. Hence the current state of affairs, where attack is relatively easy and defense is difficult or absent, leaves the balance very much on the side of the attacker.

Ongoing security R&D is pointing to ways of protecting information systems such that detecting, tracking, and identifying intruders will be possible with greater ease and certainty through collective actions by users and service providers. These include deploying new Internet protocols, level-of-service agreements making security a contractual requirement, the automation of advanced intrusion-detection systems for warning and tracking, the integration of security tools to provide more complete capabilities to meet wider ranges of needs, the creation of global incident response capabilities, third-party clearinghouses for secure and anonymous communications among incident responders, the use of digital objects to better define ownership of and appropriate uses of information, and increased capabilities for network traffic analysis.

Advances in intruder detection and tracking will aid in deterring attacks by increasing the risk of being caught.

They can also be expected to reduce intrusions on user privacy implicit in current tracking techniques. International agreements, both informal and formal, will be needed if information infrastructure users are to receive greater protection than they can reasonably provide for themselves. These include extending intrusion detection to operate across larger domains, development of new Internet protocols, coordinating international responses to global incidents, shared R&D to keep pace with evolving international threats, and collecting and providing attack information to users in a timely manner to allow them to provide for adaptive defenses.

The Draft Convention presented in this volume illustrates the kinds of steps that can assist in achieving these capabilities. National policies that encourage the introduction of information technology into critical infrastructures, thereby allowing systems of unlimited degrees of complexity and vulnerability to be constructed without corresponding increases in system security, should be examined. It is possible that nations can encourage the evolution of their infrastructure systems in ways that will make them more robust as well as more capable.

Today's information infrastructure, which has provided such dramatic improvements in access to information, can usefully be reexamined from the point of view of system architecture. What is needed is to overlay on the current information transfer network an assurance network that makes possible the definition and enforcement of standards of behavior among its users. This assurance network will involve both technical facilities to assist in protecting user rights as well as provisions for allowing operators of the assurance network to establish and maintain concomitant trust relationships that will be necessary for international cooperation. Protective actions will take time to implement. A central question then becomes one of relative rates. Since available defensive technologies have not been universally deployed, users can do a great deal in the short term to reduce their vulnerabilities.

The pace at which short term enhancements in system security can be made will depend on several elements: the acceptance by users and system operators that increased spending on security is needed, the deployment of available technologies by both individuals and organizations, improvements in current security products to make them easier to integrate, and the availability of new and more powerful security products and services. Looked at from this perspective, the picture merits some degree of optimism because there is so much "low-hanging fruit" over the next several years. The combination of defensive technology and operational process redesign can accomplish a great deal in comparatively short times.

Long-Term Prospects are Less Certain

More difficult to assess is how much society as a whole is willing to change in more fundamental ways. Will infrastructure operators realize that their rush to adopt information technology risks system failures that can only be addressed at the level of system architecture? Will utility regulators recognize that security must be on their agenda and that, without private sector initiatives, a more aggressive public posture may be called for? Will we recognize that deregulation without consideration of the architectural issues can have severe unintended consequences? Will law enforcement agencies increase their levels of investigatory and enforcement capabilities, and will legislators appropriate the required resources? And will the nations of the world agree that the protection of the information commons is a shared responsibility?

The highly dynamic nature of information technology is a further complication in the long-term outlook for protection of infrastructures. New technology creates new vulnerabilities, and it increases the power of attackers as well as that of defenders. System and network security is not a problem that can be solved once and for all; it has the measure-countermeasure and offense-defense nature of military competition. From this perspective there is less reason to be sanguine. A threshold issue for considering fundamental long-term changes in information systems will be that of weighing the cost of ignoring cyber attacks against the cost of actions to reduce the frequency and severity of their failures. There is no simple or obvious answer to this question.

Because no fatal infrastructure failures have so far been induced by cyber attack, our only evidence of catastrophic failure is indirect. The rates of attack, and computer crime of many forms, are increasing, in some cases doubling annually. Such strong exponential increases can rapidly dominate the balance. Unless it can be shown that these exponential growth rates will saturate at some comfortably low level, policymakers in both public and private sectors would be well advised to adopt conservative positions. It would seem prudent to invest now to hedge future downside risks.

Security in Cyber Space

Measures to protect information systems against cyber attacks are receiving increasing attention as the threat of attacks grows and the nature of that threat is better understood. Among these measures are sophisticated technologies for monitoring computer networks and users, detecting intrusion, identifying and tracing intruders, and preserving and analyzing. What legal standards should govern the use of these measures? What nontechnical constraints are likely to be placed, or ought to be placed, on them? What importance should be assigned to these constraints in designing and implementing technologically robust solutions, as well as international agreements to facilitate law enforcement? Specific answers to these questions will ultimately be determined by evaluating the specific measures or agreements proposed. But certain legal principles are broadly applicable, including the right to privacy, the protections against self-incrimination and unwarranted searches and seizures, and the right to due process of law.

These civil liberties are supported in international law and guaranteed in varying forms by the national laws and institutions of many countries. An international regime against cyber crime and terrorism must operate within the constraints of these principles, as defined by the legal frameworks of its States Parties. There is often a tension between protecting civil liberties and enforcing laws to maintain public safety and order. States resolve this tension differently. Agreeing upon a common global level of protection of citizens' rights is problematic owing to international variance in normative standards, legal practices, and political objectives. An international common denominator could reduce the level of protections currently afforded in some states to the level of authoritarian states. In the interest of promoting international cooperation and a timely response to the growing threat of cyber attacks, seeking measures other than agreement on a specific level of protection is more likely to succeed.

However, the differences in domestic values and rules may allow misuse of systems set up for preventing, tracking, or punishing cyber crime. The diversion of technologies for illegitimate purposes—such as unwarranted surveillance—is a real threat, especially in countries that give little weight to civil liberty principles constraining such activities. Countries may be tempted to circumvent legal constraints, moreover, when faced with a national security threat. Systems set up for international cooperation would also introduce new cyber vulnerabilities, since they may be "hacked" or "cracked" and misused by criminals or unauthorized persons. States should address these dangers in the course of developing forms of international cooperation that extend to sharing information and coordinating technology. Issues concerning search, seizure, and due process of law apply primarily to criminal law enforcement.

The world's use of and dependence on international computer networks fosters transnational computer crime. Sophisticated criminals are able to operate from a distance and cover up or confuse the origins of their attacks. To respond to attacks in a timely and effective manner, system operators need to monitor user behavior and detect intrusions in real time. To identify suspects and launch investigations once a crime is detected, large-scale screening, tracing, and analysis of electronic evidence may be required. Such methods demand substantial commitments of technological, economic, and human resources. States, as well as commercial and other public and private entities, face difficult trade-offs in allocating resources to fight cyber crime. Increased network security and investigative measures may come at the expense of network performance, privacy, and users' desire for anonymity.

States may also find their domestic laws, national security objectives, and political or economic priorities at odds with the conditions required for effective international cooperation. Restrictions on cross-border flows of information imposed for policing purposes may impede electronic commerce and other transactions. There are two basic approaches to security in cyberspace: a protective one and a reactive one. Each is constrained in different ways. The protective approach aims to deter criminals through measures that deny access or make a potential target less vulnerable to an attack. This approach is focused on defense. It involves designing more secure Internet protocols, introducing trusted routers and virtual private networks, and utilizing firewalls, encryption, automated intrusion-detection systems, and other security measures.

The reactive approach seeks to deter the threat through effective investigation, prosecution, and punishment. Both approaches involve monitoring and diagnosing abnormal and unauthorized activity. The protective approach favors automation as well as oversight and decision making by computer security experts. The reactive one depends more heavily on the participation of law enforcement and requires end user–oriented (rather than anonymous) traffic analysis, which may be as intrusive as scanning of attached files, keyword searches, and content filtering for signs of potential breaches of criminal law.

Real-time investigative capabilities may extend to creating embedded data collection infrastructures and modifying hardware and/or software to provide for confidential law enforcement access to business, governmental, and private computer networks. The two approaches can be complementary. Their relative weights depend on the preferences and capabilities of implementing parties. Although there are significant obstacles to achieving high levels of cyber security, the protective approach is likely to facilitate greater security with less intrusion. The reactive approach may be more effective in cases of inadequate defense and in safeguarding users who are unable to afford, or unwilling to implement, sufficient protective measures. However, the reactive approach is inherently more intrusive and more threatening to civil liberties.

Privacy and Data Protection

Among the issues considered in this chapter, privacy in cyberspace is the most controversial and publicly debated. Privacy concerns not only the context of law enforcement but also day-to-day business practices and an individual's ability to control the treatment of personal data made available in electronic format or accumulated during Internet use. Commercial exploitation of personal data without consent is already leading to enhanced legal protections for privacy. The enforcement of such protections will raise the issue of the desirability of using protective versus reactive methods, leading to discussions of what can be done to ensure that any method used will protect privacy interests against unwanted intrusion.

The Value, Law, and Status of Privacy Protection

Privacy is not an absolute, well-defined, or uniformly protected value. Individuals, organizations, and societies have traditionally sacrificed some privacy in exchange for greater security, economic gain, or convenience. Trade-offs between privacy and intrusion (by government, industry, etc.) reflect the different historical and social contexts in which they were made. The norm of privacy is linked to an individual's independence, dignity, and integrity. Protection of privacy has evolved historically through international and domestic law. Privacy is a fundamental human right recognized by the 1948 Universal Declaration of Human Rights and many other international and regional instruments and treaties.

The Universal Declaration proclaims that "no one shall be subjected to arbitrary interference with his privacy, family, home or correspondence, nor to attacks upon his honour and reputation", and "everyone has the right to the protection of the law against such interference or attacks". It also states that "everyone has the right to freedom of opinion and expression; this right includes freedom to hold opinions without interference and to seek, receive and impart information and ideas through any media and regardless of frontiers". These provisions create the basic international law framework for the right to privacy, which extends to cyberspace. On the national level, privacy is protected through a combination of constitutional and legislative instruments and self-regulation.

Nearly every country in the world recognizes a constitutional right to privacy, including at least the rights to inviolability of home and secrecy of communications.

Some recently written constitutions, such as those of South Africa and Hungary, contain rights to access and control of one's personal information. In countries where the right to privacy is not explicitly guaranteed by the constitution—the United States, Ireland, and India, for example—this right has been established through other legal provisions or judicial rulings. The advent of information technology provided a new context in which to consider privacy and a new legal impetus for the protection of personal data. The first modern legislation on collecting and handling personal data emerged in the early 1970s in Sweden (1973) and the United States (1974).

The Organization for Economic Cooperation and Development (OECD) was the first international organization to issue a policy, "Guidelines on the Protection of Privacy and Transborder Flows of Personal Data", adopted in 1980. The OECD's policy applies to personal data, whether in the public or private sectors, that pose a danger to privacy and individual liberties because of their nature or the manner in which they are processed and used. Development of international standards continued in the 1980s and 1990s. The Council of Europe (COE) adopted a "Convention for the Protection of Individuals with regard to the Automatic Processing of Personal Data" (1981) and "Guidelines on the Use of Computerized Personal Data Flow" (1989).

The United Nations (UN) produced "Guidelines for the Regulation of Computerized Personal Data Files" (1989). These documents establish principles of minimum privacy guarantees for personal information at all stages of its collection, storage, and dissemination by other parties. They also create new rights for "data subjects"—those whose data are collected and manipulated by government agencies, businesses, and so on—requiring that accurate and up-to-date personal information must be obtained fairly and lawfully, used only for the original, intended purpose, and destroyed after the purpose is achieved. Data subjects are granted the right to access and amend information about them.

The 1995 European Union (EU) Data Protection Directive established a regulatory framework for free movement of personal data, while allowing individual EU countries to exercise their unique approaches to implementation. "Data subjects" are guaranteed the right to know where the data originated, the right to have inaccurate data corrected, the right of appeal in the case of unlawful processing, and the right to deny permission to use data under certain circumstances.

The 1999 COE Recommendation provides guidelines for the protection of privacy on the Internet. Whereas the COE and UN guidelines are recommendations, the EU Directives are binding: member states must adopt them into their domestic law. Currently, nearly fifty countries and jurisdictions have enacted or are in the process of enacting privacy laws, designed to ensure compatibility with international standards, to address past government abuses, and/or to promote electronic commerce.

Threats to Privacy in Cyber Space

Privacy in cyberspace is threatened by businesses and other entities that collect and manipulate personal data, by criminals who steal such data or stalk people over the Internet, and by governments that pursue surveillance or allow intrusive law enforcement practices. Sophisticated electronic capabilities to collect, analyze, manipulate, and disseminate information, as well as to enable tracking, surveillance, and interference with communications, create unprecedented challenges to privacy.

Such technologies are becoming more effective, available, and affordable internationally. At the same time, globalization and growing dependence on information technology in all spheres of society have led to a dramatic increase in the level of electronically compiled and transmitted personal data. The differences in domestic legal standards and practices also endanger private data transmitted over international networks. Even if one state has robust privacy laws, it cannot currently guarantee equivalent levels of protection once the data flow beyond its borders. Gaps in protection will be created to the extent that market forces undervalue privacy, laws and law enforcement fail to keep up with technological capabilities, and international discrepancies undermine domestic levels of protection.

The U.S. Federal Trade Commission found that privacy policies, posted on many commercial websites, did not provide sufficient protection for online consumers. Businesses track online behavior, sell personal information, and misuse personal profiles built on the basis of financial, medical, and other sensitive information. Employers' intrusion into electronic communications of employees in the workplace is another area of concern. Privacy protection is often subordinated to property rights of employers as the providers of their employees' electronic communication services. In the United States, for example, legislation prohibits employers from eavesdropping on the private telephone conversations of their employees at work, but no similar protection extends to electronic mail communications.

Criminals take advantage of deficiencies in the protection of sensitive information transmitted and accumulated in electronic form. Identity theft is among the fastest-growing cyber crimes; in the U.S. alone, it has increased more than 300 percent, from 7,868 cases in 1997 to 30,115 in 1999. Pedophiles entice victims in Internet chat rooms and use electronic communications to arrange actual meetings. Spurned suitors forge vindictive e-mails inviting rape. Stalkers identify victims on the Internet and threaten them physically. The spread and growing severity of cyber crime require greater security and better law enforcement.

Where security and policing methods are intrusive, achieving these objectives may demand some limitations of privacy. Should governments treat Internet communications like a phone call, paper correspondence, or a discussion in a public place? Responses to this question determine the extent of permissible infringements, as well as the specific rules governing law enforcement functions, and responses vary among states. Even the relatively strong European Convention on Human Rights makes exceptions to the exercise of the right to privacy "in accordance with the law", when it is "necessary in a democratic society in the interests of national security, public safety or the economic well-being of the country, for the prevention of disorder or crime, for the protection of health or morals, or for the protection of the rights and freedoms of others".

Although the burden of proof to establish the need for this exception rests with the potential intruder, the scope of the exception is very broad. Many national laws have similar provisions. Such breadth can lead to abuse if police attempt to assume excessive powers or governments pursue unlawful surveillance. Caspar Bowden of the United Kingdom's Foundation for Information Policy Research has warned about the implications of improving detection, prosecution, and prevention of cyber crime at the expense of privacy: There are now traffic-analysis tools commercially available to law enforcement which can take telephone number logs in machine-readable form and draw "friendship trees", which show the grouping and relationships between parties calling each other in time, and can match patterns of association automatically using sophisticated artificial intelligence programming.

There is enormous potential for law enforcement in increased use of traffic analysis, but there are a number of fundamental distinctions between traffic analysis of telephony, and Internet traffic—especially in a fully wired Information Society. The Internet Protocol ("IP") abolishes any meaningful distinction between domestic and foreign communications intelligence. A well-funded national communications intelligence agency, which already captures large quantities of both traffic and content data and has the organization to process it and integrate it effectively with other forms of intelligence gathering, presents an enormous temptation to government simply to leverage that capability for wider domestic coverage.

Intelligence-integrated traffic analysis is phenomenally corrosive of civil liberties. If government was in a position to know which websites you visit, what you buy online, the e-mail addresses of those who-mail you and those you have e-mailed, and analyze and archive that information without hindrance, there is potential for an unprecedentedly serious abuse of power. The threat of systematic government intrusion into electronic communications has already received attention around the world. Russia's Federal Security Bureau (FSB) is implementing an Internet surveillance system that requires all Internet service providers (ISPs) to enable routine FSB monitoring of communications.

Russian human rights advocates report that many of the country's 350 ISPs have already been forced to comply; endangering secrecy of communications and other civil liberties of users and persons whose sensitive information may be transmitted over the Internet. The U.S. Federal Bureau of Investigation (FBI) is using a similar wiretapping system with specialized software that can scan millions of e-mails a second. When deployed, the system must be connected directly into ISPs' computer networks, thus giving the government potential access to all customers' digital communications. Typical Internet wiretaps last about forty-five days, after which the FBI removes the equipment. Critics contend that the system is open to abuse, raising dire privacy and security concerns.

Threatening surveillance has also taken place on the international scale. The United States, the United Kingdom,

Canada, Australia, and New Zealand allegedly engage in selective multinational screening of telephone, fax, satellite, and Internet communications for foreign intelligence purposes. This system, known as Echelon, supposedly links computers around the world to capture large volumes of information, and to sort and analyze it through sophisticated keyword searches and artificial intelligence aids. The information collected is compiled and routed according to requests of the participating parties.

Allegations of unlawful surveillance and violation of privacy, in the United States and abroad, have been raised in regard to this system. There are inherent dangers in a system for advanced monitoring, searching, tracking, and analyzing of communications. Though it could be very helpful against cyber crime and terrorism, it would also provide participating governments, especially authoritarian governments or agencies with little accountability, tools to violate civil liberties domestically and abroad. Correspondence of innocent people could be intercepted and people could be repressed as a result.

Systems set up for international policing of cyberspace could also be hacked or misused by an insider to undermine a participating government or to damage the interests of a state. The technology and know-how, which will be developed and provided to less technologically advanced countries in the course of international cooperation, could be used to enhance domestic surveillance and suppression by governments that disregard human rights. These threats exist now and they are likely to expand in the future as advanced computer networking becomes pervasive in public and private lives and methods for intercepting and analyzing information become more sophisticated, widespread, and affordable. Integrating attributed personal data from different systems could make comprehensive, detailed profiles available for retrieval, manipulation, and abuse.

Abuses by the private sector may range from inundation with unsolicited targeted advertisements to various forms of covert discrimination, such as denial of employment on the basis of prior knowledge of health conditions, or denial of medical services on the basis of financial debts. Such conglomerations of data would be vulnerable to identity theft and other cyber crimes. As for possible government abuses, the totalitarian regimes of the twentieth century—with ubiquitous informers, government controls over all spheres of society, and egregious violations of human rights—should serve as a reminder and a warning. Several models of data protection have emerged—public enforcement, sector-specific regulation, and self-regulation—reflecting different legal approaches to privacy. Methods are also used in combination.

The EU, Australia, Hong Kong, New Zealand, Canada, and many countries of Central and Eastern Europe have adopted the first model, in which a public official (a commissioner, ombudsman, or registrar) enforces a comprehensive data protection law. This official monitors compliance, conducts investigations into alleged violations, and requests legal action in case of a breach. The official is also usually responsible for public education and international interaction with respect to data protection and transfer. Alternatively, the United States has adopted sector-specific rules (covering video rental records or financial privacy, for example) rather than comprehensive laws.

Singapore, Australia, and the United States also promote a form of self regulation, whereby companies and industries establish codes of practice. Enforcement in these cases typically proceeds through private, as opposed to government, actions. Industry self-regulation will be insufficient, however, as long as market forces undervalue privacy in cyberspace. Sector-specific rules may be sufficient, but protection may also fail if data are transferred or sold to entities in sectors with lower standards. Public enforcement has provided higher levels of privacy protection, but it is vulnerable to the same problem: transmittal of sensitive data beyond the networks of the country with strong legal enforcement of privacy is likely to result in decreased levels of protection.

The countries of the European Union protect personal data more rigorously than the United States, and this discrepancy has fueled an international controversy. The 1995 EU Data Protection Directive requires that personal data may be collected only for specific, explicit, and legitimate purposes. Only relevant, accurate, and up-to-date data may be held. Member states of the EU are obliged to maintain these standards when exporting or processing information pertaining to EU citizens abroad or they must halt the movement of data in the absence of "adequate" (equivalent) protections. The United States has no similar statute, and the EU considers the U.S. industry's self-regulating approach inadequate.

To mitigate the ensuing limitations on transborder data flow, a "safe harbor" agreement was recently reached that will enable some U.S. companies to collect data about EU citizens, if the companies demonstrate safeguards that meet European approval. These companies will be required to give notice to European citizens about how their information is to be gathered and used, allow them to withhold data, and offer them reasonable access to their own records. Such partial resolution toward greater privacy standards is encouraging. Nonetheless, the dispute is alarming. If the most advanced democracies disagree on adequate protection of privacy, agreement and observance of this norm can hardly be expected in a global setting that includes less democratic and least accountable governments.

From the standpoint of security against cyber crime, the 1995 EU Data Protection Directive does not necessarily impede law enforcement activities and international cooperation in cyberspace. The directive fully applies to the first two Pillars of the Treaty of the European Union: (I) the European Community, which covers democratization of the institutions, citizenship, and economic and monetary union, and (II) the common foreign and security policy. It is the third Pillar (III), however, that addresses the issues of justice and home affairs, including police and judicial cooperation to combat drug trafficking, international fraud, and other crimes. The scope of the directive does not cover law enforcement procedures.

This means that there are opportunities for international cooperation against cyber crime and also threats to privacy in the course of such cooperation. Privacy-related law enforcement practices are being examined by the European Commission and may be subject to more intense scrutiny in the near future. To compensate for the uneven or insufficient privacy protections in commercial and public settings, and to reduce their vulnerability to cyber crime, public and private organizations and individuals can adopt existing protective measures. Encryption, anonymous remailers, proxy servers, and other technologies, described in the preceding chapter, are commercially available.

Many of these technologies offer protection against cyber crime coupled with enhancement of privacy. These include more secure network protocols and routers, encryption, firewalls, virtual private networks, secure anonymous communications, challenge response systems, and security management applications. IP version 6 (IPv6), the next generation of Internet Protocols, allows routers along delivery paths to record addresses of previous destinations in the header of the message. This feature would enable the searching and tracing of suspect messages without prior disclosure of their content or author, thus protecting the identity of the sender and the secrecy of communications. Information exchanges among computer security staff regarding modes of penetration and attack, suspected crimes, early warnings, and anomalies in computer operation can facilitate prevention and timely incident response.

Incentives for greater protection can be created by placing more legal or financial responsibility on the owners and principal operators of computers and networks—be they businesses, organizations, or individuals. Stronger cyber security would deter some cyber crimes, but not all. Moreover, technologically and economically advanced nations can enhance cyber security and privacy by making protective technologies available and affordable on the market, but citizens of less advanced countries may not be able to afford these alternatives. The United States has proposed creating an international cyber police. Such a system would need to be worldwide in both coverage and participation, and would enable police to conduct rapid investigations over global communication networks.

Although it is unclear what the United States intends beyond voluntary coordination, the European Union reacted unfavorably, citing privacy implications. A full-fledged international police force would exemplify an extreme of the reactive approach; its mere existence would pose concerns about the security and integrity of information it acquires, the reliability of its operators and users, the trustworthiness of international participants, and the possibility of its use for unlawful purposes (by member states, police officials, or criminals and terrorists). Some forms of international cooperation will nonetheless be required to combat transnational cyber crime.

The "International Convention to Enhance Protection from Cyber Crime and Terrorism", draft combines protective and reactive measures with provisions for protecting privacy and other civil liberties. This draft calls upon States Parties to establish cyber offenses as crimes under domestic law. Thereafter, investigations, extraditions, prosecutions, mutual legal assistance, and judicial proceedings are to be carried out in accordance with the laws of the States Parties. Intrusive international law enforcement procedures may be allowed, but only in accordance with domestic legal standards and mutual legal assistance treaties.

The proposed convention explicitly states that it shall not be construed to require an infringement of the privacy or other human rights of any person as defined by the laws of the requested state. To ensure systematic monitoring and implementation of this provision, the draft proposes to create a group of experts dedicated to the protection of privacy and other human rights. In some cases, especially those involving international exchanges of sensitive information and monitoring of networks by law enforcement, special procedural safeguards for privacy may also be necessary.

Domestic and international exchanges among technology and law enforcement experts of data regarding past and suspected computer crimes, anomalies in computer operation, network vulnerabilities, modes of penetration, alerts, and warnings, fall into this category. Such data—no doubt relevant and probably crucial for effective response to cyber crime—are likely to contain sensitive security and personal information, including aliases, identities, and passwords. Information about the citizens of one country may be provided to entities in other countries, whose privacy laws may not afford the same level of protection.

An agreed-upon privacy policy—whether deference to domestic practices or a reasonable minimum level of protection— acceptable to parties in the international exchange, would help guard privacy during such information exchanges. Businesses, such as information infrastructure or service providers, may also be called upon to reveal sensitive information concerning attacks, vulnerabilities, and personnel as part of investigative or preventive measures. Even though the support of commercial entities is often required, they are reluctant to share sensitive security-related information with the government.

Disclosure and attribution of such information may have the consequences of disrupting business objectives, causing economic losses, triggering unwelcome legal proceedings, and threatening individual employees. Employees are in many cases subject to loss of their jobs for unauthorized revelation of suspected criminal activity; and businesses should be concerned about the personal safety and privacy of employees when dealing with a suspected crime or perpetrator, or they should be compelled to have such concern by legislation or economic incentives. Preserving the identity of institutions and their employees in tracking, tracing, and investigating crime against them may be a crucial vehicle for building the necessary public–private sector cooperation in this area. Automation is particularly important to enhance both security and privacy.

The use of automated and semi automated tools facilitates near-real-time detection of security breaches, tracing to origin of attack, scalability of action (detecting intrusions among large volumes of data involved in normal network operations and responding to intrusions that may hop across international networks), and ultimately increased efficiency and effectiveness. Automation in searching, tracing, and tracking preserves the anonymity and privacy of innocent individuals whose messages may be subjected to search in the course of an investigation. The protection of privacy ultimately relies on a combination of automated and other protective technologies as well as laws that constrain law enforcement. Where law enforcement methods are intrusive and automation is not available or fully reliable, legal constraints are especially necessary.

Criminal Law and Constraints on Police Behavior

Constraints on police behavior in cyberspace have received far less public attention than privacy problems.

This is partly because they are narrowly focused on criminal investigation—whereas privacy interests span personal, commercial, and government realms—and partly because what is necessary and legally permissible in cyber-related investigation and prosecution procedures is still being determined. The protections against self-incrimination and unwarranted searches and seizures and the rights to due process of law apply in cyberspace as anywhere else, yet technological realities can complicate the observance of these rights.

The pursuit of crimes committed over international computer networks is also complicated by the differences in domestic procedures and the absence of a system of international criminal law. In most legal systems, the main sources of law that govern searches, seizures, and other modes of police behavior are constitutions, legislation, and case law. Investigation and seizure of evidence in democratic states are governed by laws that protect citizens *vis-a'-vis* the state and its law enforcement powers. In many states, searches and seizures must not only be legally authorized, they must also be carried out with due respect for civil liberties.

In the United States, for example, these principles are protected by the Fourth Amendment to the Constitution, which states that "the right of the people to be secure in their persons, houses, papers, and effects, against unreasonable searches and seizures, shall not be violated, and no warrants shall issue, but upon probable cause, supported by oath or affirmation, and particularly describing the place to be searched, and the persons or things to be seized". The concept of "search" can be defined broadly to include not only the search of a place or person but also other invasions of privacy such as wiretapping. Searches may be held upon consent of the individual to be searched, as long as specific consent criteria are satisfied. Many national legal systems prohibit the admission in criminal prosecutions of evidence obtained unlawfully; the rationale for and the extent of exclusion vary.

Such differences make it difficult for states to agree on a common international standard of police behavior. Sovereignty issues, addressed by Drew Arena of the U.S. Department of Justice, complicate international investigations: [T]he basic problem is presented by a nation's perception of its national sovereignty. To what extent must it assert its sovereignty to protect its citizens and enforce its criminal law? To what degree is it prepared to compromise that sovereignty for the sake of (reciprocal) international cooperation? For example, could the U.S. enter into an agreement which provided that foreign officials, armed with legal process in their country, would be searching data bases in the U.S. from abroad, unless we were satisfied that the Fourth Amendment's probable cause requirements had been met?

How would we reconcile such an agreement with the rigorous standards to be met for domestic law enforcement to obtain access and disclosure of electronically stored data in our criminal law? How would we avoid treating it as an unauthorized access under Title 18 Section 1030? On a practical level, how would we know that a foreign law enforcement access to a data base was not a hacker's attack? These challenges do not preclude international cooperation. For example, the convention proposed in this volume explicitly recognizes the priority of national laws. It also helps clarify which rules should apply in transnational investigations, extraditions, and judicial proceedings by establishing priority in jurisdiction and venues for cooperation and mutual legal assistance.

When a requested state is asked to assist—in identifying and tracing cyber attacks, executing searches and seizures, locating or identifying persons, examining objects and sites, securing and exchanging information and evidentiary items, and so on, by electronic and other means—rules of this requested state will apply. Moreover, the proposed convention requires that requests be made upon a reasonable belief that an offense has occurred and that evidence is contained in cyber systems within the territory of a requested state. The requested state will then undertake the preservation of such data, but it will not be compelled to release the data unless presented by the requesting state with adequate cause for release.

The technology of searching and seizing electronic evidence presents challenges of a different nature. Computer hardware and disks may need to be obtained as evidence. Surveillance of network and user behavior may also be necessary, along with searches and forensic investigation of e-mail messages, user files, customer or employee records, and encryption keys. Surveillance may be needed before, during, and after an incident to determine whether a crime has occurred and how to respond.

Available methods range from wiretaps on phone calls and Internet communications to various tagging and tracing techniques (user, chip or software ID, network IP address, location detector, etc.), room bugs, and cameras (possibly tied into face-recognition systems). Suspect computers can be remotely monitored by capturing keystrokes, passwords, e-mail messages, attachments, and desktop files. Police may also monitor the "computer underground"—skilled but not directly suspected hacker communities—to gain insights into the nature of the attack and possible attackers.

National laws often contain exceptions to balance protective civil liberty principles with the need to maintain public safety and order. These exceptions can help guide the police to determine the legal boundaries in computer searches and seizures in the absence, or in early stages of development, of cyber laws. Exceptions can also create opportunities for abuse of law enforcement powers. Many countries still lack specific computer-related laws and procedures, so they refer to general criminal laws in cyber cases. Alternatively, the U.S. Department of Justice has published, and regularly updates, specific "Federal Guidelines for Searching and Seizing Computers". The guidelines address the Supreme Court's strong preference for warrants in searches and seizures, as well as the limited exceptions to Fourth Amendment requirements.

As such, the guidelines provide a suitable background for the discussion of the exceptions, drawing upon technical and international realities to evaluate their application in cyberspace. The exceptions to the warrant requirement include: *(a) Lack of reasonable expectation of privacy.* The Supreme Court defines a "search" as an intrusion by police into an area where individuals have a "reasonable expectation of privacy". Generally, no one has an expectation of privacy as to something that can be observed by the public. Whether the Internet is a public space or a private space, where search warrants are usually required, is still legally unsettled.

Determinations have been made in specific cases, depending on the type of electronic transmission sent and the recipient of the transmission. For example, real-time, Internet conversations observed by an agent in a chat room lacked Fourth Amendment protection, because the defendant did not have a reasonable expectation of privacy vis-a' -vis other participants in chat room discussions. However, a determination regarding the public or private nature of the Internet cannot be made categorically, because the Internet can be used in different ways, with more or less reasonable or justifiable expectations of privacy. *(b) Informants and undercover agents.*

The use of informants or undercover agents to aid investigation is generally permitted by law. In accessing electronic bulletin boards and chat rooms undercover agents are not required to identify themselves as such, but must confine their activities to those authorized for other users. The sender of an e-mail message, like the sender of a letter, runs the risk that he is sending that message to an undercover agent. A government informant or undercover agent may capture and record the contents of electronic conversations to which he is a party, just as an agent may record a conversation in which he is a participant.

However, the inexperience of police in Internet-related cases may lead them to draw erroneous conclusions about apparently incriminating information. If an agent is to exercise law enforcement powers as a result of undercover activities, he must still demonstrate probable cause and fulfill other requirements. *(c) Plain view doctrine.* Evidence of a crime may be seized without a warrant, if a police officer is in a lawful position to observe such evidence and its incriminating character is immediately apparent. This applies to situations where police enhance their ability to observe by commonly used means, such as binoculars or a flashlight. In such cases, there is no reasonable expectation of privacy, and police observation is not considered a search.

However, creating plain view by means of "moving" or "disturbing" items, or using sophisticated electronic devices, must be justified by probable cause. If agents with a warrant to search a computer for evidence of narcotics trafficking observe a list of passwords taped to the computer monitor, the list may also be seized. The application of enhanced plain view to cyberspace is less clear. Some applications may depend on what is considered public or private space on the Internet, because government investigators can lawfully be in a public space without a warrant and they may observe illegal activity in plain view.

Discretion in using this exception is necessary because computer and multimedia communications technologies advance very rapidly, making it difficult to distinguish what electronic devices are sophisticated and uncommon enough to require probable cause. *(d) Wiretaps.* Wiretaps may be performed by federal agents only for certain specific crimes, upon application to a judge through high-level officials at the Department of Justice. State agents must gain approval of high-level state law enforcement officials. Approval may be waived in case of emergencies that involve "conspiratorial activities threatening to national security", "conspiratorial activities characteristic of organized crime", and "immediate danger of death or serious bodily injury to any person".

It may be difficult to detect and determine, in a timely manner, whether an Internet surfer is engaged in conspiratorial activity rather than electronic commerce or mere chatting. To assist such detection and determination, Bowden proposed the use of "trawling warrants". A required "trawling warrant" would specify a logical circuit or domain of capture, rather than allowing the capture of all messages on a topic or from or to a person. Signals from this specified domain would be automatically selected by computer against a "certificate" issued by a Secretary of State (or similar authority) that contains the description of the target subject matter suitable for machine searching.

To limit abuse, the issuer would need to guarantee that uncertified intercepted material would not be looked at, read, or listened to by any person. Exemptions for extended interceptions for national security reasons could be given on a case-by-case basis only. However, one must be warned that facing the difficulty of such narrow, targeted wiretapping of speedy and possibly disguised electronic communications, law enforcement may be—and has been—tempted to utilize large-scale, indiscriminate, and intrusive surveillance instead. *(e) Exigent circumstances.* "When destruction of evidence is imminent, a warrantless seizure of that evidence is justified if there is probable cause to believe that the item seized constitutes evidence of criminal activity".

Investigators must consider the degree of urgency, the time necessary to obtain a warrant, whether the evidence is about to be removed or destroyed, the destructibility of evidence, the possibility of danger, and whether suspects are aware that they are being observed or followed. This exception also justifies warrantless searches if the circumstances would cause a reasonable person to believe that an immediate search is necessary. Such circumstances involve the need for immediate aid, escape of a suspect, or another emergency or frustration of legitimate law enforcement objectives. A warrantless seizure under exigent circumstances does not automatically justify a warrantless search.

If police lawfully observe a suspect's computer screen displaying evidence of crime, and then see the suspect modifying or deleting files containing such evidence, police may justifiably download them or seize the computer. However, the application of exigent circumstances to searching and seizing data from two or more computers on a wide area network, used by individuals other than suspects, is less clear and should be determined upon a careful examination of each situation. Electronic data are generally perishable. Integrity of data can be compromised by humidity, temperature, vibrations, physical mutilation, strong magnetic fields, and computer commands to erase or re-format, and so on.

This condition may strengthen the grounds for this exception, but only in the presence of probable cause. *(f) Consent search.* Neither probable cause nor a warrant is required if a police officer obtains a suspect's consent for a search. The police are not required to inform the suspect of his right to withhold consent. The only criterion that must be satisfied is "voluntariness", defined in terms of whether a reasonable "person would feel free to decline the officers' requests or otherwise terminate the encounter". The burden is on the government to prove that the criterion is met. Defining the scope of consented search on a networked computer can be problematic when consent to search one computer does not necessarily extend to other computers or equipment that may be physically or virtually connected to it. Encryption creates another challenge.

An encrypted computer file can be analogous to a locked file cabinet (because the owner is attempting to preserve secrecy) or to a document written in a language foreign to the reader. A warranted search would authorize searching for and seizing encrypted information, as well as requesting authority to decrypt (to "break the lock" on the cabinet or to "translate" the document). If, however, the search is based on consent, a court may find that a target who encrypted his data and did not disclose the necessary decryption key has tacitly limited the scope of his consent. If police do not ask explicitly for consent to search the encrypted material, or such consent is refused, a warrant may be required for the encrypted data. *(g) Border search.* As a condition of crossing the border or its "functional equivalent", officials can search people and property without a warrant and without probable cause. Incoming baggage, persons, mail, as well as diskettes, tapes, computer hard drives, and other media, fall under this exception. This exception highlights the quintessential law enforcement problem created by cyberspace. On the one hand, cyberspace is tied to physical locations of ISPs and Internet users within some sovereign territory.

On the other hand, sending an e-mail message is categorically different from crossing a national border in person or sending a paper letter. Regular mail travels intact and enters its international destination through an established border post. E-mail travels in the form of several packets of coded information that may separate enroute and pass through servers located in various countries. The border search exception does not readily apply to data transmitted electronically because its justification, based on the sovereign's power to exclude illegal articles from the country, no longer applies once such articles have come into the country undetected.

Network monitoring, as a protective measure conducted by computer security specialists (without involvement of law enforcement) for the purposes of optimizing network performance and ensuring security, generally will not face constraints of criminal law. Cooperation among ISPs and computer security professionals could be summoned to protect hardware, software, and databases. This would serve not only the goal of combating cyber crime (which may have a lower priority in nongovernmental, for-profit organizations), but also immediate goals of meeting contractual commitments to customers, maintaining continuity of business, and guarding against liabilities that may arise from allegations of negligence.

More effective computer security and timely detection of and response to unauthorized access or use of cyber systems would help reduce both cyber crime and intrusive law enforcement. Should police investigation become necessary, the use of automated near-real-time intrusion detection, tracking, containment, response, and reporting capabilities would more readily satisfy the legal constraints imposed on this activity? Automation may not solve all problems, but where available and appropriate, it could provide grounds for probable cause, identify suspects, and collect a certain amount of evidence, while preserving the anonymity of uninvolved network users.

Some automated methods may be limited in scope to local orientation and reaction, which is ineffective in the internetworked global environment. A global response to cyber crime demands capabilities to correlate intrusion/ attack symptoms occurring seemingly independently in different parts of the network. Reaction must be coordinated and uniform. Constraints on search, seizure, and due process of law under these circumstances are necessarily more important.

Due Process of Law

International human rights agreements and many national constitutions guarantee equal and proper treatment of individuals before the law. This guarantee entitles individuals to protection against self-incrimination and arbitrary arrest, detention, or exile. If arrested, one must be informed at the time of arrest of the reasons for the arrest and the charges made. The Universal Declaration of Human Rights and the International Covenant of Civil and Political Rights entitle every person to a fair and public hearing by a competent, independent, and impartial tribunal, in the determination of the person's rights and obligations and of any criminal charge. Moreover, everyone charged with a penal offense has the right to be presumed innocent until proved guilty according to law in a public trial, and the right to call and confront witnesses and to introduce evidence.

No one may be found guilty of any penal offense that did not constitute a penal offense under national or international law at the time it was committed, nor may a heavier penalty be imposed than the one applicable at the time the penal offense was committed. States implement such provisions through national criminal justice systems. Suspects typically have the right to silence, although the levels of protection differ. Due process of law is generally interpreted to require a trial or other legal proceedings, which provide fair procedures under accepted standards of national law and international norms.

The right to qualified counsel is fairly common, but it differs in scope. Regardless of the existing domestic and international legal safeguards, violations of due process principles persist around the world. The U.S. State Department reports widespread denials of basic legal protections and due process to criminal defendants, detentions without trial or charge, prolonged pretrial detentions and trial delays, illegal searches, and infringements on citizens' privacy rights. Requirements for due process of law and accountability apply fully to computer-related cases.

They also augment technological, legal, and organizational challenges involved in combating cyber crime. Effective and timely information exchanges among ISPs, technical experts, and law enforcement can improve investigative functions. A global incident response capability may require teams of technical, legal, and police experts, linked to their respective organizations, to track trends and activities of known and potential cyber criminals and terrorists. Accomplishing such cooperation among individuals and organizations with different goals, cultures, and procedures is likely to be difficult from the operational standpoint. The legitimacy of specific methods used to accomplish such goals will be judged according to specific situations. General warnings are also appropriate.

Proposals have been made to assign a presumption of guilt to suspects who withhold decryption keys, unless the defense could somehow prove non-possession. Reversing burdens of proof in this manner may deprive an accused of the right to a fair trial. Extensive profiling of individual behaviors on the Internet may lead to self-incrimination. Once an infrastructure for policing of international networks is in place, it could be used to the detriment of private citizens. The extent of intrusion justified in a targeted and warranted police investigation is unacceptable in the general societal context. Concern over due process of law in the course of international cooperation against cyber crime and terrorism has led to a number of provisions in the proposed Draft Convention.

As a minimum level of protection, it allows States Parties to insist on the preservation of national norms. It entitles any person detained by a State Party to rights extended under national law to: communicate without unnecessary delay with the appropriate representative of the detained person's state or authority entitled to protect his or her rights; be visited by a representative of that state; have this representative physically present to observe any legal proceedings that may result in punishment; and be informed of these entitlements promptly after detention. The Draft Convention prohibits any denial or impairment of these entitlements.

The proposed convention also prohibits extradition or legal assistance if there are grounds to believe that a suspect will be prosecuted or punished on account of political offense, or on account of that person's race, religion, nationality, ethnic origin, or political belief. Although strong differences exist among states concerning restrictions on expression and political activity, this provision allows states to prevent or hinder politically motivated or unfair prosecutions by refusing or ceasing cooperation with the prosecuting state. In case of a serious and unresolvable situation of abuse of the international regime of technical and legal cooperation, effective economic and political sanctions may be imposed on the offending state.

The sanctions may extend to denial of technological and economic assistance under the regime, expulsion from the regime, and measures to limit the ability of the offending government to benefit from participating in the international information infrastructure. The extent to which the rights to privacy, the protections against unwarranted searches and seizures, and the rights to due process of law constrain an international regime against cyber crime and terrorism depends on the regime and the domestic laws of participating states. National laws often contain exceptions or special privileges for law enforcement to pursue criminal investigations.

These privileges may also threaten the protection of human rights. States have different attitudes toward privacy, law enforcement powers, and due process. However, unilateral responses to cyber crime are not likely to be effective. Confronted with the need for international cooperation, states will look for ways to reconcile these differences or attempt to justify some inappropriate behavior. Greater emphasis on protective technological and legal measures, and respect for civil liberties in the course of cooperation, will help reduce the latter outcome. Overall, protective measures, which aim to reduce cyber vulnerabilities and rely on computer security staff for initial reaction to incidents, are less intrusive than measures designed to allow extensive law enforcement presence in cyberspace.

The protective approach can be implemented through encryption, automation, and anonymous tagging and tracking—recording fields in packet header information, for example, which does not intrude on the content of messages, or router assisted fingerprinting of packets without disclosure of their originator unless sufficient evidence of crime emerges. Although better measures will need to be designed and updated continuously to keep up with offenses, this approach can afford greater protection against both cyber crime and intrusive law enforcement. The reactive approach necessarily involves the participation of law enforcement officials, who will likely scan files, review content, and engage in other surveillance of communications to collect evidence and to identify perpetrators.

Engaging in such activities on a wide "preventive" scale, rather than in specific cases with established probable cause of crime, would raise legal and moral concerns of unduly intrusive policing. Furthermore, even in specific cases of suspected crime, limiting the scope of targeted surveillance may be technologically and operationally difficult. This approach places communications of innocent people and their private information at risk. The reactive approach requires greater scrutiny. While clearly threatening to civil liberties, reactive measures would not necessarily result in fewer crimes and better law enforcement.

Even in most technologically and economically developed countries today, police lack equipment and training to meet the growing challenge of the electronic dimensions of crime. Technical experts agree that greater automation is crucial for a timely, scalable, and less intrusive response to international cyber crime. These offers hope that, in the name of both efficiency and civil liberties, relatively nonintrusive technological measures will be developed and implemented in the near future. Such solutions should provide a more suitable balance among security, law enforcement, and civil liberties in cyberspace. Reactive measures will also be enhanced, however, and will need to be fashioned and monitored so as to ensure adequate protection of human rights.

The technologies of crime and punishment are undergoing a rapid and profound evolution. But though such technologies constitute a moving target for evaluation, the legal and normative principles discussed here will endure, because they are independent of specific technological means. As such, they can provide a framework for building a global infrastructure and policy environment that balances the needs for crimefree business, government, and personal communications, with the protection of property, privacy, and civil liberties. Tensions between security and civil liberties may emerge.

These tensions should be carefully examined with the awareness of threats and social implications of measures against cyber crime and terrorism. Ensuring the protection of fundamental rights to privacy, protection against self-incrimination and unwarranted searches and seizures, and due process of law is critical. Such protections should be prominent among the design criteria for technological, policy, and legal measures, and should be enforced by law and strong economic and political incentives. Governments value liberty, privacy, and security differently. National rules concerning the intrusiveness of law enforcement, protection of citizen's rights, and international cooperation, reflect the country's normative choices about the roles of the state, market, and individual.

Constituting the basis of domestic law, these norms affect the international behavior of nation-states. An international regime can help influence these norms over time. Today, when an international regime to combat cyber crime and terrorism is becoming a reality, there is a special opportunity to promote greater respect for human rights. At the very least, methods for international technological and legal cooperation against cyber crime and terrorism should not be permitted to become a vehicle for governments to oppress society.

5

International Convention on Cyber Security

The case for international cooperation in dealing with cyber crime is overwhelming. The presentations and discussion at the Stanford Conference, distilled in this volume, demonstrate the growing threat and cost of such crime, as well as its transnational nature. The debates currently under way is over the form and scope such cooperation should take, and the extent to which the United States and other technologically advanced states should rely upon multilateral efforts to enhance cyber security. Proposals for voluntary international cooperation have been advanced and are being implemented.

The principal elements of these proposals—to train law enforcement officials to understand and cope with cyber crimes, and to establish round-the-clock emergency response teams—are widely supported. In addition, the Group of Eight (G-8) and private groups such as the Internet Alliance have issued guidelines aimed at making voluntary cooperation more effective. Although these groups recognize that international cooperation is essential, they have yet to accept the idea that an international treaty should be negotiated establishing legally mandated standards and obligations. Support for voluntary, as opposed to legally mandated, international measures rests upon several arguments.

Most cyber crime, it is argued, is conventional crime (fraud, drug dealing, and money laundering, sexual exploitation of minors), in which cyber technology happens to be used. Existing treaties and international arrangements provided for extradition and legal assistance are potentially applicable in these cases. Securing international agreement on the wording of new cyber crimes will be difficult, moreover, and vast differences exist among states regarding appropriate regulation of content, the proper scope of transnational investigation, and the bases upon which tracking information and messages should be subject to seizure and scrutiny. Furthermore, a great disparity exists among states—even technologically advanced ones—as to the scope of privacy and other rights possessed by individuals under national laws that would either operate to limit an international agreement or be compromised by one.

Finally, the Internet, many believe, has been a powerful vehicle for economic growth and enhanced communication in large part because it is controlled by the private sector rather than by governments, and this growth and creativity may be adversely affected by international legal requirements and regulation. For these reasons, Drew C. Arena, then senior counsel to the assistant attorney general, U.S. Department of Justice, commented at the Stanford Conference that achieving consensus on "the specific steps" to be taken in negotiating a multilateral treaty would be "too hard" at the present time to warrant the effort.

University of Chicago School of Law Professor Jack L. Goldsmith has argued that, in the absence of a suitable international regime, the United States should rely on unilateral measures in fighting transnational cyber crime. However, he does, in principle, favor the pursuit of such a regime. These arguments against the creation of an international legal regime to deal with cyber security are cogent, but they are based on difficulties and dangers that are avoidable. Not only is the case for a multilateral agreement to combat cyber crime and terrorism strong, the need to undertake the effort of negotiating one is becoming clearer with the increasing costs of such activity.

Though it may indeed be true that most crimes in which computers and networks are involved are conventional and potentially covered by international agreements, these are not the crimes against which a new treaty is needed. Existing international agreements provide no help in dealing with crimes related directly to the information infrastructure, including attacks utilizing viruses (such as "Melissa" and "I Love You"), denials of service, and other destructive conduct. Furthermore, the need for an international agreement to deal with cyber crime rests not merely on the fact that such acts include new types of conduct but also on the need for new methods by which cyber crimes will have to be investigated and prosecuted to provide effective protection.

Certainly it would be complicated to secure multilateral agreement on the precise wording of cyber crimes, but that effort need not be undertaken: a broad consensus exists with regard to certain conduct involving the information infrastructure that should be made criminal; and a treaty could readily be drafted that describes such conduct and requires all States Parties to make such conduct criminal through any formula they choose to utilize. The differences that exist among states concerning several key issues in developing a treaty must be taken into account and will limit and shape the arrangements that are currently feasible.

But differences concerning such issues as regulation of content, scope of extraterritorial investigation, standards of proof, and protection of privacy and other rights can be resolved, largely through a willingness to begin this effort by focusing on measures likely to secure universal agreement. The sharp differences that exist among states with regard to what can be done unilaterally demonstrate, in fact, the need to attempt to secure agreed, multilateral arrangements, rather than establishing a basis for making no effort to do so.

The notion that the United States should act unilaterally when necessary to protect its interests is in principle sound. As discussed further below, the proposed draft international convention herein (the Stanford Draft) explicitly (in Article 20) excludes from its coverage the national security activities of states. Professor Goldsmith seems to recognize, however, that unilateral activities must be legally defensible, and resort to them must be in the nation's best interests. His assumption that it will take many years to negotiate and implement a multilateral convention may turn out to be wrong, in light of the increasingly obvious need and growing momentum for such an arrangement.

Furthermore, even before a multilateral treaty is complete, the United States may be able to reach less comprehensive arrangements with other states to enhance legal protections. Unilateral conduct that offends other states, and leads them to reject or delay negotiating a desirable treaty, would harm U.S. interests. Concerns expressed by the private sector over establishing legally mandated norms and obligations stem from the fear that law enforcement considerations will adversely affect (and greatly burden) Internet businesses and freedom of expression. Government control of the information infrastructure could well have detrimental effects, and international regulation could be especially damaging if political objectives and bureaucratic requirements are allowed to interfere with the present, privately dominated Internet regime.

National governments, including the U.S. government, have sought or imposed potentially damaging restrictions on Internet users, including limitations on the use and sale of advanced encryption, demands for the power to intrude upon, hear, and record Internet traffic, and suggestions that private entities assume quasi-prosecutorial responsibilities in criminal investigations. These policies and suggestions have, however, unjustifiably evoked suspicion of all efforts to establish legally mandated obligations. If, as we believe, voluntary efforts will not provide adequate security, legal obligations to cooperate can be devised that are consistent with continued private creativity and control.

An international regime can be fashioned to satisfy the full range of cyber-security needs, in a manner that ensures continued private-sector control of Internet technology and practices. The United States is party to several international regimes encompassing the creation of consensus-based, non-mandatory measures crafted by public and private-sector experts, which a treaty for cyber security could draw on in providing a comprehensive and lasting system for international cooperation. The strong case for a legally mandated, international regime has led to several significant developments. Treaty provisions are being proposed to close loopholes in existing multilateral commitments in the specific area of civil aviation.

This approach may be feasible in other areas, particularly to protect critical infrastructures from criminal and terrorist attacks, and it seems likely to cause little controversy. The Council of Europe (COE) has taken a more comprehensive approach, publishing and refining a draft treaty on cyber crime. This proposal includes definitions of cyber activities that must be made criminal by all States Parties, as well as other features and forms of cooperation. The COE's draft assumes, correctly, that substantial consensus exists with respect to what cyber activities should be considered criminal, and that substantial benefits can be derived from a multilateral arrangement with common standards, investigative cooperation, and extradition.

This chapter seeks to demonstrate the advantages and feasibility of an even more comprehensive regime by proposing a draft international convention (the Stanford Draft) and discussing its principal elements. The Stanford Draft differs from the draft COE Convention on Cyber crime in several important respects. Most significantly, the Stanford Draft would limit the acts it covers to attacks on the information infrastructure and violations of antiterrorist conventions, whereas the COE Draft includes conventional crimes in which computers are used as well as content-related offenses but do not include violations of antiterrorist conventions.

The Stanford Draft also would establish an international agency, modeled along the lines of successful, specialized United Nations agencies, to prepare and promulgate— on the basis of advice from nonpolitical experts—standards and recommended practices (SARPs) to enhance the effectiveness of protective and investigative measures, whereas the COE proposes detailed forms of cooperation without such a process.

Covered Conduct

The basis for international cooperation rests, most fundamentally, on the combination of a demonstrable need for international agreement to combat harmful cyber conduct and the existence of an international consensus on what conduct should be considered criminal. A review of existing statutory law and proposed international arrangements reflects widespread consensus on prosecuting as criminal the conduct covered in the Stanford Draft: attacks aimed at disrupting or damaging computer operations, deliberate and unauthorized intrusions, interference with computer-security measures, maliciously altering content, intentionally and materially facilitating the commission of prohibited conduct, using a cyber system in committing violations of any of several widely adopted antiterrorist conventions, and using a cyber system to attack critical infrastructures.

Most of these forms of conduct are covered in the COE's draft proposal, although that draft attempts to classify cyber crimes into a number of specific categories: illegal access, illegal interception, data interference, system interference, and the misuse of "devices" for the purpose of committing acts in the preceding categories. The COE effort to generalize makes the categories of offenses relatively easy to comprehend, but may have created coverage on some issues that is undesirably broad. The prohibition on illegal access, for example, would prohibit intentional access to any part of a computer system "without right". Acts "without right" may include conduct not deliberately undertaken to violate adequately communicated prohibitions on entry. This vague standard is included in most of the COE's proposed offenses.

The draft then continues: "A party may require that the offense be committed either by infringing security measures or with the intent of obtaining computer data or other dishonest intent". To the extent the COE Draft permits members to vary conduct it covers, in this and many other provisions, the treaty's effectiveness will be undermined. Uniformity of commitments is in general of greater importance than any particular form or level of coverage. The introductory language to Article 3 of the Stanford Draft— specifically the concept of "legally recognized authority"—is intended to incorporate the concept of self-defense.

Efforts of governments, companies, and individuals to defend themselves from attacks may sometimes require measures that, if adopted without authorization or justification, would be criminal, such as alterations of code, or interfering with operation of computers being used by attackers. At times, such efforts may affect innocent third parties, but nonetheless may be reasonable. The complex issues that are certain to arise in applying established principles of law to this new area of technological activity will be resolved over time, on the basis of experience. The

Stanford Draft recognizes and attempts to deal with the fact that states have different standards in statutes that cover the conduct it proscribes.

Instead of attempting to list specific, commonly defined "offenses", as in most extradition treaties, the Stanford Draft refers to types of conduct, and secures commitments from all States Parties to enforce any applicable law against every form of covered conduct, or to adopt new laws necessary to create authority to prosecute or extradite for such conduct. This approach overcomes the problem of attempting to develop precise, agreed-upon definitions of offenses, and therefore the requirement that every State Party adopt particular formulations as national crimes. In addition to requiring criminal enforcement against conduct specifically aimed at the information infrastructure, the Stanford Draft requires criminal enforcement against the use of computers in the commission of offenses under certain widely adopted multilateral treaties.

These include clearly defined crimes against aircraft, ships, and diplomats, and terrorist bombings. Computers can greatly enhance the potential damage caused by crimes, and can make them especially difficult to investigate. Therefore, since most states are parties to these multilateral treaties, they should be prepared to impose more stringent punishment for the use of cyber capacities in committing the targeted offenses. Other, widely recognized forms of criminal conduct may also become more aggravated through the use of computers, such as forgery, fraud, theft, and conversion. These crimes are not included in the Stanford Draft; however, since they are in general already encompassed in extradition treaties, to the extent States Parties want such coverage.

The cyber dimension of such activities, moreover, would generally involve conduct covered in the Stanford Draft, irrespective of the crimes such conduct may have facilitated. (The COE Draft includes coverage of "computer-related" forgery and fraud, but its definitions of these offenses seem likely to cause uncertainties.) Other types of conduct, when related to the information infrastructure, have been prohibited in some states, including copyright violations and sexual exploitation of minors. Such types of conduct are not covered in the Stanford Draft because their inclusion may prove controversial. These areas are covered by the COE Draft, however, as "Content-related offences".

In fact, a sufficient consensus for including some of these offenses—especially the use of computers for sexual exploitation of minors—may exist, and the Stanford Draft's coverage could be expanded to include such offenses. The COE Draft covers offenses related to child pornography, as well as "copyright and related rights", but whether the scope of copyright coverage should be coterminous with treaties in the area, such as the Berne Convention and other copyright treaties administered by the World Intellectual Property Organization, is left unsettled, and Parties are explicitly allowed to "reserve the right not to impose criminal liability" for copyright violations, "provided that other effective remedies are available".

The Stanford Draft includes very limited coverage of "content" offenses, in part to avoid the strong differences that exist among states concerning restrictions on speech and political activity. No type of speech, or publication, is required to be treated as criminal under the Stanford Draft; if, for example, Germany were to decide to ban publication on the Internet of *Mein Kampf*, it would have to do so unilaterally and could not expect to receive enforcement assistance under the Stanford Draft. The single exception to this principle in the Stanford Draft is the narrow coverage of conduct described as the "distribution of devices or programs intended for the purpose of committing" other conduct made criminal by the Stanford Draft.

The Draft thereby makes criminal the knowing and deliberate effort to cause illegal attacks through such distribution, but not discussions of computer vulnerability intended for evaluating exposure to attacks on the Internet, or other protected speech. States Parties wishing to encourage open discussion of computer attacks and vulnerabilities could designate "safe harbor" sites at which discussion would be considered lawful. (The COE Draft would prohibit the "Misuse of Devices", defined to include the production or transfer, etc. of programs designed primarily to commit other violations, or passwords or other code used for access to computers for that purpose.) While the Stanford Draft avoids content regulation by focusing on protecting the information infrastructure and computers, the protection proposed is comprehensive.

A convention based on such coverage could be used to protect activities that some States Parties may decline to protect as a matter of policy. For example, a company could use code to design protection for information that it could not otherwise protect; a person having the right under the law to obtain such information through lawful means might be prevented from doing so because of the convention's prohibition of efforts to gain access through any proscribed form of conduct. This is a serious concern, since the convention is not intended to enable parties to create a new method for restricting otherwise permissible personal, business, or political activities. It is unclear; however, whether the scope of the Draft's proposed protection could convincingly be restricted in terms that allowed any of the proscribed activities without undermining its credibility. The Draft therefore includes a public-policy exception to its enforcement in Article 13; a similar provision is included in the COE Draft.

A final issue concerning offenses is whether a cyber crime convention should cover only those offenses that provide for penalties exceeding some minimum term of imprisonment. Extradition treaties generally contain such a limitation, usually that the crime for which extradition is sought be punishable by one year of imprisonment or more. This rule is intended to exclude minor offenses from coverage. Given the complications and the effort required to satisfy extradition requests, this consideration is at least as important in a cyber crime convention as in any other.

By having such a requirement, moreover, States Parties would in effect be required to cover prohibited conduct with potential penalties of at least one year in prison. The Stanford Draft therefore includes only crimes for which a potential penalty of at least one year's imprisonment is provided. (The COE Draft includes a separate article on this subject, which is designed to ensure serious penal and civil sanctions.)

Jurisdiction

The Stanford Draft anticipates that the conduct it covers will have effects potentially conferring jurisdiction on multiple States Parties for the same offense. It provides a set of priorities that Parties would agree to follow in performing their duties and pursuing their rights, to the extent practicable, given the difficulty of anticipating all the possible contingencies.

A State Party must establish jurisdiction to try offenders who commit offenses in its territory, who are its nationals, or who are stateless residents in its territory and whose extradition from its territory is refused. A State Party may establish jurisdiction to try offenders who attempt to harm it or its nationals, or to compel it to perform or abstain from performing an act, or whose offenses have substantial effects within its territory. (The COE Draft provides less comprehensive coverage, and fails to provide any guidance with regard to priorities, requiring only "consultation" aimed at determining the "most appropriate" jurisdiction for prosecution.)

The problem of multiple-state jurisdiction over crime is by now commonplace in international law. Transnational fraud, for example, has led to decisions by national courts assuming jurisdiction on the basis of any significant connection to the conduct involved. Among these are the states where a fraud was planned, where an effort to defraud was initiated, where individuals worked at implementing the fraud, where or through which communications were made that were intrinsic to the fraud, where the victims were located, and where the fraud had material and intended effects.

The widespread recognition of fraud as criminal activity leads states readily to find jurisdiction over such activity, despite the significant relationship particular frauds may have to other states. They tend to assume that punishing fraud will be supported by other affected states, rather than opposed as violating their sovereignty. Cyber crime is quintessentially transnational, and will often involve jurisdictional assertions of multiple states. To avoid the conflict such assertions of jurisdiction could cause, enforcement under the Stanford Draft is limited to cyber activities that are universally condemned.

The Stanford Draft does not accede to a state's jurisdiction merely because someone within its territory is able to access a website in another state; to confer jurisdiction, someone in control of the website must deliberately cause one of the covered crimes, with effects in the state seeking to assert jurisdiction. It seems likely, therefore, that states will in general accept all of the reasonably based jurisdictional claims approved in the Draft.

Cooperation in Criminal Enforcement

The Stanford Draft includes commitments by States Parties to engage in the full range of cooperative activities found in widely adopted international agreements. Under it, States Parties would agree to extradite or prosecute persons reasonably believed to have engaged in any form of the covered conduct or offenses. Where necessary, and on a proper evidentiary basis, they would arrest and hold alleged offenders for a short period pending an extradition request. They would also agree to cooperate in seizing, preserving, developing, and providing in usable form evidence for the prosecution of offenders in the courts of other States Parties. They would coordinate these activities through designated "Central Authorities", as in Mutual Legal Assistance Treaties, so that each State Party would know whom to address requests to, and would have an identified agency or person responsible for dealing with such requests in a timely and proper manner.

The COE Draft is detailed and comprehensive in the obligations it contains related to (what it terms) "Procedural Measures". It mandates prompt responses to cyber attacks and requests for cooperation, on a twenty-four-hour/seven-days-per-week basis. (The Stanford Draft incorporates a similar commitment.) The COE Draft provides, among other things, for the expedited preservation and disclosure of stored or traffic data; production orders for computer data and subscriber information from service providers; search and seizure of data; real-time collection of data from service providers; and interception of content data.

Several of these provisions are controversial. The COE Draft deals with this by requiring that all such measures be implemented in accordance with the domestic law of the requested Party, with due regard for the protection of human rights; and it also allows Parties to limit to certain cases their obligations to provide realtime collection of traffic data, and interception of content data. Although these rules may prove useful, they have evoked distrust and opposition, and may well become dated or problematic over time, with the availability of new technologies or methods. The Stanford Draft avoids these problems by providing for commitments to cooperate on each of the subjects covered by the COE Draft, but without further specification, leaving it to the Parties to develop on a consensus basis detailed standards and practices with public input.

But if the basic principles of cooperation are clear, when it comes to implementation many problems still exist, and many more are certain to arise, for which answers have not as yet been developed. What, for example, should be the scope of a state's power unilaterally to seek information in a foreign state? A state may not know whether its electronic effort to obtain information about a crime will enter or have any significant effect within another state or states; it could not avoid such uncertainty even if it tried. Some tolerance of extraterritorial effects would, therefore, seem to be imperative in any viable, multilateral cyber-related arrangement. Both the Stanford Draft and the COE Draft call for the widest possible cooperation, and both provide for reasonable unilateral action.

Another area of current uncertainty is what duties an Internet Service Provider (ISP) should have to preserve and provide information of cyber crimes. Should any such duty be enforceable by law, and if so by what means? These are sensitive issues, since states have not yet imposed duties on ISPs and other Internet participants, such as those imposed in analogous contexts. What should states be required to do to enhance the prospects of preserving evidence that could be helpful in investigating an attack; in particular, should a state be required to seize such information? As noted, the COE Draft is much more specific on these issues than the Stanford Draft, although the former contains significant room for reservations. These sorts of issues related to transnational investigation of cyber crime and terrorism raise several common questions.

The first concerns technology: What technological measures are possible and/or desirable to assist States Parties in securing cooperation that goes beyond the conventional steps currently undertaken in treaties of extradition and mutual legal assistance? Rapidly changing technological capacities and needs make it fruitless to attempt to deal definitively in a draft convention with this aspect of the cyber crime and terrorism problem. Instead, the Draft proposes general principles supporting certain existing technological objectives, and would establish an international agency (the "Agency for Information Infrastructure Protection" or "AIIP",) through which States Parties would cooperate in considering and proposing the use of particular technological measures to enhance cooperative efforts.

In addition to the technological dimension there are certain questions of principle concerning the right of States Parties to defend against or to investigate cyber crime. May a State Party, for instance, deliberately initiate investigative actions or countermeasures for law enforcement purposes that could involve sending transmissions into cyber systems located in other, sovereign territories? Based on experience to date, fast-spreading computer viruses and other cyber attacks demand prompt efforts to track down attackers, and it is difficult if not impossible to know in advance all the places to or through which any part of any cyber transmission might travel.

Therefore, both the Stanford Draft and the COE Draft approve in principle unilateral measures where they are electronic and reasonable. The Stanford Draft provides, moreover, that any law enforcement activity undertaken that knowingly affects another State Party, including any effort to seek cooperative measures from an entity located in another State Party, must be made known to the central authority of that state as soon as practicable. In addition, the Stanford Draft would require all entities, including ISPs, to comply with any standard or procedure developed by the AIIP and accepted by the State Party in which they are located, and would mandate that all States Parties enforce all such standards and procedures. Arrangements based on these principles seem likely to garner widespread support, and would be preferable to unilateral actions that some states could find objectionable (or even criminal).

The Stanford Draft includes a provision authorizing the seizure and forfeiture of equipment utilized in the commission of offenses, subject to due process protections. States could use the information contained in such equipment, or dispose of the equipment as they see fit, consistent with national law. Funds derived from forfeitures have provided resources in other areas for use in upgrading law enforcement capabilities. The seizure and/or forfeiture of cyber equipment used in committing covered offenses is consistent with the universally recognized right of governments to seize instruments of crime.

Structure for Technological Cooperation

An effective transnational response to cyber crime requires a high level of technological cooperation with regard to virtually every function expected to be performed by the States Parties. Cyber criminals exploit the technological possibilities available, including the ability to mask their identity, to hide the origin of attacks and other actions by conducting them through intermediate sites, and to find and exploit weaknesses throughout the worldwide information infrastructure. The challenges of dealing with these capacities are further exacerbated by dynamic changes in technology, the continuing development of new methods for committing cyber crimes, the current widespread sharing of information and ideas about cyber system vulnerabilities, and a culture among users of cyberspace that is skeptical of, if not outright hostile to, government involvement.

Given these circumstances, it is unrealistic to expect that cyber crime will be significantly controlled or deterred through unilateral or voluntary or purely defensive measures. Defensive measures always make sense, and will prove effective for some entities, some of the time. But the pressure to operate openly in business, education, research, entertainment, and personal activities leads users to develop or choose accessible (hence more vulnerable) technology. Governments have seemed especially unable to defend their sites and systems, and have been frequent targets of attack.

Furthermore, the objectives sought through cooperation, and simply unavailable to states acting unilaterally, require a high level of technological coordination.

Take, for example, the need to anticipate, freeze, and trace information packets that are used in cyber crime. Those measures, once devised, will need to be approved and implemented by all participants in the information infrastructure, in a technologically compatible manner, or criminals will find and use gaps in coverage. Similarly, to enable states to conduct searches and seizures, to provide for extradition, and to develop evidence that is usable in the courts of all cooperating states, will require adoption of uniform and mutually acceptable standards and technological solutions, on which all states can rely. The pressures for multilateral solutions to information-infrastructure problems are, indeed, likely to be so great that solutions will be developed without the formal, open, and accountable processes associated with established international institutions.

The story of how private and public actors developed and secured U.S. government support for a system of website domain protection illustrates both the need for and inevitability of multilateral solutions to at least some of the key issues, as well as the ad hoc and relatively undemocratic process that may occur in the absence of established, publicly accountable mechanisms. The process by which effective standards and practices are established for international cooperation in dealing with cyber crime and terrorism is likely to be the most important aspect of any multilateral agreement.

Considerable guidance can be gained in designing a structure for setting such standards from other areas in which transnational standard-setting activities occur, such as airline safety, marine safety, telecommunications, and banking. In general, standard setting and cooperation in such areas is achieved by establishing an international agency assigned clearly articulated and widely shared objectives, with the technical and material resources to achieve those objectives, a professional and nonpolitical staff, substantial reliance on the private sector (especially on highly skilled technical experts), and continuous political involvement and ultimate control by representatives of the participating states.

The history and structure of the International Civil Aviation Organization (ICAO) are instructive in this regard. ICAO is governed by an Assembly consisting of representatives from all its States Parties (185), which meets at least once every three years, establishes basic policies consistent with governing treaties, considers and recommends treaty revisions, approves the budget, which it funds through an apportionment among Member States, and elects delegates to the Council for three-year terms. The Council currently has thirty-three members, including representatives from states of chief importance in air transport, from states that make the largest contributions to international aviation, or chosen to ensure that all major geographical areas are represented.

It implements Assembly decisions, prepares the budget, administers ICAO's finances, appoints the Secretary General and provides a Secretariat, and is empowered to adopt Standards and Recommended Practices (SARPs), which are incorporated into the ICAO Convention through Annexes. The Council acts by majority vote in carrying out its functions, including the adoption of SARPs, which are only adopted after exhaustive development and "technical monitoring, evaluation and backstopping". Though it may delegate authority in any particular matter to a committee of its members, decisions of any such committee may be appealed to the Council by any interested contracting state. The subjects dealt with in SARPs reflect the Council's authority to adopt measures necessary to maintain the safety and efficiency of international air transport.

In performing these functions, the Council is assisted by the Air Navigation Commission, a body of fifteen persons with "suitable qualifications and experience", appointed by the Council from among nominees of Member States. This expert body is responsible for considering and recommending new or amended SARPs, establishing technical subgroups, and ensuring that the Council collects and disseminates to all Member States the information necessary and useful for the advancement of air navigation. Technical assistance is a major aspect of ICAO's work.

Member States license pilots in accordance with ICAO standards. Standardization of equipment and procedures is a major aim and activity, on the whole array of technical issues, including navigation, meteorology, charts, measurement, aircraft operation, air traffic services, search and rescue, accident inquiry, and security. Developing countries are actively assisted through a variety of programs, funded by ICAO, the United Nations Development Program (UNDP), and other sources. Some 80 staff members are involved in about 120 assistance projects each year, with an overall budget of $55 million. They provide training, technical advice, and help in purchasing necessary equipment.

A second international agency that performs duties analogous to those relevant to cyber security is the International Telecommunication Union (ITU). The ITU is the oldest intergovernmental organization in existence, having been formed in 1865 to implement the Telegraph Convention. It expanded its activities to radio in 1906, and currently deals with issues related to all forms of "telecommunications", including telephone, television, and telex. It operates along the same lines as ICAO, and relies heavily on private-sector expertise and involvement. In recent statements, the ITU has expressed its intent to become more involved with information-infrastructure issues.

The ICAO and ITU regimes deal with underlying technological matters that differ from each other, and from

Internet communications, in significant ways. But the needs that led to the creation of these, and of other, similar regulatory mechanisms, are largely analogous to those affecting the cyber world. The key factors behind establishment of these multilateral bodies have been safety and efficiency—the same considerations supporting a multilateral solution to the problem of cyber crime and terrorism. In addition, these multilateral entities are designed to: (1) enable all States Parties to learn of and become involved in the multilateral solutions of problems related to transnational technologies; (2) enable technologically advanced states to protect their interests; (3) ensure that solutions are based on the best possible scientific knowledge, developed with the input of expert advice; and (4) benefit from involvement and expertise of private interests (both commercial and nonprofit).

The Stanford Draft draws on the ICAO and ITU patterns in creating a proposed international institution, the "Agency for Information Infrastructure Protection" or "AIIP", to implement the objectives of States Parties with regard to protecting the information infrastructure from criminal and terrorist cyber activities. No single set of technical fixes will solve the problems that now exist, let alone those that will develop as the technological possibilities expand. The AIIP is therefore designed to play an ongoing role in formulating and revising standards and in proposing treaty revisions for enhanced safety, efficiency, and effective cooperation in light of continuing technological and political developments. Properly designed and structured, this type of agency should contribute materially to cyber security.

The Stanford Draft would require States Parties to establish the AIIP, with the following key components: an Assembly having functions similar to those exercised by the plenary bodies that operate in ICAO, the ITU, and some other specialized agencies; a Council that implements the policies set by the Assembly, through committees of experts, with heavy private-sector representation; and a Secretary General and Secretariat to implement Assembly and Council instructions and perform administrative tasks. The Council would formulate and the Assembly would adopt recommended standards and practices (SARPs) to advance the purposes of the Stanford Draft, and the AIIP would also propose amendments and additional international agreements to implement solutions to problems that require new authority from states.

Some of the UN's specialized agencies have an impressive record for developing and proposing international agreements to deal with important areas not covered by their founding instruments. The International Maritime Organization (IMO), for example, has proposed over twenty treaties to deal with important issues of maritime safety or efficiency, most of which have been widely ratified. In addition, the AIIP Council would be authorized to create and implement, with the Assembly's support, assistance programs to help needy States Parties participate effectively in the activities contemplated in the Stanford Draft. The standards and recommendations to be developed by the AIIP would be designed to have the same legal force attributed to SARPs developed by ICAO.

SARPs adopted by ICAO are not legally binding; they become part of appendices to the ICAO Convention, and States Parties are expected to implement them. States Parties are, however, required to advise other States Parties of their failure to implement SARPs, and the latter would be free to act to protect themselves from the potential consequences of a state's failure to abide by the standard or practice at issue. This type of arrangement has proved universally acceptable in civil aviation and in other areas of transnational regulation, to ensure that standards and practices proposed are thoroughly evaluated, widely supported, and accepted voluntarily on the basis of sovereign self interest and mutuality of obligation.

Authority is provided in Article 12 to the AIIP in the Stanford Draft to enable it to discipline States Parties, or states that are not parties but are participating in the information infrastructure.

Where a state acts or allows persons to act in a manner that undermines the objectives of the Draft, the Council is authorized to recommend sanctions, and the Assembly is authorized to impose them on a two-thirds vote, up to and including expulsion from the AIIP, and a recommendation to states of exclusion from the information infrastructure. Although the Draft avoids regulating state conduct, actions that undermine its purposes, such as allowing persons to use a state's territory to launch attacks affecting other states, would allow the AIIP to exclude such states from membership or to recommend punishing persons and/or non–States Parties by excluding them from participation in the international information infrastructure.

Protection of Individual Rights

Transnational regulation of the Internet raises several important issues related to privacy and other individual rights. The Stanford Draft ensures that, at a minimum, individual rights afforded by States Parties are not adversely affected. No State Party has any duty under the Stanford Draft to act in any manner that might infringe upon the privacy or other human rights of any individual or entity, as defined by the law of that state. In addition, the Stanford Draft authorizes States Parties to refuse or cease cooperation in investigations or prosecutions they consider politically motivated or unfair. It would also create a subcommittee of experts as part of the AIIP, assigned the task of following and reporting upon the protection of privacy and human rights.

Finally, the Draft provides that certain fundamental protections must be extended to persons detained for violations of any offense covered by its terms, including notice to the representative of the state of which an accused is a national, and the right to such representative's assistance. Efforts to protect privacy and other human rights will involve complications for States Parties, for private entities, and for the AIIP as an organization. Notions of privacy and the scope of procedural and human rights vary considerably among the states whose participation is needed for a workable international regime. These differences have led the Internet Alliance to conclude that a legally mandatory regime on Internet crime would likely "wreak havoc" on privacy protections.

In fact, no such result is necessary to have effective multilateral cooperation. By allowing States Parties to insist on the preservation of national norms as a minimum level of protection, the Stanford Draft would preclude its use to deprive any person of rights granted by any State Party, and the problems anticipated will be analogous to those created under the air transport and other antiterrorism conventions. Just as the United States and USSR were able to live with such differences in those contexts and still benefit from the agreements (for example, by securing extradition and prosecutions of hijackers), the Stanford Draft has been designed to enable states with radically different political values to work together on achieving mutually beneficial aims without sacrificing those values.

If, however, a serious and unresolvable situation emerged in which, for example, the regime of technical and operational cooperation developed under the Draft was abused by a state in some manner, the Assembly is empowered to impose sanctions in Articles 12, 13, and 21, including expulsion from the AIIP or a recommendation against the offending state's participation in the international information infrastructure. In some situations, the requirement that all actions requested of a State Party must be consistent with its laws may provide less than optimal protection. A State Party could, for example, establish a method for preventing information from reaching its nationals that could be breached only through conduct inconsistent with one or more of the types of activities prohibited by the Stanford Draft. If a U.S. national engaged in a prohibited form of conduct in sending information into such a state he or she would theoretically be subject to extradition or prosecution, since the U.S.

Constitution does not guarantee a right to communicate information into another state in a particular manner that is prohibited by treaty. States Parties should be able to determine, in such situations, whether compliance with a demand for cooperation would be manifestly inconsistent with established public policy, and on such a finding to decline cooperation. The Stanford Draft and the COE Draft both contain such provisions (Article 13(1) and Article 27(4)(b), respectively), which are consistent with the power explicit or implicit in all extradition treaties to decline cooperation as a matter of sovereign discretion.

National Security

The Stanford Draft makes clear, in a manner similar to other multilateral agreements, that it is inapplicable to state conduct and national security affairs. A multilateral agreement on cyber crime will have novel, complex, and important objectives apart from the possible use of cyber systems by states as military or intelligence tools. Efforts to control state conduct related to national security will be unhelpful in advancing the development of a multilateral approach to the problem of cyber crime and unnecessary as well. ICAO protects civilian aircraft from attack, and the ITU protects radio transmissions from interference. But these treaties do not attempt directly to control states in the conduct of their national security affairs.

To the extent use of cyber technology as a weapon is a concern, existing arms control agreements, and treaties incorporating the laws of war, are all potentially applicable, as are the UN Charter provisions concerning the use of force. The Draft does provide sanctions against conduct that undermines its purposes. If further measures need to be considered to limit the use of cyber technologies in areas of national security, they should be taken up separately and not used to hold hostage the development of a multilateral regime to advance the process of dealing with criminal activities harmful to all states, their peoples, and their economies.

Dispute Resolution

The Stanford Draft relies initially on consensual resolution of disputes through negotiation and mediation. States Parties unable to resolve their disputes consensually are required to submit to arbitration in any agreed form. The Stanford Draft contemplates that the Council of the AIIP will, after its creation, propose for the Assembly's consideration an arbitration mechanism through which disputes would be resolved by expert panels designated in advance to hear and decide such matters, perhaps in the relatively informal manner preferred by the industry for resolving disputes over website domain names.

Amendments

The Stanford Draft contains a standard treaty provision enabling the States Parties to propose and approve amendments as necessary and appropriate.

Draft International Convention to Enhance Protection from Cyber Crime and Terrorism

Preamble

The States Parties to this Convention, *Acknowledging* that developments in science and technology have enabled unprecedented transnational communications through information infrastructures;

Affirming the worldwide benefits enabled by those infrastructures;

Understanding the growing reliance and dependence of persons and governments upon proper operation of information infrastructures and their growing interdependence;

Recognizing the vulnerability of information infrastructures to attacks and improper utilization;

Considering the potentially grave consequences of attacks and improper utilization to persons and governments worldwide, including failures of systems and damage to critical infrastructure, economic losses, and interruption of communications;

Resolving that there is a need to protect transnational information infrastructures from attacks and improper utilization and to deter such conduct by means of appropriate penalties and technology;

Mindful also of the need to ensure appropriate protection of privacy, freedom of communication, and other human rights;

Desiring active international cooperation through voluntary and mandatory measures effectively to investigate and prosecute cyber criminals and terrorists and to develop technological standards and practices to enhance cyber security;

Desiring also the establishment of a specialized agency designed to marshal the expertise to achieve the voluntary and mandatory objectives of this Convention, through a structure based on voluntary, private-sector activities, expertise, and involvement;

Convinced that there is an emerging consensus regarding certain conduct that should be prosecuted as criminal, as well as regarding the need for agreed standards and practices to enhance security; and

Recognizing the need to ensure that all cooperating states should have the technological capacities required for participating in and benefiting from advances in communication, and that all feasible assistance should be provided by technologically advanced states;

Have agreed as follows:

Article 1

Definitions and Use of Terms

For the purposes of this Convention:

1. "cyber crime" means conduct, with respect to cyber systems, that is classified as an offense punishable by this Convention;
2. [Not used]
3. "information infrastructure" and "cyber system" mean any computer or network of computers used to relay, transmit, coordinate, or control communications of data or programs;
4. "data" is information or communications content, including speech, text, photographs, sound, video, control signals, and other formats for information or communications;
5. a "program" is an instruction or set of instructions intended or designed to cause a computer or network of computers to manipulate data, display data, use data, perform a task, perform a function, or any combination of these;
6. "transnational information infrastructures" means information infrastructures with component parts physically present in the territory of two or more States Parties;
7. "critical infrastructures" are the interconnected networks of physical devices, pathways, people, and computers that provide for timely delivery of government services; medical care; protection of the general population by law enforcement; firefighting;

food; water; transportation services, including travel of persons and transport of goods by air, water, rail, or road; supply of energy, including electricity, petroleum, oil and gas products; financial and banking services and transactions; and information and communications services;

8. a "person" may be any of the following: (a) a human being or (b) a corporation or business organization recognized as a legally separate entity under the governing domestic law of a State Party or (c) any other legally recognized entity capable of performing or contributing to the conduct prohibited by this Convention;
9. "legally recognized authority" is authority under a governing State Party's domestic law for persons to enter into private places, to examine private papers, to observe private communications, or to engage in other legally authorized investigative activities;
10. "legally recognized permission" or "legally recognized consent" is permission recognized under a governing State Party's domestic law (when given by a person with a legally recognized interest in a place, tangible property, or intangible property) to enter into private places, to examine private papers, to intercept private communications, or to engage in other legally authorized investigative activities;
11. "misrouting" of communications content or data means intentionally changing or manipulating the ordinary operation of an information infrastructure with the purpose of delaying or diverting the delivery of a protected packet en route to its intended destination, or with knowledge that such delay or diversion will result;
12. a "protected packet" is an assembly of data used to convey communications content through a transnational information infrastructure, conforming to

an international standard for transmission of data established by the Internet Engineering Task Force (IETF) or other widely accepted process;

13. a "treaty offense" is conduct prohibited by multilateral treaty, convention, or agreement (other than this Convention) for which an individual may be punished under the governing domestic law implementing the terms of that treaty, convention, or agreement.

Article 2

Enactment of Domestic Laws

Each State Party shall adopt such measures as may be necessary:

1. to establish as criminal offenses under its domestic law the conduct set forth in Articles 3 and 4;
2. to make such conduct punishable by appropriate penalties that take into account its potentially grave consequences, including possible imprisonment for one year or more; and,
3. to consider for prompt implementation through domestic laws all standards and recommended practices proposed by the Agency for Information Infrastructure Protection (AIIP) pursuant to Article 12.

Article 3

Offenses

1. Offenses under this Convention are committed if any person unlawfully and intentionally engages in any of the following conduct without legally recognized authority, permission, or consent:
   a. creates, stores, alters, deletes, transmits, diverts, misroutes, manipulates, or interferes with data or programs in a cyber system with the purpose of causing, or knowing that such activities would cause, said cyber system or another cyber system

to cease functioning as intended, or to perform functions or activities not intended by its owner and considered illegal under this Convention;

b. creates, stores, alters, deletes, transmits, diverts, misroutes, manipulates, or interferes with data in a cyber system for the purpose and with the effect of providing false information in order to cause substantial damage to persons or property;

c. enters into a cyber system for which access is restricted in a conspicuous and unambiguous manner;

d. interferes with tamper-detection or authentication mechanisms;

e. manufactures, sells, uses, posts, or otherwise distributes any device or program intended for the purpose of committing any conduct prohibited by Articles 3 and 4 of this Convention;

f. uses a cyber system as a material factor in committing an act made unlawful or prohibited by any of the following treaties:

(i) Convention on Offenses and Certain Other Acts Committed on Board Aircraft, September 14, 1963, 20 U.S.T. 2941 [Tokyo Convention]; (ii) Convention for the Suppression of Unlawful Seizure of Aircraft (Hijacking), December 16, 1970, 22 U.S.T. 1641 [Hague Convention]; (iii) Convention for the Suppression of Unlawful Acts Against the Safety of Civil Aviation (Sabotage), September 23, 1971, 24 U.S.T. 564 [Montreal Convention]; (iv) International Convention Against the Taking of Hostages, December 17, 1979, T.I.A.S. 11081 [Hostages Convention]; (v) International Convention for the Suppression of Terrorist Bombings, December 15, 1997, 37 I.L.M. 249 [Terrorist Bombings Convention]; (vi) United Nations Convention Against Illicit Traffic in Narcotic Drugs and Psychotropic Substances, December 20, 1988, T.IA.S.,

20 I.L.M. 493 [Vienna Convention on Narcotics]; (vii) International Maritime Organization Convention for the Suppression of Unlawful Acts against the Safety of Maritime Navigation [Maritime Terrorism Convention], March 10, 1988, IMO Doc. SUA/CON/15/Rev.1, 1993 Can. T.S. No. 10; (g) engages in any conduct prohibited under Articles 3 and 4 of this Convention with a purpose of targeting the critical infrastructure of any State Party.

2. Purpose, intent, or knowledge with respect to the crimes set forth in paragraph 1 of this section may be inferred from objective factual circumstances.

Article 4

Attempts, Aiding and Abetting, Conspiracy

An offense under this Convention is committed if any person unlawfully and intentionally:

1. attempts to engage in any conduct prohibited in Article 3;
2. aids or abets others in engaging or attempting to engage in any conduct prohibited in Article 3; or
3. conspires with others to engage in any conduct prohibited in Article 3.

Article 5

Jurisdiction

1. Each State Party to this Convention shall take such measures as may be necessary to establish its jurisdiction over the offenses set forth in Articles 3 and 4 in the following cases:
   a. when the offense is committed in the territory of that State or on board a ship, aircraft, or satellite registered in that State or in any other place under its jurisdiction as recognized by international law;
   b. when the alleged offender is a national of that State;

c. when the alleged offender is a stateless person whose primary residence is in its territory;
d. when the alleged offender is present in its territory and it does not extradite such person pursuant to this Convention.

2. Each State Party to this Convention may take such measures as may be necessary to establish its jurisdiction over the offenses set forth in Articles 3 and 4 in the following cases:
   a. when the offense is committed with intent or purpose to harm that State or its nationals or to compel that State to do or abstain from doing any act; or
   b. when the offense has substantial effects in that State.
3. This Convention does not exclude any criminal jurisdiction exercised in accordance with domestic law, including any domestic law giving effect to Articles 3 and 4, or any criminal jurisdiction established pursuant to any other bilateral or multilateral treaty.
4. Each State Party will exercise its rights and fulfill its obligations under this Convention to the extent practicable in accordance with the following priority of jurisdiction: first, the State Party in which the alleged offender was physically present when the alleged offense was committed; second, the State Party in which substantial harm was suffered as a result of the alleged offense; third, the State Party of the alleged offender's dominant nationality; fourth, any State Party where the alleged offender may be found; and fifth, any other State Party with a reasonable basis for jurisdiction.

Article 6

Mutual Legal Assistance

1. States Parties shall adopt such measures as are necessary to enable themselves to afford one another the widest measure of mutual legal assistance on an expedited and continuous basis (within conditions prescribed by

treaties, domestic laws, or regulations concerning such assistance) in investigations, extraditions, prosecutions, and judicial proceedings brought in respect of the offenses set forth in Articles 3 and 4, including assistance for the following purposes:

a. identifying and tracing attacks upon cyber systems by electronic and other means;
b. locating or identifying persons;
c. taking statements from persons;
d. executing searches and seizures by electronic and other means;
e. examining objects and sites;
f. securing and exchanging information and evidentiary items, including documents and records; and
g. transferring persons in custody.

2. Requests for assistance will be made in accordance with arrangements under existing agreements between or among the States Parties involved, or through Central Authorities designated by States Parties in ratifying this Convention. Requests made for emergency assistance will be dealt with by response teams that function as necessary on a continuous basis.
3. States Parties shall promote appropriate methods of obtaining information and testimony from persons who are willing to cooperate in the investigation and prosecution of offenses established in Articles 3 and 4 and shall, as appropriate, assist each other in promoting such cooperation. Such methods of cooperation may include, among other things: granting immunity from prosecution to a person who cooperates substantially with law enforcement authorities in investigations, extraditions, prosecutions, and judicial proceedings; considering the provision by an accused person of substantial cooperation as a mitigating factor in

determining the person's punishment; and entering into arrangements concerning immunities or non-prosecution or reduced penalties.

4. Any physical property of substantial intrinsic value seized by a State Party that is later delivered pursuant to the request of a prosecuting State Party to facilitate the prosecution of a suspected offense shall, upon request within a reasonable time after final resolution of all proceedings of prosecution and appeal in the courts of the prosecuting State Party, be returned to the State Party that seized the property for disposition according to the domestic laws of that State Party.
5. States Parties shall be free to engage in reasonable, electronic methods of investigation of conduct covered by Articles 3 and 4 of this Convention, over which they have jurisdiction to prosecute under Article 5, even if such conduct results in the transfer of electronic signals into the territory of other States Parties. A State Party aware that its investigative efforts will likely result in such transfers of electronic signals shall as soon as practicable inform all affected States Parties of such efforts.
6. States Parties shall consider for prompt implementation through law all standards and recommended practices adopted and proposed by the AIIP pursuant to Article 12 as methods for enhancing mutual legal assistance provided under this Article 6. 7. States Parties agree to extend on voluntary basis cooperation in all possible areas of activity bearing upon mutual legal assistance, both individually and through efforts under the auspices of the AIIP or other governmental and nongovernmental entities.

Article 7

Extradition

1. Offenses under the domestic laws of each State Party concerning any conduct set forth in Articles 3 and 4

shall be deemed to be included as extraditable offenses in any extradition treaty existing between or among States Parties. States Parties undertake to include such offenses as extraditable offenses in every extradition treaty subsequently concluded between them; however, failure to include these offenses in such treaties shall not affect the obligations undertaken herein.

2. If a State Party that makes extradition conditional on the existence of a treaty receives a request for extradition from another State Party with which it has no extradition treaty, it may consider this Convention as the legal basis for extradition in respect of the offenses covering conduct set forth in Articles 3 and 4. Extradition shall remain subject to any other requirement of the law of the requested State.
3. States Parties that do not make extradition conditional on the existence of a treaty shall recognize offenses covering the conduct set forth in Articles 3 and 4 as extraditable offenses as between themselves, subject to any other requirement of the law of the requested State.
4. Offenses covering the conduct set forth under Articles 3 and 4 shall to that extent be treated, for the purpose of extradition between States Parties, as if they had been committed in the place in which they occurred, and also in the territories of the State or States required or authorized to establish their jurisdiction under Article 5.
5. When extradition is requested by more than one requesting State Party, the requested State Party shall respond to such requests in accordance with the priorities for jurisdiction set out in Article 5, paragraph 4.

Article 8 [sh]

Prosecution [sh]

1. The State Party in the territory of which an alleged offender is found shall, if it does not extradite such person, be obliged, without exception and whether or

not the offense was committed in its territory, to submit the case without delay to competent authorities for the purpose of prosecution, through proceedings in accordance with the laws of that State. Those authorities shall pursue such prosecutions in the same manner as other serious offenses under the laws of that State. If a State Party is unable or unwilling to prosecute such cases, it must promptly inform the original requesting State Party or States Parties.

2. A requesting State Party may prosecute an alleged offender over whom it secures jurisdiction through extradition only for crimes specified in its extradition request and found legally sufficient by the requested State Party, unless the requested State Party agrees to permit prosecution for additional offenses.

Article 9

Provisional Remedies

1. Upon the request of a State Party based upon its reasonable belief that a named suspected offender engaged in conduct covered by this Convention may be found in the territory of a requested State Party, the requested State Party undertakes to apprehend the named suspected offender if found in its territory and hold the suspected offender for up to a maximum of ten (10) days, during which period the requesting State Party will supply information sufficient to show cause for continued detention pending the resolution of its request for extradition.
2. Upon the request of a State Party based upon its reasonable belief that conduct covered by Articles 3 and 4 of this Convention has occurred, and that evidence of such conduct is present in the stored data contained in cyber systems located within the territory of a requested State Party, the requested State Party will attempt to preserve or to require preservation of the stored data in such cyber systems for a reasonable period to permit the requesting State Party to supply information sufficient

to show adequate cause for release of all or part of the preserved stored data to the requesting State Party.

3. States Parties shall consider for prompt implementation through national law all standards and recommended practices adopted and proposed by the AIIP pursuant to Article 12 as methods for enhancing the capacity of States Parties to advance this Convention's purposes through provisional remedies.

Article 10

Entitlements of an Accused Person

1. Any person detained by a State Party pursuant to one or more of Articles 3, 4, 5, 6, 7, 8, or 9 shall be entitled, in addition to rights extended under the national law of such State Party, to:
   a. communicate without unnecessary delay with the nearest appropriate representative of the State of which that person is a national or which is otherwise entitled to protect that person's rights or, if that person is stateless, the State of that person's primary residence;
   b. be visited by a representative of that State;
   c. have a representative of that State physically present to observe any legal proceedings that may result in punishment; and,
   d. be informed promptly after detention of that person's entitlements under subparagraphs (a), (b), and (c) of this Article 10.
2. States Parties shall not deny any person, or impair in any way, the entitlements described in paragraph 1.

Article 11

Cooperation in Law Enforcement

States Parties shall cooperate closely with one another

through their law enforcement agencies in preventing any conduct set forth in Articles 3 and 4, by among other things:

1. taking all practicable measures to prevent preparations in their respective territories for the commission of such conduct within or outside their territories;
2. exchanging information and coordinating the taking of administrative and other measures as appropriate to prevent commission of such conduct; and
3. considering for prompt implementation all standards and recommended practices adopted and proposed by the AIIP pursuant to Article 12 as methods for deterring and preventing the crimes covered by this Convention.

Article 12

Agency for Information Infrastructure Protection (AIIP)

The States Parties hereby establish, and agree to make operational as soon as practicable after the effective date of this Convention, the Agency for Information Infrastructure Protection (AIIP), an international agency composed of all States Parties as Members, and consisting of an Assembly, a Council, a Secretariat managed by a Secretary General, and such committees and other subordinate bodies as are necessary in the judgment of the Assembly or Council to implement this Convention's objectives. The AIIP and all its component entities and functions will be funded by a mandatory assessment imposed biannually upon its Members in accordance with a formula proposed by the Council and approved by the Assembly.

1. *Assembly*. The AIIP Assembly will consist of all States Parties, each of which will be represented by an individual competent in cyber technologies, who will have a single vote on all Assembly activities. The Assembly shall meet at least once every three years and

shall make decisions by a majority of Members voting. The Assembly shall have the following responsibilities and powers:

a. to adopt objectives and policies authorized by and consistent with this Convention;

b. to instruct the Council to formulate and/or implement measures to achieve such objectives and policies;

c. to consider and approve standards and practices proposed by the Council for adoption by States Parties;

d. to consider and approve the AIIP budget and assessment formula prepared and proposed by the Council;

e. to recommend to States Parties modifications or supplementary agreements to the present Convention, including the addition of types of conduct to be considered criminal;

f. to elect no fewer than one-fifth and no more than one-fourth of its Members to the Council, which shall include at least one representative from each of the five Permanent Members of the United Nations Security Council;

g. to consider and approve proposals by the Council to provide technical and material assistance to deserving States Parties for the purpose of encouraging the safe and widespread use of the international information infrastructure;

h. to propose to all States Parties as recommendations or as proposed amendments to this Convention, standards, practices, and technological measures approved by the Council;

i. to consider and approve measures proposed by the Council to prevent any State from being used as a safe haven or otherwise in order to enable persons to secure protection from successful prevention, investigation, or prosecution for conduct set forth in Articles 3 and 4; and,

j. to adopt regulations for its own governance, which shall include authority to suspend or expel States Parties, and to recommend to States Parties the exclusion of any State from participation in the international information infrastructure, for conduct that undermines the objectives of this Convention, on a vote of at least two-thirds (2/3) of all States Parties voting.

2. *Council.* The AIIP Council will consist of representatives from Member States elected by the Assembly. The Council shall meet at least once every year and shall decide on all matters by majority vote.

The Council shall have the following responsibilities and powers:

a. to prepare the AIIP budget and assessment formula for consideration and approval by the Assembly;

b. to appoint and supervise the Secretary General, and to provide for a Secretariat to administer AIIP activities with a staff limited in number and role to the extent that reliance on nonpermanent volunteer and contract personnel is practicable;

c. to appoint standing and special committees, consisting of persons from the public and private sectors (including volunteers) who are experts in the fields of the committees' activities, which shall meet as necessary to consider and recommend to the Council standards and practices, as well as technological measures to improve the security of information infrastructures, including the capacities of States Parties and law enforcement agencies to detect, prevent, investigate, and successfully prosecute conduct set forth in Articles 3 and 4, and to prevent any State from being used as a safe haven;

d. to consider, and where the Council sees fit to propose to the Assembly for adoption as recommendations, or as proposed amendments to this Convention, standards, practices, or measures prepared by the AIIP's standing or special committees, taking into account the work of public and private entities, such as the IETF, in order to ensure consistency of standards and practices;

e. to receive, consider, and report to the Assembly concerning the annual reports filed by States Parties under Article 14;

f. to consider and to recommend to the Assembly which States Parties should be deemed eligible for technical and financial assistance to enable them to satisfy their obligations under this Convention and to participate to the extent feasible in useful activities associated with cyber systems;

g. to adopt and implement programs of technical and financial assistance to all States Parties, including training programs for law enforcement and cyber security personnel, with particular attention to reaching States Parties eligible for financial assistance, and to work with other public and private organizations in this regard;

h. to consider and recommend as appropriate to the Assembly sanctions on States Parties or other States for conduct that undermines the objectives of this Convention; and

i. to adopt regulations for its own governance.

3. *Secretariat*. The Secretariat will function as directed by the Secretary General. The Secretariat staff provided for by the Assembly, on recommendation of the Council, will be appointed by the Secretary General.

4. *Public Participation*. Meetings of the Assembly and Council of the AIIP shall be open to the public, with such public participation as is feasible. Meetings of committees, working groups, and other AIIP entities shall also be open to the public, subject to the need for confidential consideration of sensitive information.

Article 13

Protection of Privacy and Other Human Rights

1. This Convention shall not be construed to require an infringement of the privacy or other human rights of any person as defined by the laws of the State Party requested to perform any duty agreed to under this Convention. A State Party may decline to perform any duty agreed to under this Convention if it determines that doing so would be manifestly inconsistent with its established public policy.
2. As part of the obligation to establish systematic monitoring of implementation of this Convention under Article 14, a permanent subcommittee of experts shall be established by the Council to evaluate and comment upon the manner in which the Convention is being implemented with regard to the protection of privacy and other human rights, and to recommend appropriate measures to the Council and Assembly for the purpose of protecting such rights.

Article 14

Annual Reports of States Parties

1. Each State Party shall on or before the end of each calendar year commencing with the year of its accession to this Convention provide to the AIIP any relevant information concerning:
   a. the legislative and administrative measures taken by it to implement this Convention;

b. any change in its domestic laws and regulations affecting the implementation of this Convention;

c. the circumstances of any offense over which it has established its jurisdiction pursuant to Article 5;

d. the measures taken by it in relation to each alleged offender who was detained for any period of time under the Convention or under its domestic law implementing all or any part of the Convention, and, in particular, the results of any extradition or other legal proceedings; and

e. any decision not to implement a standard or recommended practice approved by the AIIP Assembly.

2. The AIIP Secretariat shall annually collate and transmit to all States Parties the information collected from them under this Article 14.

Article 15

Signature, Ratification, Acceptance, Approval, Accession and Reservations

1. This Convention shall be open for signature by any State after [DATE] at, in the State of , which shall act as Depositary.
2. This Convention is subject to ratification, acceptance, approval, or accession. The instruments of ratification, acceptance, approval, or accession shall be deposited with the Depositary State.

Article 16

Entry into Force

1. This Convention shall enter into force on the thirtieth (30th) day following the date of the deposit of the [ORDINAL NUMBER] instrument of ratification, acceptance, approval, or accession with the Depositary State.

2. For each State ratifying, accepting, approving, or acceding to the Convention after the deposit of the [ORDINAL NUMBER] instrument of ratification, acceptance, approval, or accession, the Convention shall enter into force on the thirtieth (30th) day after deposit by such State of its instrument of ratification, acceptance, approval, or accession with the Depositary State.

Article 17

Amendments

1. A State Party or the AIIP may propose an amendment to this Convention and file it with the Depositary State. The Depositary State shall communicate each proposed amendment to the States Parties. If, within four (4) months from the date of such communication, at least a [FRACTION] majority of States Parties vote for approval of the amendment the Depositary State shall so inform all States Parties, who will thereafter communicate any ratification of such proposed amendments. Proposed amendments will become effective upon their ratification by a [FRACTION] majority of States Parties.
2. When an amendment enters into force, it shall be binding on those States Parties that have ratified it. Other States Parties will remain bound by the provisions of the present Convention and any earlier amendments that they have ratified.

Article 18

Denunciation

A State Party may denounce this Convention by written notification to the Depositary State. The Depositary State shall promptly communicate the receipt of such notification to the other States Parties. Denunciation shall become effective one (1) year after the date of receipt of such notification.

Article 19

Political Offenses and Prejudicial Actions

1. None of the offenses or conduct set forth in Articles 3 and 4 shall be regarded, for the purposes of extradition or mutual legal assistance, as a political offense or as an offense equivalent to a political offense.
2. Nothing in this Convention shall be interpreted as imposing an obligation to extradite or to afford mutual legal assistance, if the requested State Party has substantial grounds for believing that the request for extradition for offenses set forth in Articles 3 and 4 or for mutual legal assistance with respect to such offenses has been made for the purpose of prosecuting or punishing a person on account of that person's race, religion, nationality, ethnic origin, or political belief.

Article 20

State Conduct

This Convention shall not apply to any state conduct undertaken for a public, noncommercial purpose, including activities undertaken by military forces of a State Party, or to a State Party's activities related to an ongoing armed conflict.

Article 21

Dispute Resolution

1. States Parties shall attempt to resolve all disputes that arise under this Convention through negotiation and mediation, with the assistance of the AIIP Secretariat.
2. Any State Party may give notice to another that it intends to seek arbitration of a specified dispute, to

commence no sooner than ninety (90) days after such notice is received by the Party to whom it is sent. If the Parties are unable to agree on an arbitral tribunal or on any other necessary aspect of the requested arbitration, the matter will be referred by the requesting Party for decision under the auspices of [ADD ARBITRATION MECHANISM].

3. The AIIP Council shall as soon as practicable develop and propose to the Assembly a dispute resolution mechanism that is informal, speedy, and based on appropriate expert involvement.

Article 22

Languages and Depositary

The original of this Convention, of which the English, French, and Russian texts are equally authentic, shall be deposited with the Depositary State, which shall send certified copies thereof to all States Parties.

6

Terrorism, Organized Crime and Cyber Crime

The merger of transnational crime, terrorism and corruption is profound. The idea that these ideas can be discussed separately is problematic. Such compartmentalization limits our ability to analyze and address the diverse forms of transnational criminal activity. Highly corrupt societies give little opportunity for legitimate social mobility and their high level corruption is a deterrent to economic growth and investment. Under these circumstances, the employment opportunities of transnational crime groups provide a desirable economic alternative to youth without legitimate opportunities. Terrorist groups flourish in environments where youths have limited chance for advancement within their societies.

The phenomena of transnational crime, terrorism and corruption are all too often viewed as separate phenomena. These phenomena have grown in tandem because the economic and political conditions that give rise to these phenomena are quite similar. The evolution of the transnational crime-ideologically based or economically based depends on specific environmental factors that have proliferated in many developing and transitional countries that have not successfully integrated into the global economy.

Terrorists and transnational criminals use many of the

same strategies to promote their operations, chief among these being the use of information technology to plan and realize their activities. The rise of greater international mobility and the proliferation of information technology throughout the world have facilitated the growth of both transnational crime and terrorism. The ease of communications in the contemporary era makes the location of groups and actors less significant than it was previously. The ability to exploit security holes in the system makes crime groups and terrorists operate out of unexpected locales rather than their home territories.

Most transnational crime and terrorist groups are based in transitional and developing countries. The illicit businesses are now the largest and most profitable to be located in the developing world. For example, the drug trade now represents about 7% of world trade according to late 1990s estimates of the United Nations. Their vast profits and enormous assets make them powerful actors in their home countries and in their regions. Because they are so large relative to the legitimate businesses based in their region or in the countries through which they operate, they have a large influence on politics and business.

The vast profits of illegal businesses allow them to hire the best specialists domestically and internationally. Facilitating this trade is an ever greater reliance on information technology to promote their activities secretly. For example, international drug traffickers are among the most wide-spread users of encrypted messages, coded messages by cell and satellite phones and use anonymizer features on computers. They also are able to hire technical specialists capable of using steganography and other means to make messages hard or impossible to decipher. This access to high level specialists allows illicit businesses and terrorist organizations to transcend borders and operate internationally without detection. Often the crime and terrorist groups do not need to go outside their region to hire such technical specialists.

Some of the leading specialists in the technical area are located in regions that house major transnational crime groups and terrorist organizations. The presence of many highly trained technical specialists in the countries of the former Soviet Union and in the Indian subcontinent means that transnational crime groups means that a vast array of specialists are available for hire. While some specialists will not work for criminal or terrorist organizations willingly, some will do it unaware of their employers whereas others will agree to provide assistance because well-paid legitimate employment is scarce in their region.

The widespread problem of corruption in many developing countries allows the proliferation of transnational organized crime and terrorism. The official corruption facilitating this activity may assume many different forms and is not just based on bribery. Top government officials provide falsified documents to smuggled criminals and terrorists restrain law enforcement from acting against suspicious groups and provide them a safe space to operate.

Because of this, criminals can use the high level technology available in the former Soviet Union and the Punjab region to facilitate not only their own crime and terrorist groups but those of other regions of the world which find save haven on their territory. In this way criminals exploit information technology to carry on their operations in a safe and secure manner. The connections between transnational crime and terrorism are not unique to developed and developing countries.

As investigations in the advent of September, 11th have shown, terrorists in developed countries use criminal activity to survive. Arrests in Spain revealed that terrorists were selling counterfeit airline tickets to survive and such groups in the United States were surviving by means of money laundering and other criminal offenses.

The worldwide information infrastructure is today increasingly under attack by cyber criminals and terrorists—and the number, cost, and sophistication of the attacks are increasing at alarming rates. With annual damage around the world now measured in billions of U.S. dollars, these attacks threaten the substantial and ever-growing reliance of commerce, governments, and the public upon the new technology to conduct business, carry messages, and process information.

At a Hoover Institution conference, more than forty members of government, industry, and academia assembled to discuss this problem and explore possible countermeasures. The Transnational Dimension of Cyber Crime and Terrorism, edited by Hoover senior fellow Abraham D. Sofaer and Seymour E. Goodman, summarizes the conference papers and exchanges, addressing pertinent issues in chapters that include a review of the legal initiatives undertaken around the world to combat cyber crime, an exploration of the threat to civil aviation, analysis of the constitutional, legal, economic, and ethical constraints on the use of technology to control cyber crime, and a discussion of the ways we can achieve security objectives through international cooperation.

"Computers and communications are increasingly being used in almost every imaginable application", warns conference participant Peter G. Neumann, principal scientist at the Computer Science Laboratory, SRI International. "However, our computer-communication systems are not dependably secure, reliable, or robust. There are fundamental vulnerabilities in the existing information system infrastructures, and serious risks that those vulnerabilities will be exploited—with possibly very severe effects".

Although much has been said about the threat posed by worldwide cyber crime, little has been done to protect against it. A transnational response sufficient to meet this challenge is an immediate and compelling necessity and this book is a critical first step in that direction. On this point, Hoover director John Raisian writes in his foreword to the book, "During the conference, a clear consensus of the conference participants emerged: greater international cooperation is required, and a multilateral treaty focused on criminal penalties for the abuse of cyber systems would help build the necessary cooperative framework".

Abraham D. Sofaer is the George P. Shultz Senior Fellow at the Hoover Institution and professor of law, by courtesy, Stanford Law School. He served as legal adviser to the U.S. Department of State from 1985 to 1990. Seymour E. Goodman is a professor of International Affairs and Computing, Georgia Institute of Technology. The Hoover Institution, founded at Stanford University in 1919 by Herbert Hoover, who went on to become the 31st president of the United States, is an interdisciplinary research center for advanced study on domestic and international affairs.

Ratification of the Palermo Convention

Building upon the commitments made at previous G8 Summits and through other international institutions, the Heads of State gathered at Genoa will seek prompt ratification of the Palermo Convention on Transnational Organized Crime and the related Protocols. Having been adopted by the UN General Assembly on November 15, 2000, the Convention was signed by 125 States in December in Palermo, under the auspices of the UN, and was heralded as the most ambitious effort to date to fight international crime. It extends well beyond the sphere of cooperation on drug trafficking and seeks to provide the basis for stronger common action against money-laundering, greater ease of extradition, and enhanced judicial cooperation. Another important goal has been to encourage the signatories to synchronize their national laws in order to increase predictability and consistency.

The UN Conference demonstrated that there is a firm and formal international commitment to take action against organized crime. Considering that the G8 States (US, Canada, Italy, Russia, Japan) harbour particularly strong criminal organizations with increasing transnational ties, it is only logical that they would be such strong proponents of the Convention. At Genoa, the States will seek to implement the assistance mechanisms foreseen by the Palermo Convention.

In addition, 80 states also signed the Protocol to Prevent, Suppress and Punish Trafficking in Persons, Especially Women and Children, and 77 the Protocol against the Smuggling of Migrants by Land, Sea and Air. The aims of the first Protocol are three-fold: to prevent and combat trafficking in persons, particularly women and children; to protect and assist the victims of such trafficking; and to promote cooperation among States parties to meet these objectives. The protocol serves as a model for national legislation, detailing provisions on conduct, the severity of punishment, and effective measures to combat and prevent trafficking.

The second one provides an effective tool to combat and prevent the smuggling of human cargo. However, while it was created to prevent smuggling, the new laws did not aim to dictate domestic migration policy and migration flow. They recognized that migration in itself is not a crime and, therefore, not liable to criminal prosecution. In the words of the former Italian Minister Fassino, these three documents constitute the first body of international law, which facilitates efficient intervention in the various signatory States. He further added that the traditional fight against organized crime, which was purely political, is in a transition to one that is conducted on a more cogent terrain, with precise legislative, normative, and organizational measures. A convention on weapon trafficking control is currently under negotiations, and the Genoa Summit will undoubtedly seek its endorsement.

Corruption

In this particular area of concern, the Ministers noted with satisfaction that they are not departing from ground-zero: an OSCE Convention is already existent, signed, and ratified by all the G8 countries; there is another one by the Council of Europe, as well as a third one at the UN level that is currently under development. The Heads of State should be expected at the Summit to work towards the goal of creating a new UN convention against corruption globally. Fassino added that such commitments are quite evidently accompanied by measures by each State to increase administrative transparency.

To this end, the collaboration among the G8 states will be intensified at all levels - investigative, police work, as well as judicial cooperation. A meeting in Rome for March 11 has been announced: a practical reunion and a meeting of experts as a follow-up to the Milan Ministers' Meeting.

Money Laundering

In the view of this problem, the following measures have been identified at the Conference to increase the effectiveness of the G8 initiative:

- transparency of financial mechanisms and removal of bank secrecy,
- codes of integrity for public officials, and
- codes of conduct for credit operators in order to manage financial flows with maximal transparency.

Fassino added that the Ministers also agreed to adopt a firmer line of persuasion/dissuasion toward the non-cooperative States, especially the ones that profit by being "tax havens" and by the enormous sums of illicit proceeds. In such cases, they intend to restrict international funding, to obligate the intermediary bank- and financial personnel to monitor operations consistently and to strike financial transactions with persons whose place of residence is in the non-cooperative states, and, finally, to exclude the firms controlled or financed by persons residing in such countries from certain public procedures.

The G7/8 will most likely praise the actions of the Financial Action Task Force on Money Laundering (FATF), created by the group, in identifying non-cooperative states. The task force, which recently met in Paris, has taken increasingly aggressive measures to penalize such states (adding Egypt, Guatemala, Hungary, Indonesia, Myanmar and Nigeria to the black list of money-launders). Some \$500-billion - \$1.5-trillion a year (equivalent of 1.5-4.5% of the world GDP), generated by illegal activities, is washed through the banking system, according to IMF estimates. Within the G8, Great Britain often takes the lead on money laundering issues and can be expected to again do so in Genoa.

Legislative harmonization on the question of confiscation of sequestrated goods in the G8 countries was also discussed and will likely be raised again in Genoa. Yet, the fact remains that only minimal visible progress has been made since a similar commitment was made in Okinawa: in Italy, for example, only 7% of all illegal assets are sequestrated and only 3% are confiscated - a clear indication that much work still remains to be done in the domestic setting.

Illegal Immigration

Illegal immigration has obviously received much attention by all the countries involved - be it those that represent the points of destinations or the transit routes. "It is a matter that requires an interdisciplinary and global collaboration", the former Italian Minister of the Interior, Enzo Bianco, declared, adding that special attention will be asked of the Heads of State and of Government at the Genoa Summit concerning this theme - with measures which stimulate the development of the States of origin in order to try to arrive at the root of the problem.

Individual States are already seeking to curb this growing problem: the Italian Prime Minister Silvio Berlusconi will push for a crackdown on illegal migration - an issue, which he pressed during his election campaign, by advocating that no immigrant be allowed to enter Italy until he or she secured a job and a work permit. Tens of thousands of immigrants sneak into Italy every year. Italy has become one of the key entry points into Western Europe for migrants from Albania, Turkey, Eastern Europe, as well as Africa and Asia.

Many agree that Italy is at an impasse; with one of the lowest birthrates in the industrialized world and one of the largest retirement age populations, it needs to import both skilled and unskilled workers to keep its economy going. It aiming to curb illegal migration, it is faced with an economic dilemma. Yet, Italy is not alone; the EU estimates are that 500,000 illegal immigrants arrived in 2000, an increase from 40,000 as recently as 1993. Bianco also added that the Ministers are conscious that the legal immigration constitutes an opportunity for the G8 States, with high levels of economic development yet low birth rates.

The Ministers have reaffirmed their mutual decision to counteract the actions of criminal groups that organize human trafficking with every legal means available and with a maximal firmness, while possibly extending concessions on regular immigration quotas to countries of origin that apprehend illegal immigrants found on their territory. Since Okinawa, the European G8 States, notably Germany and Italy, have engaged in bilateral and regional talks to reduce the porousness of their borders and to cut off the illegal flows of immigration.

For instance, government officials from Canada and the United States have engaged in talks to intensify law enforcement cooperation to decrease human trafficking, as evidenced at the crime forum held in Ottawa (20 June, 2001). John Ashcroft, the U.S. Attorney-General, said that "alien smuggling is relatively new at the scale we are seeing it" and, while praising the ongoing efforts by Canadian and American law enforcement officials, emphasised that more must be done. The two G8 governments have increased patrols along Ontario and British Colombia borders as a part of their strategy to catch smugglers.

Yet, as Mr. Ashcroft recognized, a bilateral effort will hardly be sufficient to solve this massive and quickly growing problem; rather, it will have to be fought using increased international enforcement cooperation. Smuggling from areas such as Korea and China is estimated to be a US$6.5-billion industry. Considering the magnitude of human smuggling in the G8 States, the Leaders will undoubtedly seal their previous agreements and extend the level of cooperation among their police forces at the Summit in Genoa. Under the Italian Presidency, it may be expected that the formation of an EU border police, based on a German and Italian idea, will be saluted. The functionaries of different States are currently developing this proposal, while Italy has furthermore presented to the EU a project for financing a study to determine the feasibility of a community police.

International Terrorism

Another projected theme will be the fight against terrorism - which is becoming all the more relevant with the alleged reports of a terrorist attack on the Genoa Summit this July. It has occupied a large part of the G7 Summit agenda in the past, aircraft hijacking being the first non-economic issue discussed at a G7 meeting in Bonn 1978. Mr. Bianco indicated that there is a widespread concern regarding regionalist and nationalist types of terrorism, in particular if linked to Islamic fundamentalism.

A way of intensifying the fight against terrorism would be carried out through juridical channels - notably the EU and the Commissar Antonio Vitorino-that will promote a unitary and homogenous definition of terrorism for the member-states. Mr. Bianco also announced certain concrete measures to intensify the circulation of information, which is essential for the efficiency of action and collaboration. Italy promoted a Convention on cyber-terrorism and technological crime, which constitute the new frontier of criminality, to be held in Rome on March 18/19.

It is likely that the commitment to seek ratification of the UN International Convention for the Suppression of the Financing of Terrorism will appear in the final communiqué, as well as to support the work of Anti-terrorism Experts and the Lyon Group. Recent threats by Osama bin Laden, the most prominent anti-American terrorist, to assassinate President George W. Bush, combined with his admitted bombing of the US warship Cole in Yemen last year, make terrorism a prominent issue and an assured agenda topic, especially with the US.

High-tech and Internet Crime

The final theme at the Ministers' meeting, expected at Genoa, is the fight against high-tech crime and Internet-based child pornography. Minister Bianco stated that Italy promoted the creation of a new Databank of sites and Internet addresses concerning this specific sector. If the results are satisfactory, this Databank will be enlarged to also allow access to non-G8 countries in order to counter the use of the new technologies for the sexual exploitation of children. The Summit will address and support the Japanese initiative to host the 2nd World Congress against Commercial Sexual Exploitation of Children.

It was the Clinton administration that, in its final term, set the stage for the fight against high tech crime, their stance being that a sophisticated, well-connected network of international criminals are a real and growing national security threat. The Summit will also seek to finalize the Cyber crime Convention of the Council of Europe, as cyber crime is particularly alarming to the G8 countries. To this end, a G8 Workshop was held in Berlin (October 2000), where many concerns were voiced. For instance, the German Minister of Foreign Affairs, Joschka Fischer, indicated that the Net is becoming a common ground for information espionage, theft of data, credit card frauds, child pornography, right extremism and terrorism.

He added that the monetary losses due to cyber crime exceed DM 100 million annually, and that this is only the beginning. Joint action is needed in an area where the threat is mainly external - in the case of Germany, 80% of cyber crime could be traced to the US, Canada, Japan, Australia, and Russia. At Genoa, they will most likely seek a consolidation of national laws to prosecute hackers regardless of their place of residence; yet, fear of running into the age-old debate about privacy is already present. Germany will be a stark proponent of bringing the Internet under control, starting with a domestic "Offensive against Right-extremism", being the first G8 State to develop a DM 10 million fund for the victims of hate crime.

The unrelenting problem of illegal drugs and its magnitude at the international level, albeit ignored at the Ministers' Meeting in February, should be expected to appear in the final communiqué but will probably play only a limited role. Despite the fact that an effective strategy in the fight against drugs would involve a multilateral effort, illegal drugs and law enforcement still remain predominantly a unilateral initiative, in which the G8 states seem to prefer not to make concrete (or quantifiable) commitments. This is particularly true of the US, especially in regards to South America (Plan Colombo).

The US anti-drug forces' shooting down of a civilian plane over Peru has renewed domestic debate and criticism of the current US war on drugs strategy. Furthermore, the European G8 states are not supportive of an increased American military presence in Colombia, as espoused by the Bush Administration and the newly appointed drug "tsar", John Walters, but prefer a more holistic approach - both in the producer countries and in their domestic settings. This will make illegal drugs a sensitive subject to bring up in Genoa, and the countries will, at best, only reaffirm the commitments made in Okinawa. Note might be taken of the UN anti-drug campaign, including the success of the anti-drug day, but a light condemnation of China for the misuse of the occasion in order to publicly execute 65 drug criminals could be expected. Despite the fact that the G8 collectively perceive this issue-area to be a major concern, because of the differences in approach between the US, with its more hard-line, Walters-led initiatives, and the remaining G8's softer, more liberal policies, it is not likely that any specific initiatives will be announced.

A Proposal

The information infrastructure is increasingly under attack by cyber criminals. The number, cost, and sophistication of attacks are increasing at alarming rates. Worldwide aggregate annual damage from attacks is now measured in billions of U.S. dollars. Attacks threaten the substantial and growing reliance of commerce, governments, and the public upon the information infrastructure to conduct business, carry messages, and process information. Most significant attacks are transnational by design, with victims throughout the world. Measures thus far adopted by the private and public sectors have not provided an adequate level of security. While new methods of attack have been accurately predicted by experts and some large attacks have been detected in early stages, efforts to prevent or deter them have been largely unsuccessful, with increasingly damaging consequences.

Information necessary to combat attacks has not been timely shared. Investigations have been slow and difficult to coordinate. Some attacks are from States that lack adequate laws governing deliberate destructive conduct. Such international cooperation as occurs is voluntary and inadequate. Some significant enhancement of defensive capabilities seems essential. Cyber crime is quintessentially transnational, and will often involve jurisdictional assertions of multiple States. Agreements on jurisdiction and enforcement must be developed to avoid conflicting claims.

The need and methods for effecting international cooperation in dealing with cyber crime and terrorism was the subject of a conference sponsored by the Hoover Institution, the Consortium for Research on Information Security and Policy (CRISP) and the Center for International Security and Cooperation (CISAC) at Stanford University on December 6-7, 1999 (the "Stanford Conference"). Members of government, industry, NGOs, and academia from many nations met at Stanford to discuss the growing problem. A clear consensus emerged that greater international cooperation is required, and considerable agreement that a multilateral treaty focused on criminal abuse of cyber systems would help build the necessary cooperative framework. (A synthesis of the Stanford Conference papers and discussion will be published by the Hoover Press.)

This monograph summarizes and presents the Stanford Draft International Convention to Enhance Security from Cyber Crime and Terrorism (the "Stanford Draft" or the "Draft") and commentary on the Draft. The Draft acknowledges and builds upon the draft Convention on Cyber Crime proposed by the Council of Europe (the "COE Draft").

Why a Multilateral Convention

Cyber crime is transnational, and requires a transnational response. Cyber criminals exploit weaknesses in the laws and enforcement practices of States, exposing all other States to dangers that are beyond their capacity unilaterally or bilaterally to respond. The speed and technical complexity of cyber activities requires prearranged, agreed procedures for cooperation in investigating and responding to threats and attacks.

A multilateral convention will ensure that all States Parties:

- adopt laws making dangerous cyber activities criminal;
- enforce those laws or extradite criminals for prosecution by other States;
- cooperate in investigating criminal activities and in providing usable evidence for prosecutions; and
- participate in formulating and agree to adopt and implement standards and practices that enhance safety and security.

An international agency created pursuant to the draft Convention will provide a forum for international discussion, ongoing response to technological developments, and technical assistance to developing States.

Offenses Defined

The Stanford Draft is designed to encourage universal recognition of basic offenses in cyberspace and universal agreement to cooperate in investigating, extraditing, and prosecuting perpetrators. (The Draft specifically excludes State conduct, addressing only conduct by individuals or groups.) Article 3 describes the conduct it covers, including: interfering with the function of a cyber system, cyber trespass, tampering with authentication systems, interfering with data, trafficking in illegal cyber tools, using cyber systems to further offenses specified in certain other treaties and targeting critical infrastructures. States Parties would agree to punish all the forms of conduct specified. Article 3 was drafted with the goal of securing speedy agreement among nations to adopt uniform definitions of offenses and commitments, despite having different network capabilities and political interests. Offenses related to more controversial issues, including protection of intellectual property and regulation of political, ethical or religious content, are therefore omitted. Implementation of treaty offenses will be effected in domestic law of signatories in accordance with Article 2.

International Cooperation in Investigation and Prosecution

Participants at the Stanford Conference debated technical, legal, policy and diplomatic concerns, and many from these disparate disciplines agreed that the most important need in the battle against cyber crime and terrorism is to develop cooperative, personal relationships among government law enforcers and technical experts around the world. Successes have flowed from existing informal networks of experts, who cooperate to resolve transborder incidents as they occur. Even greater successes could result from harmonization of laws, technical standards setting, cooperative international emergency response mechanisms, and intelligence sharing.

The Stanford Draft requires State Party cooperation in investigation through the mutual legal assistance and law enforcement provisions specified in Articles 6 and 11. States Parties are required to exchange information, assist in gathering and preserving evidence, arrest alleged offenders, prosecute or extradite them, and to implement agreed international standards dealing with security and law enforcement.

Jurisdiction and Extradition

Article 5 of the Draft confirms prescriptive and enforcement jurisdiction in States where offenses are committed; where alleged offenders are citizens, reside or are present; or where the conduct of offenders has substantial effects. Priority in jurisdiction is established, resting first where the offender is physically present when the offense occurs, second where substantial harm is suffered, and third in the State of the offender's dominant nationality. Article 7 of the Draft requires all States in which an alleged offender is present either to prosecute or to extradite.

An International Agency

Article 12 of the Stanford Draft proposes an international Agency for Information Infrastructure Protection (AIIP). The AIIP is intended to serve as a formal structure in which interested groups will cooperate through experts in countries around the world in developing standards and practices concerning cyber security.

The structure of AIIP representation is inspired by treaties establishing the International Civil Aviation Organization (ICAO) and the International Telecommunication Union (ITU). All States Parties are represented in the AIIP Assembly, which would adopt objectives and policies consistent with the Convention, approve standards and practices for cooperation, and approve technical assistance programs, among other responsibilities. The AIIP Council, elected by the Assembly, would, among other duties, appoint committees to study particular problems and recommend measures to the Assembly. The Draft also provides for a Secretariat to perform administrative tasks. The AIIP would build upon and supplement, not attempt to modify or substitute for, private-sector activities.

Privacy and Human Rights

Article 13 of the Stanford Draft permits States Parties to set and maintain their own standards for privacy and human rights. Consular notification and other procedural protections are provided for all persons detained pursuant to the Draft. In addition, Article 13 establishes a standing committee of the AIIP to study and recommend to the Council measures to protect privacy and other human rights.

Commentary

A substantial commentary precedes the Draft. The commentary discusses the emerging consensus against certain, destructive cyber activities, and the advantages and drawbacks to using a multilateral approach to address this problem. The commentary explains why certain provisions are included in the Draft, and why certain issues, such as copyright infringement and speech-related content offenses, are omitted. It compares the Stanford Draft to the COE Draft, and discusses the expected role and influence of the private sector in the development of standards, and the other work of the proposed AIIP.

Methods of information infrastructure attack are neither mysterious nor difficult to foresee; at the Stanford Conference, Thomas Longstaff of the Carnegie-Mellon Computer Emergency Response Team ("CERT") predicted that, in late 1999 or early 2000, a new and very harmful distributed form of denial-of-service attack would become prevalent. He based his predictions on observations of public hacker exchanges that shared attack strategies and software to implement those strategies. Longstaff predicted precisely the method that was used by hackers in the subsequent, worldwide, February 2000 attacks on CNN, eBay, Yahoo!, Amazon.com, online investment firms and others.

Despite being able to anticipate attacks of this type, law enforcement personnel were unable to prevent them, and security personal employed by the targeted cyber systems were unable to defend against them. These troubling failures stem from serious weaknesses in the capacities of states to protect valuable cyber systems from attacks that pose a rapidly escalating danger. As Longstaff stated, effective methods to protect against distributed denial of service attacks may be best addressed by regional, national and international cooperation.

The open and defiant manner in which attackers currently operate reflects the weakness of the legal, defensive, and investigative capacities of the current system. Some attackers are snared after long, expensive investigations, but most go unpunished. The incapacities stem ultimately from the fact that the information infrastructure is transnational in nature. Attackers deliberately fashion their efforts to exploit the absence of internationally agreed standards of behavior and cooperation. For example, attackers can avoid prosecution or greatly complicate investigations simply by initiating attack packets from countries with inadequate laws, and routing them through countries that with different laws and practices, and no structures for cooperation.

The lack of an adequate international response to these weaknesses is puzzling, given the huge and growing financial impact of cyber attacks and crimes. Even if some estimates of damages are inflated, the problem has grown undeniably expensive to businesses, governments, and individual users around the world. Multilateral action is required to build security into the underlying technical and social architecture. History has shown that when nations agree upon a common malicious threat, be it piracy on the high seas centuries ago or aviation terrorism of the 20th century, a cooperative, treaty-mediated regime can contribute substantially in addressing the problem.

The challenge of controlling cyber crime in its most critical dimensions requires a full range of responses, including both voluntary and legally-mandated cooperation. A consensus exists concerning many forms of conduct that should be treated as cyber crime. Common positions are developing or can be crafted to facilitate cooperation in investigation, the preservation of evidence, and extradition. Cooperation is also essential in the development and implementation of technological solutions and standards to enhance the capacity of states and users effectively to protect computers and systems from future attacks.

The nature and culture of the cyber world demand that these responses be fashioned to maximize private-sector participation and control, as well as to ensure that privacy and other human rights are not adversely affected. Certain elements of an effective program against cyber crime will require state control or approval, however. In addition, to develop and secure the universal adoption of technological and policy standards to defend against, prosecute, and deter cyber crime and terrorism will require an international forum with the necessary authority and capacities.

This can be achieved by creating an international Agency for Information Infrastructure Protection (AIIP), an agency designed to reflect the particular needs and nature of the largely self-regulated cyber world and modeled after the International Civil Aviation Organization (ICAO) and the International Telecommunication Union (ITU). While recent growth and reliance on the information infrastructures has occurred in the absence of substantial government involvement, the notion that voluntary activities alone can create adequate security for cyber activities that now involve 300 million people on the Internet alone is simply untenable. At the national level, cyber crime would likely be even more prevalent and costly than it has been had governments left the area unpoliced.

The laws thus far adopted that make cyber attacks criminal have at least provided a vehicle by which to arrest – and thereby to stop, punish, and deter – cyber criminals. The great majorities of users – commercial, educational, personal – favor law over anarchy when it comes to cyber attacks designed to steal, defraud, and destroy. The same is true on the international level, where only through government action can laws be passed setting universal standards for misconduct, authorizing investigatory cooperation, extradition, and the adoption of technologically-advanced methods for detecting, blocking, tracking, and deterring prohibited conduct. Multilateral leadership must not mean the subordination of private leadership and influence over cyber technology and operations. The cyber revolution has been uniquely successful and rapid because it is led and largely controlled by the private sector. Government has, however, played a pivotal role in supporting and giving legal authority to private institutions.

This distribution of power and responsibility can continue, and indeed be enhanced, by the continuing support and authority of the AIIP. Governments cannot responsibly expect the private sector to solve the cyber security problem. Business stakeholders in the information infrastructure have made clear that the private sector cannot be expected to perform the roles traditionally performed by law enforcement. But an enhanced government role need not be one that requires significantly greater domestic powers or more intrusive measures; rather, the need is for international cooperation to create common standards and practices. These objectives can be achieved without conferring inappropriate or unnecessary powers on governments to regulate and to intrude upon cyber systems, while at the same time preserving private-sector control of this uniquely productive and dynamic sector.

Commentary on the Draft Convention

The case for international cooperation in dealing with cyber crime is overwhelming. The debate currently under way is over the form and scopes such cooperation should take, and the extent to which the United States and other technologically advanced States should rely upon multilateral efforts to enhance cyber security. Proposals for voluntary international cooperation have been advanced and are being implemented. The principal elements of these proposals – to train law enforcement officials to understand and cope with cyber crimes and to establish round-the-clock emergency response teams – are widely supported.

In addition, the Group of Eight (G-8) and private groups such as the Internet Alliance have issued guidelines aimed at making voluntary cooperation more effective.

While these groups recognize that international cooperation is essential, they have yet to accept the idea that an international treaty should be negotiated establishing legally-mandated standards and obligations. Support for voluntary, as opposed to legally-mandated, international measures rests upon several arguments. Most cyber crime, it is argued, is conventional crime (e.g., fraud, drug dealing, and money laundering, sexual exploitation of minors), in which cyber technology happens to be used.

Existing treaties and international arrangements those providing for extradition and legal assistance, are potentially applicable in these cases. Securing international agreement on the wording of new cyber crimes will be difficult, moreover, and vast differences exist among States regarding appropriate regulation of content, the proper scope of transnational investigation, and the bases upon which tracking information and messages should be subject to seizure and scrutiny. Furthermore, a great disparity exists among States – even technologically advanced ones – as to the scope of privacy and other rights possessed by individuals under national laws that would either operate to limit an international agreement or be compromised by one.

Finally, the Internet, many believe, has been a powerful vehicle for economic growth and enhanced communication in large part because it is controlled by the private sector, rather than governments; and this growth and creativity may be adversely affected by international legal requirements and regulation. For these reasons, Drew C. Arena, then Senior Counsel to the Assistant Attorney General, U.S. Department of Justice, commented at the Stanford Conference that achieving consensus on "the specific steps" to be taken in negotiating a multilateral treaty would be "too hard" at the present time to warrant the effort. University of Chicago School of Law Professor Jack L. Goldsmith has argued that, in the absence of a suitable international regime, the United States should rely on unilateral measures in fighting transnational cyber crime.

However, he does, in principle, favor the pursuit of such a regime. These arguments against the creation of an international legal regime to deal with cyber security are cogent, but based on difficulties and dangers that are avoidable. The case for a multilateral agreement to combat cyber crime and terrorism is strong, and the need to undertake the effort of negotiating one is becoming clearer with the increasing costs of such activity. While it may be true that most crimes in which computers and networks are involved are conventional and potentially covered by international agreements, these are not the crimes against which a new treaty is needed. Existing international agreements provide no help in dealing with crimes related directly to the information infrastructure, including attacks utilizing viruses (such as "Melissa" and "I Love You"), denials of service, and other destructive conduct.

Furthermore, the need for an international agreement to deal with cyber crime rests not merely on the fact that such acts include new types of conduct but also on the need for new methods by which cyber crimes will have to be investigated and prosecuted to provide effective protection. To secure multilateral agreement on the precise wording of cyber crimes would, in fact, be complicated; but that effort need not be undertaken. A broad consensus exists with regard to certain conduct involving the information infrastructure that should be made criminal; and a treaty could readily be drafted that describes such conduct and requires all States Parties to make such conduct criminal through any formula they choose to utilize.

The differences that exist among States concerning several key issues in developing a treaty must be taken into account and will limit and shape the arrangements that are currently feasible. But differences concerning such issues as regulation of content, scope of extraterritorial investigation, standards of proof, and protection of privacy and other rights, can be resolved, largely through a willingness to begin this effort by focusing on measures likely to secure universal agreement. The sharp differences that exist among States with regard to what can be done unilaterally demonstrate, in fact, the need to attempt to secure agreed, multilateral arrangements, rather than establishing a basis for making no effort to do so.

The notion that the United States should act unilaterally when necessary to protect its interests is in principle sound. Professor Goldsmith seems to recognize, however, that unilateral activities must be legally defensible, and resort to them must be in the nation's best interests. His assumption that it will take many years to negotiate and implement a multilateral convention may turn out to be wrong, in light of the increasingly obvious need and growing momentum for such an arrangement. Furthermore, even before a multilateral treaty is complete, the United States may be able to reach less comprehensive arrangements with other States to enhance legal protections. Unilateral conduct that offends other States, and leads them to reject or delay negotiating a desirable treaty, would harm U.S. interests.

Concerns expressed by the private sector over establishing legally-mandated norms and obligations stem from the fear that law enforcement considerations will adversely affect (and greatly burden) Internet businesses and freedom of expression. Government control of the information infrastructure could well have detrimental effects, and international regulation could be especially damaging if political objectives and bureaucratic requirements are allowed to interfere with the present, privately dominated Internet regime. National governments – including the U.S. government – have sought or imposed potentially damaging restrictions on Internet users, including limitations on the use and sale of advanced encryption, demands for the power to intrude upon, hear, and record Internet traffic, and suggestions that private entities assume quasi-prosecutorial responsibilities in criminal investigations.

These policies and suggestions have, however, unjustifiably evoked suspicion of all efforts to establish legally-mandated obligations. If, as we believe, voluntary efforts will not provide adequate security, legal obligations to cooperate can be devised that are consistent with continued private creativity and control. An international regime can be fashioned to satisfy the full range of cyber-security needs, in a manner that ensures continued private-sector control of Internet technology and practices. The United States is party to several international regimes encompassing the creation of consensus-based, nonmandatory measures crafted by public and private-sector experts, on which a treaty for cyber security could draw in providing a comprehensive and lasting system for international cooperation.

The strong case for a legally-mandated, international regime has led to several significant developments. Treaty provisions are being proposed to close loopholes in existing multilateral commitments in the specific area of civil aviation. This approach may be feasible in other areas, particularly to protect critical infrastructures from criminal and terrorist attacks, and seems likely to cause little controversy. The Council of Europe (COE) has adopted a more comprehensive approach, recently publishing a draft treaty on cyber crime. This proposal includes definitions of cyber activities that must be made criminal by all States Parties, as well as other features and forms of cooperation. The COE's draft assumes, correctly, that substantial consensus exists with respect to those cyber activities that should be considered criminal, and that substantial benefits can be derived from a multilateral arrangement with common standards, investigative cooperation, and extradition.

We undertake in this monograph to demonstrate the advantages and feasibility of an even more comprehensive regime by proposing a draft international convention (the Stanford Draft) and discussing its principal elements. The Stanford Draft is largely consistent with the draft COE Convention on Cyber crime, but differs in some respects. Most significantly, the Stanford Draft would establish an international agency, modeled along the lines of successful, specialized United Nations agencies, to prepare and promulgate – on the basis of advice from non-political experts – standards and recommended practices (SARPs) to enhance the effectiveness of protective and investigative measures.

Covered Conduct

The basis for international cooperation rests, most fundamentally, on the combination of a demonstrable need for international agreement to combat harmful cyber conduct, and the existence of an international consensus on what conduct should be considered criminal. A review of existing statutory law and proposed international arrangements reflects widespread consensus on prosecuting as criminal the conduct covered in the Stanford Draft: attacks aimed at disrupting or damaging computer operations; deliberate and unauthorized intrusions; interference with computer-security measures; maliciously altering content; intentionally and materially facilitating the commission of prohibited conduct; using a cyber system in committing violations of any of several widely-adopted antiterrorist conventions; and using a cyber system to attack critical infrastructures.

Most of these forms of conduct are covered in the COE's draft proposal, although that draft attempts to categorize cyber crimes into a number of specific categories: illegal access; illegal interception; data interference; system interference; and the possession or transfer of "illegal devices" under specified circumstances. The COE effort to generalize may have created coverage on some issues that is undesirably broad. The introductory language to Article 3 of the Draft – specifically the concept of "legally recognized authority" – is intended to incorporate the concept of self-defense. Efforts of governments, companies, and individuals to defend themselves from attacks may sometimes require measures which, if adopted without authorization or justification, would be criminal, such as alterations of code, or interfering with operation of computers being used by attackers.

At times, such efforts may affect innocent third parties, but nonetheless may be reasonable. The complex issues that are certain to arise in applying established principles of law to this new area of technological activity will be resolved over time, on the basis of experience. The Stanford Draft recognizes and attempts to deal with the fact that States have dissimilar standards in statutes that cover the conduct it proscribes. Instead of attempting to list specific, commonly defined "offenses", as in most extradition treaties, the Stanford Draft refers to types of conduct, and secures commitments from all States Party to enforce any applicable law against every form of covered conduct, or to adopt new laws necessary to create authority to prosecute or extradite for such conduct.

This approach overcomes the problem of attempting to develop precise, agreed definitions of offenses, and therefore the requirement that every State Party adopt particular formulations as national crimes. In addition to requiring criminal enforcement against conduct specifically aimed at the information infrastructure, the Stanford Draft requires criminal enforcement against the use of computers in the commission of offenses under certain, widely-adopted multilateral treaties. These include clearly-defined crimes against aircraft, ships, diplomats, and terrorist bombings. Computers can greatly enhance the potential damage caused by crimes, and can make them especially difficult to investigate.

Therefore, since most States are parties to these multilateral treaties, they should be prepared to impose more stringent punishment for the use of cyber capacities in committing the targeted offenses. (The COE Draft currently does not include such provisions.) Other, widely recognized forms of criminal conduct may also become more aggravated through the use of computers, such as forgery, fraud, theft, and conversion. These crimes are not included in the Stanford Draft; however, since they are in general already encompassed in extradition treaties, to the extent States Parties want such coverage. The cyber dimension of such activities, moreover, would generally involve conduct covered in the Stanford Draft, irrespective of the crimes such conduct may have facilitated. (The COE Draft includes coverage of "computer-related" forgery and fraud, but its definitions of these offenses seem likely to cause uncertainties.)

Other types of conduct, when related to the information infrastructure, have been prohibited in some States, including copyright violations, and sexual exploitation of minors. These offenses are covered by the COE Draft, along with the use of computers to commit fraud. These types of conduct are not covered in the Stanford Draft because their inclusion may prove controversial. In fact, a sufficient consensus for including some of these offenses – especially the use of computers for sexual exploitation of minors – may exist; the Stanford Draft's coverage could be expanded to include such offenses. (The COE Draft covers offenses related to child pornography, as well as "copyright and related offences", but whether the scope of coverage should be coterminous with treaties in the area – such as the Berne Convention and other copyright treaties administered by the World Intellectual Property Organization – has been left unsettled.)

The Stanford Draft also includes very limited coverage of "content" offenses, to avoid the strong differences that exist among States concerning restrictions on speech and political activity. No type of speech, or publication, is required to be treated as criminal under the Stanford Draft; if, for example, Germany were to decide to ban publication on the Internet of *Mein Kampf*, it would have to do so unilaterally and could not expect to receive enforcement assistance under the Stanford Draft. The single exception to this principle in the Stanford Draft is the narrow coverage of conduct described as the "distribution of devices or programs intended for the purpose of committing" other conduct made criminal by the Stanford Draft.

The Draft thereby makes criminal the knowing and deliberate effort to cause illegal attacks through such distribution, but not discussions of computer vulnerability intended for evaluating exposure to attacks on the Internet, or other protected speech. States Parties wishing to encourage open discussion of computer attacks and vulnerabilities could designate "safe harbor" sites at which discussion would be considered lawful. (The COE Draft would prohibit a broad range of conduct involving the transfer or possession of "illegal devices", defined to include certain computer programs.) A final issue concerning offenses is whether a cyber crime convention should cover only those offenses that provide for penalties exceeding some minimum term of imprisonment. Extradition treaties generally contain such a limitation, usually that the crime for which extradition is sought be punishable by one year of imprisonment or more.

This rule is intended to exclude minor offenses from coverage. Given the complications and effort required to satisfy extradition requests, this consideration is at least as important in a cyber crime convention as in any other. By having such a requirement, moreover, States Parties would in effect be required to cover prohibited conduct with potential penalties of at least one year in prison. The Stanford Draft therefore includes only crimes for which a potential penalty of at least one year's imprisonment is provided. (The COE Draft includes a separate article on this subject, which is designed to ensure serious penal and civil sanctions.)

Jurisdiction

The Stanford Draft anticipates that the conduct it covers will have effects potentially conferring jurisdiction on multiple States Parties for the same offense. It provides a set of priorities that Parties would agree to follow in performing their duties and pursuing their rights, to the extent practicable, given the difficulty of anticipating all the possible contingencies. A State Party must establish jurisdiction to try offenders who commit offenses in its territory, who are its nationals, or who are stateless residents in its territory and whose extradition from its territory is refused. A State Party may establish jurisdiction to try offenders who attempt to harm it or its nationals, or to compel it to perform or abstain from performing an act, or whose offenses have substantial effects within its territory. (The COE Draft provides similar coverage, but fails to resolve aspects of this problem in a definitive manner.)

The problem of multiple-State jurisdiction over crime is by now commonplace in international law. Transnational fraud, for example, has led to decisions by national courts assuming jurisdiction on the basis of any significant connection to the conduct involved. Among these are the States where a fraud was planned, where an effort to defraud was initiated, where individuals worked at implementing the fraud, where or through which communications were made that were intrinsic to the fraud, where the victims were located, and where the fraud had material and intended effects. The widespread recognition of fraud as criminal activity leads States readily to find jurisdiction over such activity, despite the significant relationship particular frauds may have to other States. They tend to assume that punishing fraud will be supported by other affected States, rather than opposed as violating their sovereignty.

Cyber crime is quintessentially transnational, and will often involve jurisdictional assertions of multiple States. To avoid the conflict such assertions of jurisdiction could cause, enforcement under the Stanford Draft is limited to cyber activities that are universally condemned. The Stanford Draft does not accede to a State's jurisdiction merely because semeone within its territory is able to access a website in another State; to confer jurisdiction, someone in control of the website must deliberately cause one of the covered crimes, with effects in the State seeking to assert jurisdiction. It seems likely, therefore, that States will in general accept all of the reasonably-based jurisdictional claims approved in the Draft.

Cooperation in Criminal Enforcement

The Stanford Draft includes commitments by States Parties to engage in the full range of cooperative activities found in widely adopted international agreements. Under it, States Parties would agree to extradite or prosecute persons reasonably believed to have engaged in any form of the covered conduct or offenses. Where necessary, and on a proper evidentiary basis, they would arrest and hold alleged offenders for a short period pending an extradition request. They would also agree to cooperate in seizing, preserving, developing, and providing in usable form evidence for the prosecution of offenders in the courts of other States Parties. They would coordinate these activities through designated "Central Authorities", as in Mutual Legal Assistance Treaties, so that each State Party would know to whom to address requests, and would have an identified agency or person responsible for dealing with such requests in a timely and proper manner.

The COE Draft is particularly impressive in mandating prompt responses to cyber attacks and requests for cooperation, on a 24-hour/7-day-per-week basis, and the

Stanford Draft incorporates a similar commitment. The COE Draft also provides detailed rules concerning seizure of data, production orders, expedited presentation, and disclosure. A provision (Article 28) regarding "interception" is contemplated but under discussion. These rules are currently useful, but may become problematic with the availability of new technologies or methods. The Stanford Draft, for this reason, provides a commitment to cooperate on each of these subjects that is not further specified.

The basic principles of cooperation are clear. When it comes to implementation, however, many problems exist, and many more are certain to arise, for which answers have not as yet been developed. What, for example, should be the scope of a State's power unilaterally to seek information in a foreign State? A State may not know whether its electronic effort to obtain information about a crime will enter or have any significant effect within another State or States; it could not avoid such uncertainty even if it tried. Some tolerance of extraterritorial effects would seem, therefore, to be imperative in any viable, multilateral cyber-related arrangement. Both the Stanford Draft and the COE Draft call for the widest possible cooperation; the former's provision for unilateral action is more narrowly drawn in some respects, but the latter's is still not agreed upon by COE Members.

Another area of current uncertainty is what duties an Internet Service Provider (ISP) should have to preserve and provide information of cyber crimes. Should any such duty be enforceable by law, moreover, and if so by what means? These are sensitive issues, since States have not yet imposed duties on ISPs and other Internet participants, such as those imposed in analogous contexts. What should States be required to do to enhance the prospects of preserving evidence that could be helpful in investigating an attack; in particular, should a State be required to seize such information?

These sorts of issues related to transnational investigation of cyber crime and terrorism raise several questions. The first concerns technology: what technological measures are possible and/or desirable to assist States Parties in securing cooperation that goes beyond the conventional steps currently undertaken in treaties of extradition and mutual legal assistance? Rapidly changing technological capacities and needs make it fruitless to attempt to deal definitively in a draft convention with this aspect of the cyber crime and terrorism problem. Instead, the Draft proposes general principles supporting certain existing technological objectives, and would establish an international agency through which States Parties would cooperate in considering and proposing the use of particular technological measures to enhance cooperative efforts.

In addition to the technological dimension are certain questions of principle concerning the right of States Parties to defend against or to investigate cyber crime? May a State Party, for instance, deliberately initiate investigative actions or countermeasures for law-enforcement purposes that could involve sending transmissions into cyber systems located in other, sovereign territories? Based on experience to date, fast-spreading computer viruses and other cyber attacks demand prompt efforts to track down attackers, and it is difficult if not impossible to know in advance all the places to or through which any part of any cyber transmission might travel. Therefore, the Stanford Draft approves in principle unilateral measures where they are electronic and reasonable.

The Stanford Draft provides, moreover, that any law enforcement activity undertaken that knowingly affects another State Party, including any effort to seek cooperative measures from an entity located in another State Party, must be made known to the Central Authority of that State as soon as practicable. In addition, the Stanford Draft would require all entities, including ISPs, to comply with any standard or procedure developed by the AIIP under the Stanford Draft and accepted by the State Party in which they are located, and would mandate that all States Parties enforce all such standards and procedures. Arrangements based on these principles seem likely to garner widespread support, and would be preferable to unilateral actions that some States could find objectionable (or even criminal).

The Stanford Draft includes a provision authorizing the seizure and forfeiture of equipment utilized in the commission of offences, subject to due process protections. States could use the information contained in such equipment, or dispose of the equipment as they see fit, consistent with national law. Funds derived from forfeitures have provided resources in other areas for use in upgrading law-enforcement capabilities. The seizure and/or forfeiture of cyber equipment used in committing covered offenses are consistent with the universally-recognized right of governments to seize instruments of crime.

Structure for Technological Cooperation

An effective transnational response to cyber crime requires a high level of technological cooperation with regard to virtually every function expected to be performed by the States Parties. Cyber criminals exploit the technological possibilities available, including the ability to mask their identity, to hide the origin of attacks and other actions by conducting them through intermediate sites, and to find and exploit weaknesses throughout the worldwide information infrastructure. The challenges of dealing with these capacities are exacerbated, moreover, by dynamic changes in technology, the continuing development of new methods for committing cyber crimes, the current widespread sharing of information and ideas about cyber system vulnerabilities, and a culture among users of cyber-space that is skeptical of, if not outright hostile to, government involvement.

Given this context, it is unrealistic to expect that cyber crime will be significantly controlled or deterred through unilateral or voluntary or purely defensive measures. Defensive measures always make sense, and will prove effective for some entities, some of the time. But the pressure to operate openly in business, education, research, entertainment, and personal activities leads users to develop or choose accessible (and hence more vulnerable) technology. Governments have seemed especially unable to defend their sites and systems, and have been frequent targets of attack. Furthermore, the objectives sought through cooperation, and simply unavailable to States acting unilaterally, require a high level of technological coordination. Take, for example, the need to anticipate, freeze, and trace information packets that are used in cyber crime.

Those measures, once devised, will need to be approved and implemented by all participants in the information infrastructure, in a technologically-compatible manner, or criminals will find and use gaps in coverage. Similarly, to enable States to conduct searches and seizures, to provide for extradition, and to develop evidence that is usable in the courts of all cooperating States, will require adoption of uniform and mutually acceptable standards and technological solutions, on which all States can rely. The pressures for multilateral solutions to information-infrastructure problems are, in fact, likely to be so great that solutions will be developed without the formal, open, and accountable processes associated with established international institutions.

The story of how private and public actors developed and secured U.S. government support for a system of domain protection illustrates both the need for and inevitability of multilateral solutions to at least some of the key issues, as well as the ad hoc and relatively undemocratic process that may occur in the absence of established, publicly accountable mechanisms. The process by which effective standards and practices are established for international cooperation in dealing with cyber crime and terrorism will likely be the most important aspect of any multilateral agreement. Considerable guidance can be gained in designing a structure for setting such standards from other areas in which transnational standard-setting activities occur, such as airline safety, marine safety, telecommunications, and banking.

In general, standard setting and cooperation in such areas is achieved by establishing an international agency assigned clearly-articulated and widely-shared objectives, with the technical and material resources to achieve those objectives, a professional and nonpolitical staff, substantial reliance on the private sector (especially on highly-skilled technical experts), and continuous political involvement and ultimate control by representatives of the participating States. The history and structure of the International Civil Aviation Organization (ICAO) are instructive in this regard. ICAO is governed by an Assembly, consisting of representatives from all its States Parties, which meets at least once every three years, establishes basic policies consistent with governing treaties, considers and recommends treaty revisions, approves the budget, which it funds through an apportionment among Member States, and elects delegates to the Council for three-year terms.

The Council currently has 33 members, including representatives from States of chief importance in air transport, from States that make the largest contributions to international aviation, or chosen to ensure that all major geographical areas are represented. It implements its decision, prepares the budget, administers ICAO's finances, appoints the Secretary General and provides a Secretariat, and is empowered to adopt Standards and Recommended Practices (SARPs), which are incorporated into the ICAO Convention through Annexes. The Council acts by majority vote in carrying out its functions, including in the adoption of SARPs, which are only adopted after exhaustive development and "technical monitoring, evaluation and backstopping". While it may delegate authority with respect to any particular matter to a committee of its members, decisions of any such committee may be appealed to the Council by any interested contracting State.

The subjects dealt with in SARPs reflect the Council's authority to adopt measures necessary to maintain the safety and efficiency of international air transport. In performing these functions, the Council is assisted by the Air Navigation Commission, a body of fifteen persons with "suitable qualifications and experience", appointed by the Council from among nominees of Member States. This expert body is responsible for considering and recommending new or amended SARPs, establishing technical sub-groups, and ensuring that the Council collects and disseminates to all Member States the information necessary and useful for the advancement of air navigation.

Technical assistance is a major aspect of ICAO's work. Member States license pilots in accordance with ICAO standards. Standardization of equipment and procedures is a major aim and activity, on the whole array of technical issues, including navigation, meteorology, charts, measurement, aircraft operation, air traffic services, search and rescue, accident inquiry, and security. Developing countries are actively assisted through a variety of programs, funded by ICAO, the United Nations Development Program (UNDP), and other sources. Some 80 staff members are involved in about 120 assistance projects each year, with an overall budget of $55 million. They provide training, technical advice, and help in purchasing necessary equipment.

A second international agency that performs duties analogous to those relevant to cyber security is the International Telecommunication Union (ITU). The ITU is the oldest intergovernmental organization in existence, having been formed in 1865 to implement the Telegraph Convention. It expanded its activities to radio in 1906, and currently deals with issues related to all forms of "telecommunications", including telephone, television, and telex. It operates along the same lines as ICAO, with heavy reliance on private-sector expertise and involvement. In recent statements, the ITU has expressed its intent to become more involved with information-infrastructure issues.

The ICAO and ITU regimes deal with underlying technological matters that differ from each other, and from Internet communications, in significant ways. But the needs that led to the creation of these, and of other, similar regulatory mechanisms, are largely analogous to those affecting the cyber world. The key factors behind establishment of these multilateral bodies have been safety and efficiency – the same considerations supporting a multilateral solution to the problem of cyber crime and terrorism. In addition, these multilateral entities are designed to: (1) enable all States Parties to learn of and become involved in the multilateral solutions of problems related to transnational technologies; (2) enable technologically-advanced States to protect their interests; (3) ensure that solutions are based on the best possible scientific knowledge, developed with the input of expert advice; and (4) benefit from involvement and expertise of private interests (both commercial and non-profit).

The Stanford Draft draws on the ICAO and ITU patterns in creating a proposed international institution, the "Agency for Information Infrastructure Protection" or "AIIP", to implement the objectives of States Parties with regard to protecting the information infrastructure from criminal and terrorist cyber activities. No single set of technical fixes will solve the problems that now exist, let alone those that will develop as the technological possibilities expand. The AIIP is therefore designed to play an ongoing role in formulating and revising standards, and proposing treaty revisions for enhanced safety, efficiency, and effective cooperation in light of continuing technological and political developments. Properly designed and structured, this type of agency should contribute materially to cyber security.

The Stanford Draft would require States Parties to establish the AIIP, with the following, key components: an Assembly having functions similar to those exercised by the plenary bodies that operate in ICAO, the ITU, and some other specialized agencies; a Council that implements the policies set by the Assembly, through committees of experts, with heavy private-sector representation; and a Secretary General and Secretariat to implement Assembly and Council instructions and perform administrative tasks. The Council would formulate and the Assembly would adopt recommended standards and practices (SARPs) to advance the purposes of the Stanford Draft, and the AIIP would also propose amendments and additional international agreements to implement solutions to problems that require new authority from States.

Some of the UN's specialized agencies have an impressive record for developing and proposing international agreements to deal with important areas not covered by their founding instruments. The International Maritime Organization (IMO), for example, has proposed over twenty treaties to deal with important issues of maritime safety or efficiency, most of which have been widely ratified. In addition, the AIIP Council would be authorized to create and implement, with the Assembly's support, assistance programs to help needy States Parties participate effectively in the activities contemplated in the Stanford Draft.

The standards and recommendations to be developed by the AIIP would be designed to have the same legal force attributed to SARPs developed by ICAO. SARPs adopted by ICAO are not legally-binding; they become part of appendices to the ICAO Convention, and States Parties are expected to implement them. States Parties are required, however, to advise other States Parties of their failure to implement SARPs, and the latter would be free to act to protect themselves from the potential consequences of a State's failure to abide by the standard or practice at issue. This type of arrangement has proved universally acceptable in civil aviation and in other areas of transnational regulation, to ensure that standards and practices proposed are thoroughly vetted, widely supported, and accepted voluntarily on the basis of sovereign self interest and mutuality of obligation.

Authority is provided in Article 12 to the AIIP in the Stanford Draft to enable it to discipline States Parties, or States that are non-Parties but are participating in the information infrastructure. Where a State acts or allows persons to act in a manner that undermines the objectives of the Draft, the Council is authorized to recommend sanctions, and the Assembly is authorized to impose them on a two-thirds vote, up to and including expulsion from the AIIP, and a recommendation to States of exclusion from the information infrastructure. While the Draft avoids regulating State conduct, actions that undermine its purposes, such as allowing persons to use a State's territory to launch attacks affecting other States, would allow the AIIP to exclude such States from membership or to recommend punishing persons and/or non-Party States by excluding them from participation in the international information infrastructure.

Protection of Individual Rights

Transnational regulation of the Internet raises several important issues related to privacy and other individual rights. The Stanford Draft ensures that, at a minimum, individual rights afforded by States Parties are not adversely affected. No State Party has any duty under the Stanford Draft to act in any manner that might infringe upon the privacy or other human rights of any individual or entity, as defined by the law of that State. In addition, the Stanford Draft authorizes States Parties to refuse or cease cooperation in investigations or prosecutions they consider politically motivated or unfair. It would also create a subcommittee of experts as part of the AIIP, assigned the task of following and reporting upon the protection of privacy and human rights. Finally, the Draft provides that certain, fundamental protections must be extended to individuals detained for violations of any offense covered by its terms, including notice to the representative of the State of which an accused is a national, and the right to such representative's assistance.

Efforts to protect privacy and other human rights will involve complications for States Parties, for private entities, and for the AIIP as an organization. Notions of privacy and the scope of procedural and human rights vary considerably among the States whose participation is needed for a workable international regime. These differences have led the Internet Alliance to conclude that a legally-mandatory regime on Internet crime would likely "wreak havoc" on privacy protections. In fact, no such result is necessary to have effective multilateral cooperation. By allowing States Parties to insist on the preservation of national norms as a minimum level of protection, the Stanford Draft would preclude its use to deprive any person of rights granted by any State Party, and the problems anticipated will be analogous to those created under the air transport and other antiterrorism conventions.

Just as the United States and USSR were able to live with such differences in those contexts, and still benefit from the agreements (for example, by securing extradition and prosecutions of hijackers), the Stanford Draft has been designed to enable States with radically different political values to work together on achieving mutually beneficial aims without sacrificing those values. If, however, a serious and unresolvable situation emerged in which, for example, the regime of technical and operational cooperation developed under the Draft was abused by a State in some manner, the Assembly is empowered to impose sanctions in Articles 12, 13, and 21, including expulsion from the

AIIP or a recommendation against the offending State's participation in the international information infrastructure.

National Security

The Stanford Draft makes clear, in a manner similar to other multilateral agreements, that it is inapplicable to State conduct and national security affairs. A multilateral agreement on cyber crime will have novel, complex, and important objectives apart from the possible use of cyber systems by States as military or intelligence tools. Efforts to control State conduct related to national security will be unhelpful in advancing the development of a multilateral approach to the problem of cyber crime and unnecessary as well. ICAO protects civilian aircraft from attack, and the ITU protects radio transmissions from interference. But these treaties do not attempt directly to control States in the conduct of their national security affairs.

To the extent use of cyber technology as a weapon is a concern, existing arms control agreements, and treaties incorporating the laws of war, are all potentially applicable, as are the UN Charter provisions concerning the use of force. The Draft does provide sanctions against conduct that undermines its purposes. If further measures need to be considered to limit the use of cyber technologies in areas of national security, those should be taken up separately and not used to hold hostage the development of a multilateral regime to advance the process of dealing with criminal activities harmful to all States, their peoples, and their economies.

Dispute Resolution

The Stanford Draft relies initially on consensual resolution of disputes through negotiation and mediation. States Parties unable to resolve their disputes consensually are required to submit to arbitration in any agreed form. The Stanford Draft contemplates that the Council of the

AIIP will, after its creation, propose for the Assembly's consideration an arbitration mechanism through which disputes would be resolved by expert panels designated in advance to hear and decide such matters, perhaps in the relatively informal manner preferred by the industry for resolving disputes over website domain names.

Amendments

The Stanford Draft contains a standard treaty provision enabling the States Parties to propose and approve amendments as necessary and appropriate.

Bibliography

Adams, James. *The Financing of Terror,* New York: Simon & Schuster, 1986.

Alexander, Yonah and Richard Latter, eds. *Terrorism and the Media: Dilemmas for Government, Journalists & the Public,* Washington, DC: Brassey's, 1990.

Andersan, Sean and Stephen Solan. *Historical Dictionary of Terrorism,* 2nd ed. Lanham, MD: Scarecrow, 2002.

Atkins, Stephen E. *Terrorism: A Reference Handbook,* Santa Barbara, CA: 1992.

Bell, J. Bower. *Transnational Terror, Washington,* DC: American Enterprise Institute, 1975.

Burton, Anthony. *Urban Terrorism: Theory, Practice, Response,* London: Cooper, 1975.

Chaliand, Gerald. *Terrorism: From Popular Struggle to Media Spectacle,* Atlantic Highlands, NJ: Saqi, 1987.

Comb, Cindy C. *Terrorism in Twenty-First Century,* 2nd ed. Upper Saddle River, NJ: Prentice Hall, 2002.

Crelinsten, Ronald D. and Denis Szabo. *Hostage- Taking,* Lexington, MA: Lexington Book, 1979.

Crenshaw, Martha. *Terrorism, Legitimacy, and Power,* Middletown, CT: Wesleyan University Press, 1983.

Gay, Kathleen. *Encyclopedia of Political Anarchy,* Santa Barbara, CA: ABC-CLIO, 1999.

George, Alexander, ed. *Western State Terrorism*, New York: Routledge, 1991.

Gurr, Ted Robert. *Handbook of Political Conflict: Theory and Research*, New York: Free Press, 1980.

Harmon, Christopher C. *Terrorism Today*, London: Frank Cass, 2002.

Hoffman, Bruce. *Inside Terrorism*, New York: Columbia University Press, 1998.

Jenkins, Brian. *International Terrorism: The Other World War*, Santa Monica, CA: RAND, 1985.

Kushner, Harvey W. ed. *The Future of Terrorism: Violence in the New Millennium*, Thousand Oaks, CA: Sage, 1998.

Laqueur, Walter. *History of Terrorism*, New York: Transaction Publishers, 2001.

Lesser, Ian O. et al. *Countering the New Terrorism*, Santa Monica, CA: RAND, 1999.

Lewis Bernand. *The Political Language of Islam*, Chicago: University of Chicago Press, 1988.

Miller, Abraham H. *Terrorism and Hostage Negotiations*, Boulder, CO: Westview, 1980.

Moss, Robert. *Urban Guerrilla Warfare*, London: International Institute for Strategic Studies, 1971.

Netanyahu, Benzamin. *The Terrorism Reader*, New York: Meridian, 1986.

O'Neill, Bard E. *Insurgency and Terrorism: Inside Modern Revolutionary Warfare*, Washington, DC: Brassey's, 1990.

Peters, Rudolph. *Jihad in Classical and Modern Islam*, Princeton, NJ: Markus Wiener, 1996.

Picard, Robert G. *Media Portrayals of Terrorism: Functions and Meaning of News Coverage*, Ames: Iowa State University Press, 1993.

Pillar, Paul R. and Michael H. Armacost. *Terrorism and U.S. Foreign Policy, Washington,* DC: Brookings Institution, 2001.

Rashid, Ahmed. Jihad: *The Rise of Militant Islam I Central Asia,* New Haven, CT: Yale University Press, 2002.

Rosie, George. *The Dictionary of International Terrorism,* New York: Paragon House, 1987.

Schamis, Geraldo Jorge. *War and Terrorism in International Affairs,* New Brunswick, NJ: Transaction Publishers, 1980.

Segaller, Stephen. *Invisible Armies: Terrorism in the 1990s,* San Diego, CA: Harcourt Brace Jovanovich, 1987.

Sofaer, Abraham D. and Seymour E. Goodman. *The Transnational Dimension of Cyber Crime and Terrorism,* Stanford, CA: Hoover Institution, 2001.

Sonn, Richard D. *Anarchism,* New York: Twayne, 1992.

Stern, Jessia. *The Ultimate Terrorists,* Cambridge, MA: Harvard University Press, 1999.

Tanter, Raymond. *Rogue Regimes: Terrorism and Proliferation,* New York: St. Maytin's, 1998.

Tucker, Jonathan B. *Toxic Terror: Assessing Terrorist Use of Chemical and Biological Weapons,* Cambridge, MA: MIT Press, 2000.

U.S. Department of State, *Patterns of Global Terrorism,* Washington, DC [Annual].

Venzke, Ben N. *First Responder Chem- Bio Handbook,* Alexandria, VA: Tempest, 1998.

Wardlaw, Grant. *Political Terrorism: Theory, Tactics, and Counter-Measures,* New York: Cambridge University Press, 1989.

White, Jonathan R. *Terrorism: An Introduction,* 3rd ed. Belmont, CA: Wadsworth, 2001.

Whittaker, David J. *The Terrorism Reader*, London and New York: Routledge, 2001.

Zinn, Howard. *Terrorism and War*, New York: Seven Stories, 2002.

Index

H

I

J

L

M

N

O

P

R

S

T

V

W